Our War Stories

Marvin Harper

Copyright © 2003 by Marvin Harper

ISBN 0-7414-1709-X

Published by:

PUBLISHING.COM

519 West Lancaster Avenue
Haverford, PA 19041-1413
Info@buybooksontheweb.com
www.buybooksontheweb.com
Toll-free (877) BUY BOOK
Local Phone (610) 520-2500
Fax (610) 519-0261

Printed in the United States of America

Printed on Recycled Paper

Published September 2003

Contributors

FOREWARD

Marvin Harper

The 50 stories in this book were written by friends of mine who served our country in wartime. Although stories from Vietnam and the Korean conflicts are represented, most of the stories are set during WWII.

I have sought to preserve each person's unique, wartime experience, and in so doing, pass on a deep feeling of that particular period. To this end, and to avoid copycat, cookie-cutter styles, no one had the opportunity to read another person's story.

Although the WWII generation is being referred to as "The Greatest Generation," I do not think the people of that generation (myself included) were one bit greater than our forebears who served in our country's other wars and fought courageously to obtain and then preserve our freedom. Nor do I think their actions were any greater than those demonstrated by the American people after September 11, 2001. We can all be proud to call ourselves members of a great American generation.

I thank each one who contributed a story for this book. Several of these stories came from spouses of deceased men and some contributors have died since sending me their stories. The attack on Pearl Harbor occurred more than 60 years ago, so for most of us represented in this book, the curtains have already come down or are descending fast.

Each generation represented in this book inherited a great nation, but along with the privilege of inheriting comes the responsibility of preserving. All of those whose stories are represented here have done their jobs with valor as, I am sure, the present and future generations will do to preserve our nation and maintain our freedom.

"A MAN CAN'T HAVE
TOO MANY FRIENDS"

Randall Challen Berg

This is a great long-to-be-remembered line of the actor Elwood P. Dowd in the great play "Harvey." I'll never forget it.

In March 1941, eight months before Pearl Harbor, I applied for a commission in the Navy. The Navy was looking for qualified college graduates. I couldn't pass the physical (which was tough at the time) because of my eyes.

Late in June when I was a traveling salesman with A H Pond Co, my dad called me and said the local draft board had drawn my number and that I should be ready to report as a private in the Army in three weeks.

I was determined not to go into the Army so I went to Macon, Georgia, the next day and applied for a commission in the Marine Corps. They gladly accepted my request but said I had to "Buck Private" training at Paris Island, South Carolina. If I "survived" that, they would send me to officer candidate school at Quantico, Virginia. I agreed to do so. They told me I would receive orders in three weeks.

That weekend I went to Charleston, South Carolina to visit a fraternity brother at Chapel Hill. I told him of my future career in the service. He said if I really preferred to get a commission in the Navy he had a cousin who was a lieutenant Commander on the admiral's staff there in Charleston and he could probably get me in.

On Monday morning I met his cousin and was ushered in to meet a Captain Edward H. H. Old, in starched white uniform, rows of medals etc.

The Captain said, "Sit down Mr. Berg. I have your file here from last March. I note you graduated from the University of North Carolina."

I said "Yes, captain, I did graduate there. In fact I had a very good friend there with the same last name as yours."

"What was his name, Mr. Berg?" I replied "Bruce Old. He was a teammate with me on the Carolina freshman tennis team."

"Oh really," he replied. "Bruce is my son. We need people like you in the Navy. I understand you have signed up for a commission in the Marines. We'll cancel that and also notify your draft board in Jacksonville. You will have a temporary commission as an ensign in two weeks with orders to take training as an officer candidate for permanent commission."

In two weeks I received orders addressed to Ensign Randall C. Berg USNR (temporary).

Twenty-one years later, after five years continuous sea duty and 16 years reserve duty, I retired with full benefits as a captain.

Yes, a man can't have too many friends!

"MR. BERG IS
AN HONEST MAN!"

So read the headlines of the weekly newspaper published aboard the battleship USS Wyoming, where I had just reported aboard for duty.

I was ordered to report aboard the USS Wyoming for my first sea duty early in February 1942. Shortly afterwards the captain received a message from Admiral Alex Sharp that he would give the ship and personnel a surprise inspection the next morning. Admiral Sharp was known to be a very tough admiral throughout the fleet.

The exec called in all the division officers and instructed us how to line up our divisions topside in dress blue uniforms with pea coats (it was 30 degrees and cold) and what to say to the admiral as he approached our division. The admiral had our captain and exec accompany him.

2

With the division at stiff attention the admiral walked down in front of them and asked individual sailors certain questions like, "Who is our Secretary of the Navy?", and to another, "That is a good looking uniform you are wearing. Do you have your name printed in your pea coat?" The sailor responded, "Yes sir." The Admiral asked where it was printed and the sailor said, "Right inside, here sir," pointing to his chest.

The admiral turned to me and said, "Sir is that the proper place for the name to be?" I had never held a bag inspection of the division. I had no idea where the name should be. I said, "Admiral, I'm new in the Navy and I have no idea where that name should be." "You don't know," said the admiral. "No sir, I really don't." "What's your name again," inquired the Admiral. "Berg sir, Randall C. Berg," I replied. My captain and exec were all frowns.

The Admiral said, "Mr. Berg you are an honest man. You will make a fine naval officer. If you don't mind, find out from one of your chiefs where the name should be and join me and your Captain for coffee after the inspection is secured and advise me where the name should be." I did and had a nice welcome.

In the ship's printed weekly newspaper two days later the headlines ran "Mr. Berg is an honest man" and printed the story.

When I was ordered to transfer to a ship in the Pacific my captain gave me a 4.0 fitness report, I believe based in part, on my honesty.

"SPLASH ONE!
SPLASH TWO!"

Pre-dawn, April 4, 1945, aboard the USS Ann Arundel APA (Attack Transport #15), preparing to land, 2500 Marines right off Yon Tan airstrip, Okinawa.

Together with four other APAs and a protective destroyer division we approached our designated landing area with plans to invade Okinawa at dawn.

The destroyers plus two heavy cruisers were supposed to clear the beach with their heavy guns before our troops were supposed to climb aboard our 36 landing craft for the landing.

Troops from another APA had heavy losses in landing so we were instructed to delay our landing until the beach was secured, which was about 10 a.m.

Just after the last landing boat left the ship, a force of about 100 Kamikaze planes attacked us. Our destroyer and cruiser anti-aircraft gun crews were effective in knocking down most of the attacking planes. Over the radio came the report "Splash One," "Splash Two," "Splash Three" etc. as our ships knocked down the Jap planes.

I was anti-aircraft gunnery officer with my battle station on the bridge with the captain. We had been previously instructed not to open fire for fear we would fire into our own ships as we lowered guns to meet the low flying Kamikaze planes.

Just as we thought the attack was over one Kamikaze appeared and dove toward our ship or the heavy cruiser Birmingham anchored next to us. When it came within firing range, one of my 20-mm gun crews opened fire and hit the plane. Instead of hitting us the plane hit the Birmingham just aft of its #2 turret. As instructed I had not given the order to fire.

After the hit my captain turned to me in rage, saying I had ordered the crew to open fire without his order to me to do so. I told him I had not given the order, that the trigger happy gun crew (manned by steward mates) had done so on their own instincts.

The captain said, "Randy Berg you will get a negative fitness report for this failure to obey orders."

4

Three hours later the captain received a signal message from the admiral aboard the Birmingham. "My congratulations and well done to your gunnery officer and gun crew for hitting the Kamikaze." Everybody on the ship soon knew about the congratulatory message. The Captain said nothing to me but when he left the ship two months later on a change of  command I got a 4.0 on my fitness report with comments on how good a gunnery officer I had turned out to be.

You just never know!

Randy Berg was born in Jacksonville, Florida on January 27, 1916. He was commissioned an Ensign USNR in July 1941. He retired as Captain USNR. After World War II he returned to Jacksonville and was engaged in sales and marketing.

LIFE
IN THE PEACETIME
NAVY

Benjamin Clyde Bishop, Jr.

As I served in the peacetime Navy on the USS Columbus (CA-74), I offer my experiences as a "black shoe sailor" as a contribution from those of us who didn't have the opportunity to fly airplanes.

I had the good fortune of being selected for the Navy's ROTC Holloway Plan, which provided an engineering scholarship for my four college years at Georgia Tech. Under the terms of the Holloway Plan, we midshipmen had to commit to three summer cruises between our college years and to serve a minimum of 36 months on active duty as a regular naval officer as a requirement of the scholarship.

My freshman cruise in the summer of 1950 consisted of a voyage to Hawaii from San Francisco on the heavy cruiser, the USS St. Paul (CA-73), which was a sister ship to the Columbus. The Korean War was beginning that summer, and we helped ship's company load live ammunition at Port Chicago, which is located in the most remote area of San Francisco Bay for good reason. We sailed for Honolulu not knowing whether or not we might bypass the Hawaiian Islands and sail direct to Korea. Fortunately, we midshipmen were disembarked at Pearl Harbor and ultimately returned to the United States on the USS Saipan, which was a small aircraft carrier. The Saipan had a variety of propeller-driven aircraft consisting primarily of the A-4D, which I remember was a very large airplane with a powerful engine.

At the end of the cruise, a fellow midshipman by the name of Raymond McLeod from Albany, Georgia, and I decided to save money by hitchhiking back to Atlanta. We accomplished this in six days and met delightful people. I don't believe that it is safe to do this today!

In the summer of my sophomore year, the Navy took us to Little Creek, Virginia, to indoctrinate us in amphibious warfare and to introduce us to the Marine Corps. This included a landing with full gear and rifles in the surf from a landing craft. I really didn't appreciate the dangers involved in amphibious landings until later I visited Normandy in France. Our landing at Little Creek was a piece of cake. The landings at Normandy with the hostile weather and hostile gunfire were unbelievable.

We traveled to Pensacola, Florida, after Little Creek for naval air indoctrination and I was introduced to the SNJ. I enjoyed flying very much, and the Navy gave us flight physicals to see if we were prospective aviators. I failed to pass the hearing test, which was probably a good thing, as I am not sure I could have landed on aircraft carriers. In the summer of my junior year in 1952, we went to England and Ireland on the USS Saipan again.

Upon graduating from Georgia Tech in June 1953, I was assigned as a newly commissioned ensign to report to the USS Columbus, which was based in Boston at the Charlestown Navy Yard. This was extremely good fortune, in my opinion, as most of my fellow ensigns were assigned to ships based in Norfolk. I reported to the Columbus on June 10, 1953, and she became my home for the next 37 months.

Boston was a great homeport not only because of its culture and sports (we watched Ted Williams and Bob Cousey often), but Boston had great restaurants including Durgen Park, Lockober's, Jimmy's Harborside, Anthony's Pier Four, as well as great watering holes including the bar at the Hotel Tremont.

Immediately after reporting to the Columbus, we took a short cruise over the 4th of July to Bar Harbor, Maine. Senator Margaret Chase Smith apparently had requested a Naval ship to help celebrate the 4th. For some unknown reason, the Navy sent the Columbus rather that a smaller ship such as a destroyer. Even though the executive officer of the Columbus allowed one-third of the ship's company ashore at one time, the Bar Harbor experience was not dissimilar to the movie, Mr. Roberts. I suspect that only small ships have been invited, if any, to Bar Harbor subsequently.

We went into dry dock in the fall of 1953 in the Charlestown Navy Yard, and subsequently spent many hot months during our "shake-down" trials in Guantanamo Bay and its neighboring liberty ports. One of our liberty ports was pre-Castro Havana, which was truly a beautiful and fascinating city. Once Castro leaves, Havana should become a world-class city again.

One of my fellow junior officers during our monotonous days in Guantanamo Bay decided that a constructive idea would be to solicit the assistance of all his fellow officers to purchase as much Scotch as possible at $1.00 per bottle of Johnny Walker and to carry and store it aboard the ship. His idea was to have a huge party for crew and anyone else upon his discharge some 12 months hence. Everyone cooperated, none of us were put in the brig, and I understand that he had one heckuva party as I missed it.

We sailed for the Mediterranean in September 1954 to become the flagship for the Sixth Fleet. The admiral was Admiral "Thirty-One Knot" Arleigh Burke, who needs no introduction. We were based in Ville Franche when we were not launching aircraft at 31 knots, and in between we toured the Mediterranean. When we were in Oran , Algeria, I received a message that my father had passed away and I was granted emergency leave to return to the United States. Upon my return to the ship, I was ordered to catch a MATS plane out of Westover Field, Massachusetts, which I did. I returned to the ship in Naples, and the officer of the deck looked at me when I reported back with the comment, "We thought you were dead." It turned out that the plane from Pax River crashed with no survivors.

We returned to Boston in the spring of 1955, and the ship received orders to be assigned to the Pacific Fleet with a new homeport of Long Beach, California. We sailed for

Long Beach, went through the Panama Canal, and took a side trip to Lima, Peru, to "fly the flag." We played golf at the Lima Golf and Country Club where the weather was so dry they flooded the golf course every Monday to provide water for the fairway and greens.

When we arrived in Long Beach, we were greeted by Hollywood starlets, including Linda Crystal, who was married to Tyrone Power. As Bob Hope often said, "The ladies were there to show us what we were fighting for."

We sailed to Yokusaka, Japan, by way of Pearl Harbor in January 1953, and over the next sixth months, we visited Bangkok, Manila, Sasebo, Singapore, Kuala, Lumpur, and last but not least, Zamboanga, which is located in Mindanao in the Philippine Islands. One of my favorite 35MM slides is a picture of our golf foursome standing in front of "The Zamboanga Golf and Cock Fighting Club" with a small sign suggesting that golfers may search for golf balls that have been hit out of the fairway at their own personal risk.

One very dark night when we were steaming with the Seventh Fleet, including two large aircraft carriers, in the South China Sea off the coast of Taiwan, the task force commander for training purposes imposed wartime communications procedures on the Task Force such that radio messages were transmitted and executions were given without the normal acknowledgements from each ship in the Task Force. When the signal was given to turn into the wind to launch aircraft, every ship executed smartly with the exception of one destroyer. That destroyer failed to receive the signal and maintained its prior heading. This sequence of events put the destroyer directly in the path of the Columbus, and our OD and the captain had only a few moments to take corrective action. We hit the destroyer at 30 knots just forward of its number one five-inch gun turret, and the collision sliced off the bow of the destroyer. Ten men on the destroyer drowned. A good friend of mine, who was OD, received a reprimand and he resigned from the Navy. I'll always remember that I could have had the deck watch that night.

The Columbus is now scrap iron, but its memories endure. The flag quarters on the Columbus had a trophy case for the ship's silver, which had been transferred to the Columbus from the USS Tennessee, which was one of the battleships sunk at Pearl Harbor. I do not know where the Tennessee's silver is today.

Thanks to the men and women who won WWII and the Korean War, I and many others enjoyed the peace-time Navy. I met great people and I saw most of the civilized world. I learned about the virtues of leadership, responsibility and discipline.

The draft was in effect during the 1950's, and there is simply no dispute that its effect on the character of America's youth was positive in every way. Not only did the draft serve its primary purpose to provide trained reserves for the military, it provided an environment of discipline and responsibility that simply is not available in today's lifestyle. Military service allowed young people to meet their contemporaries from all over the country, and it inculcated in them a strong sense of patriotism. As a result, the service men and women of  the 1950's were far better qualified as citizens, workers, students, and parents than those who were products of the 1960's and later years.

It would be a good thing if Congress would reinstate the draft.

Ben Bishop was born in Greenville, South Carolina, November 30, 1931, and moved to Jacksonville, Florida in 1972. He has been a successful investment banker for over 30 years and has been president of Allen C. Ewing & Co. for that period of time. He is married to Starke Hagood Bishop, has three children, and four grandchildren.

THE BEGINNING
OF THE WAR-
1942 IN THE ATLANTIC

Farris Bryant

My first assignment in the Navy after joining in early 1942 was to proceed to Galveston and accept from the Port Authority the command of 27 young sailors who knew even less that I about what we were doing. It was our duty to repel any German attack on our ship by firing the armaments that we had aboard our ship.

We joined the company of the Paul Harlow, an oil tanker, under the command of a Norwegian who was in command of the ship in addition to having a responsibility for his wife who was going to make the voyage with us. We left Galveston almost immediately for Aruba where we took on a load of oil to be delivered to Bristol, England. As we crossed the Gulf, we had no particular security for the ship but relied upon the Navy to advise us if submarines were in the vicinity. After loading at Aruba, we headed northeasterly to go around the southern tip of Cuba. On that course we could expect German submarines as we headed north towards our destination of New York harbor. Our course set for us was close along the eastern boundary of the United States, which was populated with many submarines.

I did not know it at the time but my wife and our baby were housed in Daytona where she could see the ships that were attacked by the German subs explode and burn. I learned later that was a tense post, which she had not realized she would fall into. The submarines lying off the coast of Florida would attack at night when the lights of the shore would make for the German subs an easy target.

We zigzagged up the coast to Carolina and had no unfortunate accidents along the way but we realized that we were in increasingly dangerous territory and most of the crew did not mind standing watch for long hours to give us the best protection we could have. We arrived in New York and under orders reported to the commodore of the convoy that we were to join to go to England.

After several days of waiting for the convoy to fill up, we found we had been assigned a position on the port quarter of the commodore's ship. At this point we could still rely to some extent upon the naval air vessels, which tried to keep the commodore advised of the location of any of the wolf pack that might be there.

Not far short of Iceland and Greenland, the submarines became evident and we were on alert. The guns of the ship consisted of a five-inch cannon and a three and one-half inch cannon which had to be manned in full alert until the commodore signaled that the danger was passed, if that happened. It didn't happen. The German subs were very aggressive and were determined that oil should not arrive in England and at an early date the Germans found their targets and several ships were destroyed. Under the rules of engagement, we could not stop to assist anyone who might have been subject to attack because our duty was to get the oil to England not to try to defend the ships in the convoy, which were about 40 in number. The subs at night were extremely difficult to see with the best glasses we had so that our first notice of the subs whereabouts would be when one of their targets were struck by their torpedoes and the ship began to go down.

All crew members and I were heavily dressed for stormy weather and 40-foot waves which were normal for the North Atlantic at that time of year, but we all knew that the clothing and the life boats that we had prepared to throw over when needed would not be of much use in that weather. I don't remember how many ships went down in our convoy, but it was several and it was a terrible sight to see your shipmates on other ships flame and disappear.

That was the nature of our travel and each trip across the Atlantic until we came to almost Ireland where we came under the protection of British aircraft and sailed on to Bristol where we unloaded our oil.

THE MED AND
THE PACIFIC
1943 – 1945

After we unloaded, I was detached from the Paul Harlow oil tanker and was assigned to a liberty ship, which headed for the Mediterranean Sea and the North African coast. We were under German attack two or three times but we anchored in North African waters. We then discovered that we had supplies for the attack on Salerno on the coast of Italy. We had no combat battle assignment but lay passively so that our military supplies could be utilized by the armed forces. I don't recall how we left there. That was my last armed guard duty. My next order was for an assignment to Comdespac (Command of Destroyers, Pacific).

Late in 1943, I was assigned to the Pacific Command Office in Hawaii for further duty as an antisubmarine officer. I found in Hawaii a number of my friends of earlier assignments and was assured by my friends that if war ended shortly, I would be one of the first people recalled from that duty. That was a laugh. I was assigned to Guam Naval Station to command a school to instruct the officers of destroyers, most of whom had been in the Navy some time but had not been exposed while on the Pacific coast to any significant warfare.

I proceeded to Guam and established a school for the teaching of antisubmarine warfare to the Pacific officers. That involved establishing quarters in Quonset huts and having the officers in training join one or two destroyers or destroyer escorts in leaving Guam at four in the morning in pursuit of some friendly subs that we needed to organize the Pacific antisubmarine effort. We went through the nets behind the subs and gave the subs a head start. Then we would continue firing dumb weapons and close the nets

14

behind us as we chased the friendly subs. As the European war slowed down, the German subs moved to the Pacific and the training of officers in our school quickly increased. That went on for one year and a half with different levels of intensity until the war ended.

I waited for a telephone call from my friends in Hawaii and, not getting it, I called to arouse them. They had already gone home. I went to see the commanding officer on the island to explain to him that I had planned a political career immediately after the war and I had to get home to pursue it. That apparently was persuasive to the vice admiral, who was probably an Annapolis man, that the Navy needed this politically oriented officer more in the Congress than they needed him in the Pacific. The next morning I was on a ship for Mobile and was discharged from the Navy on January 1, 1946.

All the above is to the best of my knowledge and remembrance.

Farris Bryant was born in Ocala, Florida on July 26, 1914. He grew up in Ocala and he was Governor of Florida, 1961-1965.

MY LIFE
AS A NAVAL
AVIATOR

William Shuler Burns

This is William Shuler Burns the First speaking. Your dad told me about your telephone conversation last night and now I'm going to undertake to weave a story from which you may be able to garner the facts that you need to write your report on the history of World War II.

First of all, let's start with a little background. Think first of Junes. Junes were very important in my life and my directions when I was a young man. In 1938 in June, I graduated from Washington & Lee with an AB degree. In June of 1939, I took and passed the Virginia Bar and thus became a young lawyer at age 21. In June of 1940, I graduated from Washington & Lee Law School and I'm now ready to practice law in the normal world.

I did not wind up practicing law in a normal way, however, because in June of 1941 I reported to the Naval Air Station at Anacostia, Washington, D.C., to go into training to be a Navy flyer. During all those years from 1938 to 41, the war in Europe was growing and growing and it became obvious to me that our participation in it was not only necessary but it was becoming inevitable. For that reason, I put aside any current thoughts of normal life and decided to pick the place I wanted to be during a wartime experience.

Now, back to Anacostia in June of 1941. At this point, Anacostia was what they called an elimination base. That meant that applicants to be Navy flyers went there to determine whether they were qualified to go on with some Navy flight training. The requirements, very basically, were that you had to have a college degree to apply, you had to be just about perfect physically and pass an exam to prove it, and then you had to be able to solo a training plane and demonstrate that you had the aptitude for further training and investment by the Navy in making you a full-fledged wearer of the golden wings.

As history will establish, I did make the cut at Anacostia. I soloed a plane. I took my first airplane ride there--I'd never been up before--and eight hours later I soloed a training plane out of the Anacostia Naval Air Station.

I then got my orders to Jacksonville, Florida, Naval Air Station for further training as a naval aviation cadet. That training was comprised of four chapters. There was the primary phase where we flew the same type planes we had at Anacostia. There was a basic phase where we were introduced into bigger, faster planes more like we would have in operations. There was the instrument phase in which we had to learn to fly under the hood, blind, using instruments only. And then there was the final squadron phase, which in my case was done in PBY's, the big sea planes, off the St. Johns River right out in front of this apartment.

I started this training the first of August 1941 and was well along in it at the time of Pearl Harbor, at which time we were all ordered into uniform for the duration and the training became a very serious matter. I went on and received my wings fairly early in 1942 and, to my surprise, received orders to come back to Jacksonville as an instructor in the primary phase of training. The three air stations at Jacksonville -- which were the Mainside Station at Navy Jax, Cecil Field and Lee Field -- were all involved in training pilots before they got their wings at that time. They were programmed and beginning to switch over by stopping this kind of training and concentrating only on operational training for pilots that had already gotten their wings and were being prepared for special assignment in the Fleet. As a result of this, I taught primary at Lee Field first until we phased it out; I taught primary at Cecil Field until we phased it out, and then I taught instrument flying at Mainside until phased it out.

At that point, I received orders along with eight other naval aviators, who happened to be junior to me by a few weeks, to go to Miami for special training in torpedo planes and tactics. We went to Miami and were introduced to the old TBD, the torpedo bomber made by Douglas, and received some instructions in tactics. Mainly, however, we were on our own, and I and my eight friends flew the required amount of hours in the old TBD to have said to have completed the course. I can remember especially that we were down thee on Christmas Eve night because we were flying over Miami, which although it was blacked out, shown brightly under a full moon.

After leaving Miami, we went to Fort Lauderdale to receive the first TBF's, the new torpedo plane, that were being delivered to our Navy. There were two English flyers there because they had used them a little bit before and they were there primarily to check us out and show us what the instruments all meant and that sort of thing. We repeated our tactical hours at Fort Lauderdale in the new plane and then returned to Jacksonville as instructors for operational training classes that were going to come through the Naval Air Station. The students in these classes were anywhere from newly graduated ensigns with bright new wings to full Commanders who had come from desk jobs or whatever else. We were the teachers, and I had maybe a dozen classes of 12 to a class over the period that I remained in Jacksonville.

Finally, in August or early September of that year, 1943, I received orders to the Fleet. I wound up at Westerly, Rhode Island, where Torpedo Squadron 15 was being formed. Elsewhere on the Atlantic Coast, the other squadrons of Air Group 15, the fighter squadron and the dive-bombing squadron, were being formed.

At Westerly, a number of important things happened. My aircrew, my gunner and my radioman, were assigned to me and they were with me for the duration of my experience in Torpedo 15. Also, my wingman and the rest of my section, four planes in all, became permanently assigned to me. Most important, I met your grandmother and that turned out to be sort of important for you, too.

We wound up our training at Westerly somewhere before Thanksgiving of that year and went down into the Norfolk area to await a carrier to go to the Pacific. We finally got our carrier and took it out on a shakedown cruise off of Bermuda in the Atlantic in January of 44. From there, we went through the Panama Canal and out to the Hawaiian Islands, where we transferred again to the island of Maui, and waited on our final assignment, which developed to be the carrier Essex. The Essex was the carrier that we went into combat with.

I think it may be of interest at this time to know that the Essex was a CVL-type carrier and it was the name of the class of that type carrier that was in the Fleet at the time I was out there. There were eight such carriers in the Fleet and there were eight other carriers of the Princeton class, which were CVL's or converted cruisers. The difference lay in the size and complement of those ships. On the Essex we had 90 planes and on the other carriers there were 60, as I recall.

The Essex air group, Air Group 15, had 18 torpedo planes, 36 dive-bombers, and 36 fighters. The torpedo planes were originally made by Grumman, although as the war heated up, General Motors took those plans and turned out an identical clone, which we used a lot of, also. Grumman also made the fighter plane that we had. It was an F-6, while the dive-bomber was made by Curtiss, an SB2C.

Also, it may be of interest to know that the Fleet to which we were attached was sometimes called the 3rd Fleet, and sometimes called the 5th Fleet, depending on whether Admiral Spruance or Admiral Halsey was in over-all command, which they exercised from the battleship New Jersey, which was in my task group.

There were four carrier battle groups, each with two Essex-type carriers and two Princeton-type carriers. Each had two battleships, four cruisers, and I believe 24 destroyers. It was a very big operation. The format or general plan that was exercised as we began our assault and attack mission in the Pacific was one where three of those battle groups would be on the line while the fourth was back meeting supply ships like the oilers, the ammunition ships, and the baby flattops, which would bring in replacement planes and replacement pilots, which unfortunately we needed quite a few of as the war progressed.

When we began our advance, you have to remember that our Navy had been on the defensive pretty much. The Japanese were on the offensive up until the Battle of Midway. That corner had been successfully turned before I got out there and so we were beginning to take back the territories and islands and so forth that were lost earlier in the war. Our attacks and our missions included names like Saipan, Tinian, Guam, Palau, Mindanao, Cebu, Leyte, Luzon, Iwo Jima, Formosa, Okinawa, and I'm sure I've left out a few.

I only had occasion to carry a torpedo one time and that occasion was detailed in the letter that was sent to you in the last few weeks.

Our general mission, the way it worked out, was bombing. We were going into islands like Saipan for the first time and we were able to catch their planes on the ground. I recall that on the first strike in Saipan I led a group of torpedo planes, each loaded with a dozen 100-pound bombs, which we could drop in a stick along the runways where the parked planes of the Japanese were. When you take eight torpedo planes and drop 12 bombs apiece on a flight line, you can bet your Betsy that none of those planes flew anymore during World War II. A more unusual load for us was four 500-pound bombs with delayed-action fuses. These were used on shipping other than the heavy ships of the Japanese Navy. Oilers or troop ships or something of that nature were very susceptible to the skip-bombing operation with 500-pound bombs. That was fairly rare opportunity, too, as we were mainly knocking out airfields, putting airplanes out of commission, and that sort of thing.

Last week, my gunner came by to visit me and reminded me that we had flown 39 missions together in the Pacific. These began, oh, I would say March of 1944, and by November 1944 our relief squadrons came aboard the Essex and we returned home on the Bunker Hill, which was an Essex-type carrier, but it had been banged up pretty much by the kamikaze, the Japanese suicide planes, and had to go back for refurbishing. In any event, we got back to the states and I made it home for Christmas.

My next assignment was, as I had requested, to form a new group, again on the Atlantic Coast. I was assigned to Torpedo Squadron 151 in Boston. We repeated the same program as we had in Westerly a couple of years before. Everything was finally in readiness and we moved the squadron to the Pacific Coast in preparation for going aboard another carrier and going back to the Pacific. It was about the time we were to go aboard our new carrier when the bombs were dropped on Hiroshima and the Japanese quickly surrendered.

With all the time and all the points that I had for my medals and so forth , I had the privilege to go on inactive service immediately and I took that privilege for a number of reasons. I wanted to get back to civilian life but, most important, your grandmother was seven months' pregnant with your father and I wanted to get her home to her doctor so that your dad could be born where we wanted him to be born.

Well, to make a long story short, we made it home again. And during this whole time--and I guess I missed telling this part -- but some of my efforts were rewarded by things like the Navy Cross, Distinguished Flying Cross, seven air medals, and a lot more unit citations and things of that nature. My Navy experience was a valuable one to me. I rate it along with my college experience as being high points in my past that I now can look back on with pleasure.

And I think I made an important point there, William. When you reach my age and the future is getting shorter and shorter, the past becomes more and more important. And it's been very heartening to me to be able to look back at my past with some sense of accomplishment in school where I was entered in the Law Review, in the Navy where I had played a fairly prominent role, and in business where hard work paid off, and we made it to retirement and here we are looking back the way someday I hope you'll look back. But stay in there, old buddy, and keep it rolling so you can.

THE TURNING POINT
IN THE PACIFIC

Perhaps the best way to evaluate the effect which the Second Battle of the Philippines Sea had upon the course of the Pacific War, and therefore upon the course of American history, would be by using a before and after example.

Before the Second Battle of the Philippines Sea, the imperial Japanese Navy was intact. It, therefore, had to be reckoned with as a potentially effective force against which our Pacific strategy had to provide. After the Second Battle of the Philippines Sea, the Japanese Navy had been reduced to ineffectiveness and impotency. It was no longer a major factor to be reckoned with in our conduct of the Pacific campaign.

Our landings on Leyte were most certainly a part of the construction of our "island highway" toward Japan. We had followed the system methodically, taking some Japanese-held islands and bypassing, and therefore neutralizing, others. Our landings on Leyte were certainly not conceived with the single thought of luring the Japanese Navy into action. This was, however, the incidental effect of those landings.

From June 20 to October 20, 1944, the Japanese fleet remained in ports from Japan to Singapore, and much advantage was taken of this time for repairs and general battle readiness preparations.

During the First Battle of the Philippines Sea, the Japanese Navy launched from its carriers the best of its naval air force. This was done from extreme range and the fleet then retreated. Those planes which survived the now famous Mariana "turkey shoot" went on to Guam to Japanese bases there. While we did not make contact with the Japanese fleet during this operation, we certainly skimmed the cream from the top of the Japanese naval air force.

Leyte was evidently the point at which the Japanese were willing to risk their fleet by committing the entire force to action. Much of what went on in the Second Battle of the Philippines Sea I only know through the inexhaustible scuttlebutt which somehow gets around in the navy. Studies of the history of the battle will point out everything in much greater detail. The part that I do know first-hand is the part that the Third Fleet played in general; our Task Group in a little more detail;, the U.S.S. Essex air craft carrier in particular, and Torpedo Squadron 15 in detail.

The Third Fleet under the command of Admiral Halsey was composed of four task groups. Admiral Fredrick A. Sherman was in command of my task group and his flagship was the Essex, my carrier. Task groups were built around four aircraft carriers each. After the landings in Leyte on October 20, 1944, which we had covered, we ranged north while Admiral Kincaid's Seventh Fleet took over close support of the landing operations. At this time, as I learned later, three enemy naval forces were approaching Leyte Gulf from three directions. The one that I was introduced to personally was the strong central force coming east through the Sibuyan Sea. It originally included five of the Japan's biggest, most modern battleships, eight cruisers and 15 destroyers. It was to come through San Bernardino Straits and turn south to attack the Seventh Fleet off Samar and Leyte.

From the south the Japanese World War I navy was coming from the Sulu Sea toward the Leyte Gulf. Without the Third Fleet in attendance, Admiral Kincaid was reduced to our older ships and a complement of Kaiser carriers or "baby flat tops" as we called them. Their disadvantage lay in their slow speed and light armament.

On the morning of October 24, I took off from the Essex and made the usual right, then left turn to clear the deck of my slip-stream. As I did I could see the aircraft carrier Princeton just off the port quarter. At that very moment I saw a Japanese suicide plane dive into the Princeton. A huge cloud of black smoke made it clear that the ship was in trouble. To say the least, this was not a very encouraging start. We proceeded to rendezvous our group and headed westward on a scouting mission, 16 torpedo planes supported by perhaps a dozen dive-bombers and a dozen fighters. We were loaded with torpedoes. The depth setting of the torpedoes in the division which I led were calculated for maximum vulnerability for a heavy Japanese cruiser. The other 12 torpedo planes were loaded for battleships. We were just at the point of "must return" fuel-wise, when we spotted the central force of the Japanese navy.

Because of a narrow channel through the Sibuyan Sea, the Japanese fleet was drawn into a very tight formation and was unable to take the evasive action normal against a torpedo attack. While this gave us targets that were easier to hit, it also had the effect of concentrating the firepower of all of those ships in one relatively small area. I sincerely believe that the time has yet to come when any group will face the total firepower that opposed us on our torpedo runs that day.

The Musashi and Yamato, with their 17.7-inch guns, the largest naval guns then afloat, were firing everything they had at us including those big guns. I can remember the sound of shrapnel ticking against the wings and fuselage of my plane. I never made an attack against the enemy that I did not feel a tightness in the throat and have an empty feeling in the pit of my stomach. This time was different. There was a feeling of hopelessness attached to this one and hopefulness that we could at least launch our torpedo first.

Our attack was successful. There were many hits; mine was on the lead cruiser. I don't remember what our losses were exactly. I do remember that of the four planes which I led in an attack on their starboard bow, two were shot down. I can also remember after dropping my torpedo, that I followed a line of retirement, which I had decided upon previously, while watching the Japanese attack against our fleet.

I stayed low and retired in the same direction the enemy was headed, changing altitude and direction in a jinxing pattern. There were geysers of water all about me but my plane was unharmed and was flyable the next day.

Upon return to the Essex, we found the Task Group still under Japanese air attack but they took us aboard any way. I was no sooner out of my plane than I was called to report to Admiral Sherman's station at Flagplot. It was the only time I ever talked with Admiral Sherman. I remember he was very pleasant and calm about the whole thing. As requested, I gave my estimate of the strength and composition of the central force. In reply to his direct question, I stated flatly that I though the force was heading for the San Bernardino straits and that I did not believe that we had been able to cause sufficient damage to deter the force from its determined objective.

I do not wish to be yet another voice in the much publicized argument over the decision Admiral Halsey made a short time later to leave the area with the Third Fleet and go to meet the Japanese carrier force which was coming in on the north. The essence of my report, however, obviously did not effect his evaluation of the tactical situation.

We had a comparatively easy day the next day against the Japanese carriers.

In spite of the fact that our Seventh Fleet had a close call when it came in contact with the Japanese central force on October 25, this did not alter the course of the battle and, therefore, did not alter the course of the war and American history. This also renders Admiral Halsey's decision interesting only from a tactical standpoint.

DEO-DÉCOR

Where did God get that
Color of green
When He did the grass
And the forest scene
For his springtimes, His Young
His "Beginnings" theme.

And, where did He get that
Color of gold
Which He saves for His autumns
And reserves for His old
For the beautiful endings
Of stories long told.

And most, where did God get that
Color of blue
When he fashioned the sky
In so breathless a hue
A window of Heaven
Each may seek to look through.

I mused as I looked
And I wondered aloud
On a face that was formed
In a wandering cloud
It was there. Now it's gone
(At least, gone from my sight)
But, where did He get
That color -- of white.

PRINCE PELICAN

In flights of two
To flights of dozens
These aristocratic creature cousins
Soar in review
That all may see
Their coastline claim to royalty.

In echelon, precision spacing
Each one attuned to leaders pacing
Their grace so effortless, untrying
These masters of formation flying
Slip to a line, then to a "V"
And turn their squadron out to sea.

Now back to line in one smooth motion
They drop to skim the crest of ocean
Too close to measure, bird to tide,
In seemingly an endless glide
Til' on command their wings as one
Propel them upward in the sun.

Then diving headlong to the sea
They crash and splash in obvious glee
And feed and float, and look to say
"It's easy...we're designed this way."

They were "designed" to complement
And cope with their environment
In such detail...in such dimension
To strain, then pass my comprehension
I sit in silent awe and ponder
The whats, the hows, the whys....
The wonder.

William Shuler Burns was born in Lebanon, Virginia on August 30, 1917. He died in Jacksonville, Florida on March 20, 1999.

SANDBLOWER

William Carrier, Jr.

Captain Bill Carrier (then Cdr.) C.O. of VA-85 aboard USS Forrestal, 100 miles East of Cape Hatteras approximately 0500, 2 May 1961 launches with his wingman, Lt. Jack Fellowes, into stormy predawn weather. He is carrying a "shape" on his trusty AD-6 (BV #139672) and is to simulate an actual delivery mission called for by Cold War Doctrine. He is wearing his infamous "poopy" suit and has been wearing it for two hours prior to launch due to launch delays. His provisions are on soggy bologna sandwich and one canteen of water. The two "Spads" go "fleet dry" over Cape Hatteras just at dawn (appropriately near Kitty Hawk, N.C.) where they split and go their separate routes.

Carrier's target is the Deep Creek Lake Dam in extreme Western Maryland. He arrives at the target within plus or minus 30 seconds, as required, and performs his labs maneuver, having navigated a sinuous route at tree-top level across North Carolina, Virginia, the hills and "hollers" of West Virginia and Western Maryland. From the target, he proceeded down the spine of the Appalachians and Smokies to Northern Georgia and reverses directions back to N.A.S. Norfolk where he lands, taxis to FAETU to have the "ship" returned to storage, never shutting down the engine. He takes off for the ship cruising in the operating area.

As he approaches Forrestal, approximately 1710, he requests recovery at the tail end of recovery in progress. Signal "Dog for 45 minutes." (Inconvenient for flight Deck Officer to accept one more aircraft!) He lands aboard approximately 1800, 12.9 hours after launch. Tim in "poopy" suit 15 hours. Perspiration in suit boots up to top of ankles.

This mission was a testament to the durability of the human mind and body, to the fantastic design of the AD-6's and to the magnificent crews who maintained them. P.S. The officer with back turned in the picture of Jim Reid's spring article is Cdr. N.O. Scott, one of the many top-notch officers in VA-85 at that time. (Not the least of which was LTJG "Zip" Rausa.)

Captain Carrier was born in Indianapolis, Indiana on November 21, 1921. He is a graduate of the U.S. Navy Academy. He had 152 Carrier landings; 4,500 flying hours and flew 42 aircraft types. He and Grace live in Orange Park, Florida.

SUB HUNTING
IN THE
NORTH ATLANTIC

Ewing Carruthers, Jr.

My name is Ewing Carruthers Jr., date of birth March 14, 1917, born and raised in Memphis, went in the Navy July 22, 1942, and processed out January 8, 1946.

I was in VPB 201 the entire time. I was the Reserve Squadron VPB727 for eight years, based at NAS Memphis, flying everything they had on the field that had two engines and some SNJs in addition. The most exacting one was the PV2 that had those wonderful Pratt Whitney 2500 horsepower engines in it. To get to 110 Kts to get us off the ground in the summer time, you had to roll off the end of the runway. Once they got up, the engines made a lot of airplane.

An amusing story took place in the middle of March 1943 in the North Atlantic and it was cold as the devil. We had alert duty number two. When Carl Ahee's crew got the call about 11 o'clock at night, he took off and headed northeast about 600 miles up to the shipping lane from a direct course, England to Norfolk, through iceberg country. A destroyer had its bow blown off by a sub in the English Channel and the English people had shored it up with heavy timbers, etc., so the ship could make about eight knots maximum cruising.

They were going to take the ship back to Norfolk to rebuild the bow. Every one of those sailors on that skeleton crew should have been given a Medal of Honor for being on that ship. If a sub came close, saliors could have been picked off with a .22 rifle!

Since the ship was outside the British Coastal Command, we were told to go up and give the ship some coverage and be there for dawn to come. Carl Ahee and his crew got the first run.

About 3 a.m. they decided the weather was stinking and the ship would be in danger after the critical time of dawn as far as subs were concerned. So we were told to get going. As you may know, alert duty meant that you had to be briefed, warmed up, crew aboard, etc., in 30 minutes. We made it and took off.

As dawn broke, we actually found the ship and Carl. I mean that literally, because with an overcast sky in the North Atlantic in March, it is black as I have ever seen anything black. It was great to have some good radar. With radio silence and no navigational aids, what it really took was luck.

When we got there, Carl was doing a close search about 10 miles ahead of the poor destroyer, that was being pounded in swells 30 or 40 feet high. Every other minute the waves and swells were going over the bow. I do not think the ship was making more than five or six knots at best. It just broke your heart to see their position and be glad you were not on board!

When we got there, communicated by an Aldus light, Carl being the first on the scene was the senior man proceeded to do a slow search north of the destroyer's course. I did one south, going out and back, so that a sub could not possibly get in position for a good shot at the destroyer.

This went on for awhile. We were running around just below the cloud ceiling, around 1,000 feet. We began to feel better because the haze of dawn was over and we were just sitting there going about our job.

Carl then picked up the mike and broke the radio silence to tell me he had a conning tower on his radar, right in front of the projected course of the ship. When I turned around that way, I picked it up, too.

We were both excited and both crews went to battle stations. When we did that, the radioman on Carl's plane sent out a three-letter identifying message. It indicated to

Norfolk, Bermuda, Washington, London and everywhere that we were at battle stations, about to make an attack on a sub.

In gambit number one, Carl was to come in right at the base of the clouds, on instruments and radar, then break out of the clouds and jump down on the sub with depth charges dropped in a stick. This involved three depth charges, 100 feet apart, with the hope of straddling the sub and crushing the hull.

My job was to continue a big search to keep another sub out of the way. There we were, barely breathing, and the first time I had ever been in battle stations. My heart was really pounding.

We waited and watched the radar with that target down there. We knew where he was. When Carl started his dive, the radioman put the key down. The routine was to hold it down until you called it off or were killed so they would know what was happening all over the Atlantic Command.

We waited for what seemed like half an hour, but it was just a few minutes. Then Carl called, furious as the devil and said, "The damn thing went down under water and we have lost contact. Now it was our turn to make the attack and let him continue the search we had been making.

We were pretty excited and envisioned a DFC, 31 days leave and a lot of fun and games.

We cleared the guns and proceeded with our assignment, to stay in the clouds, get in proper position, then make a dive on the sub. There it was on the radar again on the surface. I had it on my radar and on the big radar, as well as my remote at my knee, and so did Carl. You can understand we were furious and excited at the same time!!! We were going to get him this time!

We got in position and were doing our job right. Everybody was on the ball, the guns were cleared, the bow turret was instructed not to shoot at the sub, but into the water in front as they had been trained. The job was not to kill people on the sub; it was to distract them from killing

33

me. If I am killed that will kill us all. That was the communication so we were ready to go. Down we went out of the clouds right on the radar target. Just as we cleared the clouds the target disappeared.

You can be sure we were really frustrated and excited. We pulled back up into the clouds and told Carl we had the same experience he had. By the time we flew around five to ten minutes more, there again comes this target on radar. We felt like absolute imbeciles because that German skipper was making a nut out of us both. If we did not get him, and he was only about eight nautical miles from the destroyer, he was going to get that destroyer and we would be disgraced.

It was now Carl's turn again and he proceeded with his procedure. He went into the clouds, got ready in position and started diving down. The radio key was down indicating he was attacking. With that, Carl called on the radio and said, "Carruthers, you will not believe it. Come over here and see what I have."

I asked "What are you talking about?" He said, "Just come on over."

We flew over there. We dived down and there was the target. What would you guess the target was? A great big fat mother whale with a baby flopping around. It gave exactly the same target on the radar that the Conning Tower on a sub would give.

Needless to say, we did not get any DFC, we did not get 31 days of leave and we were not heroes. But the ship got back to Norfolk unharmed, so that was reward enough.

Carl was running very low on fuel after we looked at the whole and he had to return to base before he ran out of gas. I stayed two to three more hours protecting the sub during the late morning, then started home.

Remember now, we had not seen the sun or had any direction but dead reckoning, for 600 miles. We did the best we could, but nothing worked out.

Frankly, as the afternoon wore on, I was getting ready mentally to prepare to ditch. The crew was getting nervous, because our DR and wind drift every 15 minutes were telling us we had a ground speed about 100 Kts not 145!

We finally found the signal that Bermuda sent out on the hour for one minute. We figured that we were on track by that complicated directional radio deal that was on the overhead. We figured we were on course, but could not figure out why we were not getting back. We were getting low on gas, too.

We finally got to where we could get a message, and found out we had a 50-knot wind that we had not been able to predict and could not do it by drift sights. We were now on top of the clouds, trying to get a sun line. We finally got home because there was one tank up in the nose that was not supposed to be used. We thought we were going to run out of gas, but the flight engineer confessed that he always kept 125 gallons in that tank even though that was illegal. He figured it was for "wife and family."

You can be certain I did not put him on report for breaking squadron regulations. That 125 gallons sure made a big difference.

"YOU CAN'T BEAT
A LITTLE
GOOD FORTUNE"

Arthur Ralph Chambers

Life on an aircraft carrier during an all-out war can be very exciting but can also be very dull at times. My personal observations and experiences as a fighter pilot on the Yorktown taught me many things not acquired in university classes or textbooks. Even today, I reflect back on events that have shaped my life, and some of these are recorded here.

One event that I recall was an approach to land on the carrier. The landing was controlled by the LSO (Landing Signal Officer). He would hold the paddles and extend his arms to indicate whether your approach was too high \O/, or too low /O\. A cut (cut off power completely) was mandatory! This was indicated by the LSO bringing one paddle up across his chest.

When I received the "cut" signal, I cut off the power as required. Unfortunately, my Hellcat fighter was a little too "low." I hit the aft end of the ship and my plane broke in two just behind the cockpit. In a matter of a split second, my plane became a helicopter as the tail separated and I slid up the deck! I may be the only naval aviator to taxi up to the first arresting cable! It's rather funny now, but it could have been disastrous.

Now the rest of the story. The LSO realized his mistake and "cut" the next plane about 40 feet too high. When he hit the deck his landing was so hard the tires burst and the wheels came up around his ears, I think. Needless to say, we acquired a new signal officer.

Many people think of aerial combat in World War II as being the most dangerous or death defying thing we encountered. While it was no Sunday picnic, most of our losses were due to bombing or strafing runs on enemy ships or land bases. Antiaircraft fire in some places was so intense; I often wonder how any of us survived. Maybe it was due to the tactics we used.

High altitude was our ally. We learned to fly over an enemy airfield high and watch for flashes from the antiaircraft guns on the ground. Then we would push over as a group and strafe one single antiaircraft placement with four or eight fighters, each one with six 50-caliber machine guns blazing. Needless to say, the hail of bullets on one placement would knock it out. After regrouping, we would do the same procedure on the next "victim" at another corner of the airfield.

With no further resistance from antiaircraft fire, we then would strafe aircraft on the field or anything else we felt like blasting. On one occasion we wound up flying so low across the field, we were shooting into the windows of the barracks. People were jumping out of the windows as we flew by. We were able to destroy some enemy planes in the hangars before they could get them airborne.

We also used the weather to our advantage along with the element of surprise. One morning, at dawn, after a snowfall during the night, we attacked a military base in Japan. The snow had blanketed the entire base and the runways, being covered, were difficult to find. As a result, their planes were taking off in every direction in mass confusion. You can imagine how easy it was to follow tracks in the snow and shoot down a plane about the time he left the ground and got his landing gear up.

Naturally, we lost planes in this type of warfare but most of our losses were operational. Landing or taking off a carrier is hazardous. Fifty years ago we had no satellites to give us a weather forecast. Sometimes the conditions would change while we were airborne, but we could only stay in the air just so long, with no alternate airfield to fly to. This made it hazardous to land if the weather had worsened.

Landing after dark was a real thrill, since we were in a war zone and no lights were permissible. The only aids were four or five smudge pots on each side of the deck that could be seen only from the rear of the carrier. The LSO (Landing Signal Officer) would use neon lighted wands instead of paddles to guide us in.

As I have mentioned, no satellite information was available and we were constantly on the lookout for enemy warships or shipping. One way to locate these was to fly "search patrols." These patrols consisted of two aircraft -- one fighter and one bomber -- flying out 400 hundred miles together, then flying a short cross leg (usually 40 or 50 miles) and returning to the carrier. Each of the two flew a slightly different heading, thus enabling us to search an area between 800 to 1,000 miles from the carrier.

Navigation was extremely important in flying such a mission. Since we were airborne around six hours, the carrier had traveled some 80 to 100 miles from the spot where we took off. Our only navigational aids were a plotting board, a clock, and an airspeed indicator. By keeping track of the time and airspeed, we could estimate our position and that of the carrier. Of course, in six hours the wind direction could change and this would affect our course and position.

In order to fly out and search as large an area a possible, the planes were equipped with a droppable, or disposable, belly tank. These were strapped underneath the fuselage and when all the fuel was depleted, a tug on a "toggle wire" would jettison the tank. This meant that all the fuel to return to the carrier was now in the regular wing or fuselage tanks.

On the return leg, after five hours in the air and gas running low, you can bet we started looking for the carrier, hoping our dead reckoning was correct. If we were within 20 or 25 miles of the ship, we could pick up a beep on the radio -- the beep consisting of one letter in Morse code. By identifying the letter, we could tell which direction to fly to intercept our carrier. With fuel running low, the volume knob on the radio suffered lots of stress from almost frantic twisting, hoping to pick up a "beep."

Several years ago, my wife and I heard Guy Lombardo's orchestra in New York. She commented that it was the sweetest music this side of heaven. I said I thought the sweetest music was when I heard that first faint "beep" after flying a search mission.

Dead reckoning navigation can be surprisingly accurate. On one occasion, it saved the life of a pilot down in the ocean. Returning from a photographic mission over the Philippines, my escort's plane started belching smoke. He apparently had taken some flack while we were taking pictures of the airfields around Manila. At any rate, he had to ditch his plane and was in the water with only his life vest for flotation.

After circling him until my fuel ran low, I had to head back to the carrier. Upon landing, the plane captain said the admiral wanted me on the bridge. Knowing I was probably in deep trouble for being late with the pictures needed for the next strike, I reluctantly went up to the Combat Information Center or CIC room. Handed a pin, I was told to insert it into a 6 foot. by 8 foot chart of the area where I thought the pilot was down. I don't claim to be that renowned a navigator, but luckily, when the rescue submarine surfaced at the spot where I inserted the pin, they spotted my pilot friend and picked him up. The admiral thought I was a navigating genius. You can't beat a little good fortune or old-fashioned luck!

Ralph Chambers, DVM, was born in Quitman, Georgia on April 15, 1921. He grew up in Ocala, Florida. He served in the U.S. Navy from April 1942 until August 1946. Then he immediately entered Auburn University, where the received a Doctorate in Veterinary Medicine in 1949. He has been in practice in Jacksonville, Florida since 1951. Doctor Chambers died in Jacksonville on December 31, 2002.

SOLVING A MYSTERY-
49 YEARS LATER

Robert E. Clancy

The date is May 1, 1952. I was platoon leader of the 3rd Platoon, Charlie Company, 1st Battalion 1st Marines of the First Marine Division. My C.P. was Hill 121 on the west flank of a position called the "Hook." In early April we took over Hill 121 from the "Princess Pats" of the British Commonwealth Division.

We could occupy an outpost about 700 yards from our MLR from first light to last light. The Chinese would occupy the outpost at night.

On May 1st, a warm day, a reinforced squad (17 men) left before dawn from the 3rd Platoon.

About noon I heard this tremendous noise -- more of a roar -- coming toward me at my C.P. Bunker. It was a Marine Corsair coming in for a crash landing. On top of Hill 121, he came by at eye level. I could see the pilot clearly. He seemed to be trying to open his canopy. The plane was carrying a suspended Napalm bomb. I took my field glasses and was appalled to see the Marines on the outpost up and watching the plane.

I immediately got on the radio and screamed, "Get the 'F' down!" At that very moment, the Chinese dropped a mortar on the outpost, wounding 11 of the 17 men.

Because every position was zeroed in, they sent three mortars to our C.P. The Chinese knew Marines always bring back their wounded and dead and that we would soon be on open ground crossing that 700 yards, through the rice paddy, to rescue our patrol.

I can't remember any orders being given. We just did what we were trained to do. Most of the men were walking wounded and four had to be carried back. My Gunnery Sgt. Wolan, Sgt. Burke and I covered the evacuation. We had to set up in minefields to provide covering fire. We got them all back within an hour.

When we got back to the MLR, we all wondered why we hadn't been killed. The outpost was closer to the Chinese line than to our line. The trail and all positions were zeroed in. If the situation was reversed, we would have killed them all, as quickly possible. It was a complete mystery!

In late January 2001, we think we arrived at the answer -- forty-nine years later! Two of the men on that patrol (Corporal Bob Hedger and PFC Jim Fitchett) and I met for a reunion in Las Vegas. They had located me on the Internet, and I immediately accepted an invitation for a get-together after all of these years.

We marveled about that pilot's skill in passing our line with a dangling Napalm bomb. We know he sacrificed his life to save ours.

We decided the Chinese did not shower us with mortars, artillery, and small arms fire because other Marine pilots would come back and destroy them for their lost comrade. Riddle solved.

We don't know who our savior was, but he sure should have received the Congressional Medal of Honor.

Robert E. Clancy was born March 23, 1927. U.S.M.C. April 15, 1951 to October 13, 1952.

"FATE IS NOT
ALWAYS UNKIND
OR CRUEL"

DeWitt Clinton Dawkins, Jr.

I had always wanted to be an Army pilot (there was no U.S. Air Force until several years later) and I was fortunate enough to get a second chance after deciding against such a move in 1939 in favor of starting my business career. At my request, my application and supporting papers were returned from MacDill Air Base, lacking only the pre-induction physical. The lure of a chance at making significant money was the deciding factor as well as marriage and starting a family.

On January 15, 1942, my mother called me at my office to tell me she had just read in the paper that applications for married men were being accepted by the Air Corps. The difference between 1939 and 1942 was that we were at war. Withdrawing the file from my desk drawer (the one returned by MacDill) I went to the Federal Building recruiting office and left as a private in the Air Corps with an appointment as an aviation cadet.

A small group of us boarded a train from Jacksonville Union Terminal Station bound for basic military training in Montgomery, Alabama on January 20, 1942. These were exciting and unprecedented days. Our nation was certainly not prepared for war on the scale we rapidly achieved.

On a Saturday afternoon in February, I was summoned to Headquarters, which was as unlikely as my being called by the President of the United States. When I returned I was besieged by the men. Even the cadet company commander wanted to know what was up. Being bored and anxious to get out of basic military training and on to flying as we all were, I decided to have some fun. I told them I had a hard decision to make. Since we all wanted to be pilots, I said I had been offered an immediate transfer to the school for bombardiers in Albuquerque, New Mexico and that in 90 days I would graduate and become not a 2nd lieutenant but a 1st lieutenant. That's just how bad the Army wanted bombardiers as well as pilots.

I was promptly sought out by numbers of the cadets, including some of the cadet officers, who asked if I would speak on their behalf to the base commanding officer. In one day this swept through all 10,000 trainees and in two days an assembly in full dress uniform was ordered for the parade ground, whereupon the commanding officer personally read us the 104th article of war (I think it was) which promised a courts martial for anyone who was found guilty of starting a rumor.

For the rest of his stay there the most eager of the prospective "bombardiers" was called "Albuquerque Al." Oh yes, my call to headquarters was for some new fangled psychological testing which I apparently passed.

After learning to drill and do basic things of importance to the military, I was sent from Montgomery to a contract flying school, the Lodwick Aviation Military Academy in Avon Park, Florida. How memorable it was to fly over hundreds of acres of orange trees in full bloom in the early spring of `42. Never having been in the air except for a limited time in a giant Curtis Condor, a new passenger plane inaugurating service to Jacksonville, I was plenty scared in my first ride in the open cockpit (with goggles and leather helmet) of a "Yellow Peril," the famous Stearman PT-17, in which so many of us, army and navy, airmen trained.

One day in primary school, well after we had "soloed," our instructors took all of us to an outflying airfield. On the landing end of the strip a white line had been placed across the grass runway. We were instructed to fly a normal pattern (around the field) and to reduce power to 1,000 RPMS on the downwind leg, so as to land just beyond the line one time and just short the next time, for several cycles. Our instructors were grouped near the line to grade our performance. This was valuable training in case we had to make an emergency "forced landing" after an engine failure. Once the power was reduced to "idle" we no longer could use the engine to "stretch our glide" if we were short.

I reasoned that the instructor's pride was involved and maybe even a bet or two has been placed among them. Accordingly, I decided to land astride the line, main gear (wheels) across, tail wheel short of it. I wasn't even close. Afterward, while returning to the main field with my instructor, he cussed me every way he could. He said he knew what I was trying and he would show me how to fly that crate. He would land in a small circle that was painted on the home field! He had been a co-pilot for National Airlines before the war. When he didn't even come close, it did nothing for his anger at me but nothing more was said about my "stunt."

He was only 27 years old himself and an all-around good guy. I would have done anything for him. After 60 hours of dual and solo training, those who survived went to basic training in Greenville, Mississippi. We flew the more complicated "Vultee Vibrator" there, a low-wing, all-metal plane with fixed gear and manually controlled wing flaps. Some fellows just quit and more "washed-out." They were then privates in the Army Air Corps. Those lucky enough to pass ground school and the flying went on to either twin engine advanced school or single engine pursuit planes. I selected twin engine and went to Columbus, Mississippi, for 60 days, I think it was, and was commissioned and received my "wings" on October 9, 1942.

FLYING THE R-26

My first duty station was a B-25 outfit (the B-25 Mitchell Bomber that was subsequently made famous by Colonel Doolittle's Raiders who bombed Japan with B-25's flown from an aircraft carrier) in Columbia, South Carolina. Quickly I was sent to a B-26 Martin Marauder base in Fort

Myers, Florida. I served under a tough little kid who was the engineering officer.

To get off early to go to town (where we married men lived) we had to go through pop quizzes on the airplane's systems. This may have saved more lives than mine. The B-26 was a formidable light bomber, with little room for error. It was very advanced with a pressurized hydraulic system for the landing gear and flaps. This system was always leaking, it seemed, so emergency procedures were of utmost importance to memorize. Rarely did you get a second chance in this plane.

In short order we were transferred to the Avon Park Bomb Range, 14 miles from Avon Park, Florida, in the deep pinewoods. After 20 hours in this very complicated, genuine twin-engine bomber we were made "instructor pilots" and given our first "students" (themselves graduate pilots), flying at night after having been "checked out" ourselves by our instructors only the night before.

It was the first night as an instructor pilot that I landed a B-26 bomber at MacDill Air Force Base near midnight with the left engine fire hardly extinguished and the engine shut down with a first-time-in-the-aircraft student officer co-pilot. I made a nighttime single engine landing at a "strange field" with a pickup inexperienced crew.

This marked the last time soldiers at Avon who were guarding our plane asked for a ride on a plane they were assigned to guard. They were in the back of the plane and those flames shooting from the left engine fire were very exciting for them, and me. They gladly waited on the ground for the plane's return thereafter.

Because, or in spite of this, I was selected for temporary duty at the home of the Air Force in Dayton, Ohio, as a test pilot on a newer model B-26. The title "test pilot" was more glamorous than the job; but how fabulous this was for a young pilot to be in this historic place, even if only for 90 days. During this brief period, several of our instructor pilots back at Avon were killed practicing formation flying, which was not a part of the regular schedule of their duties. Fate is indeed fickle.

At Avon we instructor pilots were assigned three officer-pilots per class with orders to produce two first pilots and one co-pilot. I figured they had all been trained as I had, so why not produce three first pilots, and I always did. I got a real charge one day in Naples, Italy, when a B-26 crew, coming back from a mission where they had been shot up pretty good, crash-landed on the field while I happened to be there. The pilot did a great job and they all walked away from the crash. He was one of the pilots I had taught to fly the B-26 while in Avon Park.

Very shortly after my return to duty in Avon, not quite a year after my graduation in '42, a TWX came from our headquarters at MacDill calling for 10 of our most experienced instructor pilots to be assigned to B-24 school for immediate assignment overseas. A few days prior to this a Colonel Hugh Mason was assigned to our base as the deputy commanding officer.

Hugh had been in the Pacific when war came and had made a great record as a combat pilot flying the B-26 and rapidly became a full colonel. He retired a major general after staying in the service. I knew Hugh's dad, an executive with Mason Lumber Company, as I too was in the same type of business. His younger brother Peter and I were classmates through high school. Trading on this, I went in to see the Colonel. He said I had the record for the new assignment but was married and doing a needed job where I was. I told him I wanted to be more involved. When the list came out my name was on it and, rightly or wrongly, I have always credited my visit to the colonel.

We jumped from the twin engine medium bomber (B-26) to the newest heavy bomber available, the four engine B-24 heavy bomber, the Liberator, successor to the highly acclaimed (and justly so) B-17, the Flying Fortress. Both contributed to winning the war in Europe, the B-17 having been longer at the job and serving spectacularly in 1942 and beyond in the famous 8th Air Force.

Our small group, joined by many more from other bases, took a nine-week course in only three weeks at Smyrna, Tennessee, just outside Nashville. I still remember the first time in the left seat of this monster looking out along that very long left wing with those two large engines (two on each side of me) and how small I felt.

When I took my son-in-law and grandson one day to see a visiting B-24 at Craig Field in Jacksonville it seemed so small and cramped, but that's what flying as a passenger in 747's does to you. However, the B-24 was the biggest we had until the B-29 came out toward the end of the war in Europe.

Then we went to Clovis, New Mexico, where we were assigned our 10-man air crews and I got a great one as it turned out. Here we began the task of learning to fly as a team. We went to our last stateside duty station in Alamogordo, New Mexico, prior to going overseas. Here we practiced as squadrons and as a heavy bombardment group, which, consisted of four squadrons.

After Thanksgiving we started the long trek overseas, flying pretty much on our own. In Florida, near West Palm Beach, we received sealed orders and departed for South Africa via South America. Enroute our orders were changed from more training in South Africa to Manduria, Italy -- the real thing. Our commanding officer, then Colonel John Mills, a West Pointer, had pulled strings to get us into the war.

WELCOME TO ITALY

We landed before Christmas 1943 in Manduria, in the heel of Italy's boot. It was raining; the field had been an Italian base for single engine fighters; it was short for us, and it was NOT paved. When I got the aircraft stopped in the parking space, I called the crew chief up to the flight deck (our ground crew flew over with us) and told him our brakes were out! He replied, "Sir, they looked pretty good the last

50 feet; the wheels were locked." That's just how muddy the field was.

Our detachment of engineers attacked this and other problems. Its detachment's commanding officer was a West Pointer from my hometown, though it took us years to find that out.

My first job after landing was to report to headquarters. The huge army truck that met us took us there. I ran through the rain to the building to find Colonel Mills standing in the doorway, looking out at the rain and the wet ground. I drew up and saluted my best, rattling off as fast as I could, "Lieutenant Dawkins and crew reporting for duty as ordered, sir." He gave me a dismissive wave and said, "Hell, son, scatter out and find a place to stay." I can hear it now as though it was yesterday.

Not knowing when I would again have transportation, I told the driver to take us around the base. This is a good time to tell anyone who may read this that we were sent overseas with fold-up canvas cots exactly like you would find in 1920 in an Army-Navy surplus store because that's what was used in World War One. I directed the driver to stop in front of a frame building, an Italian barracks. I entered into a long central hall, with rooms on each side, and before I heard Italian voices coming from a room in the rear, I saw steel double-decker beds fully made with pillows, mattresses, springs, blankets and sheets. I called the driver and told him to get hold of one end and we went out to the truck with the double-decker.

Upon seeing this, my 20-year-old co-pilot said, "D.C., what you got there?" So I told him while loading it onto the truck. His next question was, "What are those guys going to do for a bed tonight?"

I explained they had lost (the war) and we were winning! He said, "That's a dirty trick". But I and one of my fellow officers slept better that night, at least until we were awakened about 9:30 p.m. and not by the rain. We had flown across the Mediterranean that day from Africa and into combat, found new and strange quarters, fought uncertainty and apprehension, eaten a warm meal in the early evening fog and gloom, and gone to bed, after finding a place for our crew to sleep. And all in the presence of the enemy.

You see, just the very southern tip of Italy had fallen and our eager colonel had heard about this soon-to-be-captured base while we were en-route and snagged this base from Washington even before it had fallen to our troops. The first troops to overrun our new base ordered the Royal Italian Marine Officers and men to stay in their quarters until our P.O.W. people could collect them up. Thus the strange voices in the rear of the barracks.

Our sleep was broken by the young co-pilot who called out to me inquiring as to whether I thought we might be able to get another one of those beds. I knew then he was a fast learner and bound to do well. Later my first assignment back stateside was Mitchell Field, Long Island, my former co-pilot's home. His family invited me to dinner one evening and I told his father the story of the bed. He knew his son well -- a top flight, first rate citizen of whom he was justly proud, but who was not very experienced in life. I can still see and hear this dynamic, peppery small man laughing at this absolutely true story.

We celebrated Christmas soon thereafter with turkey and the works as dark-eyed and pitiful little Italian boys and girls begged for food. More stomachs than the soldiers were filled that night. I gave a huge leg and more attached to it to one of them but this was easy for me, all I had to do was get back in line. This ended very soon thereafter when the base was secured.

In our first weeks we improvised a lot, but we also started on our mission of what we came to do. In January 1944 my crew flew its first mission. We were allowed to go home if we could survive 50 missions; I got in 51 plus one not on my record. Ours was among the first crews to be sent for a brief rest camp break. The flight surgeon, Major Thorpe (from Kansas) directed this. I always thought he was a bit crazy himself. We didn't need a rest.

During our absence our Air Force (the 15th) drew some German and Austrian targets that were murderous. Remember what has been said about "fate." We ultimately drew our own share of tough targets, which was only fair. There were no easy targets; we were shot at every time by antiaircraft fire or M.E. 109's and 110's and many times both. There were, however, long missions and shorter missions. Once we bombed Rome! Well not really; it was a railroad marshaling yard and boy, were we briefed not to cross the Tiber River along the south edge of Rome. But we were very close to that great city. The 15th Air Force was a strategic force, not a tactical force. As a strategic force our mission was to affect the ultimate outcome, not the daily battles. Our targets were key bridges, rail yards (marshaling yards to the British), factories, refineries, docks, submarine pens and the like. Among the factories were aircraft factories and Ploesti was our favorite refinery target. Pilots had to fly in very tight formation as we neared the target! Horsing a heavy loaded B-24 around in the thin air of 25,000 feet above sea level and keeping in tight formation was a full time job, and very demanding physically.

DISTINGUISHED FLYING CROSS

I arrived overseas as a 25-year-old, first lieutenant, married, and used to supporting a family from a position in our family company. I had been identified in late training as an officer who was capable of responsible conduct and always was picked to lead the "second wave," or fly the number two spot (deputy lead) on the group leader's wing. I led the second wave of 21 planes one day over Ploesti, Romania's oil refineries, when enemy fighters shot down my entire lower left box of seven bombers. In spite of all we could do and our fighter escort as well, we lost 7 planes and 70 men. Not all of them perished. Some parachuted and escaped through the active underground or were imprisoned.

Because of the ever present threat of being shot down we wore stout shoes (for walking), had basic gear (a compass), and carried a 45. caliber Colt pistol on our side at all times. We wore heavy flack vests and steel helmets, exactly like our soldiers in the infantry for some protection from anti-aircraft fire and enemy aircraft guns. I'll tell an amusing story about a certain steel helmet later.

Believe me, some native Romanians (and others) mercilessly (and brutally) beat our men. We couldn't recognize some of them we got back after Russian troops had liberated them. Also, not something talked about much, was that during the late stages of the war we bombed Germany and neighboring countries around the clock. I don't think many military targets were hit during the night attacks, but we kept the people up and going to bomb shelters all night. Try to work the next day after being in and out of a bomb shelter all of the night before. We were told farmers took pitch forks to some of our fallen airmen in the late stages when even Hitler could not convince them they were winning.

Shortly after taking off on a mission one day, and while maneuvering into position with several hundred other heavy bombers from nearby bases, I was told that one of our crew men (a waist gunner) was sick. I couldn't leave the controls and relied on the word of other crew members. We were the deputy lead plane that day for our entire group, a force of some 42 planes among hundreds more. We had always completed our missions and we took fierce pride in not returning early as was sometimes done by less dedicated crews.

I debated having the sick man "bail out," since we were still "forming up" our vast formation and over friendly territory. Finally, putting my career on the line, I left my position in the still forming formation and went back to base against all orders not to return with a full load of fuel or bombs. I called for a jeep with a replacement crew member to be available when we landed, quickly exchanged crew members on the ground and took off again.

When worked of our return reached our crew chief, a very fine young farmer from Iowa, responsible for the maintenance (on the ground) of our plane, I am told he cried. You see, he, too, had his goals. His determination was never to send us out in a deficient aircraft, and he thought we were coming back because of a mechanical problem. What a genuinely modest, dedicated, top notch technician this man was. Thanks to him and our dedication, we never failed to complete our assigned mission a single time.

With the aid of our navigator we were able to catch up with our group before the target and joined up in the rear to add our bombs to theirs -- or so we thought. About the time we rejoined the group something happened to the lead plane, and he called on the replacement for us (after we had left) and, for whatever reason, he declared he could not take over for the leader. He had never led a mission and had no experience as a leader which no one had expected of him when the mission was planned.

Our group's part in the over-all mission was in jeopardy and a very dangerous situation was rapidly developing as we were now over enemy territory. I broke radio silence and ordered everyone to hold position and that I would climb up, over-fly the formation, drop into the lead position and they should then close in on us. Which they all did.

Our very excellent bombardier was suddenly and then unexpectedly now in the role of the lead bombardier, almost solely responsible for the bombs of our entire formation.

Though his bomb sight was not sufficiently warmed up (it's very cold at 25,000 feet) he put our group's bombs beautifully on the target and the mission was saved. The various orders that were violated were never mentioned on our return.

I was decorated with the Distinguished Flying Cross and, I have always felt bad that the superior performance of the bombardier was not recognized in a more tangible way. In my mind, he and our crew chief were every bit as "distinguished." I made captain and became the squadron operations officer.

I have spoken about how very cold it is at 25,000 feet above sea level and the waist gunners (and their 50-caliber machine guns) were cold indeed. They had no heat in the rear area of the plane and, worse, had to fire through large open "windows" in each side of the plane. One day while leading a mission it was discovered as we neared the target that the bomb bay doors would not open. I assumed they were frozen but whatever the reason we were in trouble. All of the planes in our command dropped their bombs off the lead plane. If we didn't drop ours, they didn't drop theirs. This meant we really dropped a concentrated load of bombs on the target, or we pretty much missed it, which placed a large responsibility on the lead crew and its bombardier. Accordingly, I ordered our bombs dropped through the closed bomb bay doors. Of course, the doors they went with the bombs. I was relieved to learn the doors had not struck any of our sister planes, who were drawn into very tight formation on us.

One day I was called to headquarters of the group (a heavy bombardment group consists of four squadrons of about 30 planes each) and was told I was being promoted to deputy group operations officer. In this job I was shortly promoted to major. This was a big vote of confidence by the group commanding officer, a fearless combat leader, a physically imposing red-haired young West Pointer who was all business and as direct as a shot in the heart.

He went overseas as deputy group commanding officer and when "the old man" of about 42 years of age was justly promoted to 15th Air Force headquarters (he retired a major general). Colonel Robert R. Gideon was promoted into the job of Group Commanding Officer and there I was on his staff and living in the old Italian Villa (now that's a stretch - but that's what they called it) and eating in Group Mess. In this new job, I was in charge of group training. The older (in experience, not really old in age) guys were being shot down or just getting to 50 missions and going home. My recollection is our group lost over 40% of our air crews during 1944. Fresh (make that "green") new air crews were pouring in as replacements and had to be trained. My new immediate boss was the group operations officer, and a good one he was. He was also a respected officer and a fearless flyer. I had 34 missions at this time but lost my wonderful crew with this promotion.

We in group flew missions all right, but we had no regular crews. When we flew we picked a crew from one of the squadrons, bumped their regular pilot and flew in his place. I, of course, always went to my squadron and flew with my former crew. You may guess from this why well-trained crews were of a high interest to those of us in "Group".

My immediate boss and I developed a strong training program that was cited by Wing Headquarters (47th Bomb Wing, consisting of four heavy bombardment groups). Actually our group commanding officer was cited for the excellence of our training work and he very graciously scrawled across a copy of the citation his compliments to us with the notation to "keep on chewing," meaning chewing the posteriors of the air crews to exhort them to greater care in their work. Part of the training was working on our non-combat accident rate, and we were pretty lucky with this. I think I still have a copy of this letter of citation somewhere. How many times since have I scribbled a note like that to a key employee by way of appreciation and encouragement.

I loved the Air Force, created by President Roosevelt and the Congress as a separate branch, carved out of the Army Air Corps. I was offered sponsorship by my commanding officer for a permanent commission in the regular Air Force after the war. I became the group operations officer when my immediate boss went home. He stayed in the Air Force after the war. Though not a West Pointer he was a college graduate and retired as a Major General. I told you earlier what a fine officer he was.

SAVING THE
FLIGHT ENGINEER

The flight engineer from my original crew came over to headquarters to see me one day and he was very agitated. He said according to his records he had completed his required missions but the official records showed he was one short. He sought my advice on whether to refuse to fly anymore. He was 20 years older than the rest of us, an expert flight engineer and a top notch man and airman. He died soon after World War II ended and I never got to tell him how highly I regarded him and of my admiration.

But I did tell him that day long ago, that since I knew in advance what the missions were, I would pick a short one for myself and take him along. This satisfied him, though I had not been honest with him in the interest of continuing his spotless career. We certainly did not get to pick our missions. Missions were carefully planned by the 15th Air Force, sent down to wing headquarters for refining, and sent by wing to the groups in their command who were to participate.

We were told the target, and the times and number of planes required of us. Group then called on its squadrons for the number of planes required and the crews were selected "blindly," that is to say, randomly, without regard to individuals. We crews sometimes flew five or six days consecutively while others had a day or so off.

When not on the mission for the day, the newer, less experienced crews were being further trained. The crews who were to fly the mission the next day were informed in the early evening and told what time to be at the next morning's briefing. Those flying the mission were awakened at the appropriate time to allow for dressing and eating, then we all trooped into the heavily guarded briefing room. This was a tense and exciting experience since it was the first time any of the participating crews knew where or what the target was.

During the night the Group Navigator and others had planned the mission on a huge floor to ceiling map permanently mounted on the wall showing our area of operations. A very large area it was, too, from France on the west arching up to Germany and east to the Black Sea. The planners would put a red ribbon on this map from base to target and they did this each raid, for each target, removing the ribbon immediately after the briefing.

A prominent landmark was always selected about 10 miles from the target and designated as the "initial point," usually requiring a turn toward the target. From the initial point on, things were very precise as to, timing, altitude, and course. From the initial point to the target was called the bomb run. We drew the formation in especially close on the bomb run to concentrate our fire power against enemy planes and our bomb pattern on the target.

Enemy aircraft would usually attack us head on, flying right through our formations in the hope of diverting us from our target, or scattering us to diminish our effectiveness. We had to continue to fly close and on course and on the assigned altitude on the bomb run to maximize our chances of hitting the target.

When our fighter cover got into the fray, it became a maelstrom of diving, firing pursuit planes near and around the bombers. Holding our precise altitude gave the anti-aircraft gunners an advantage but we had to do it to give our bombardiers a reasonable chance to do their job to good effect.

The navigators of the lead crews were given precise information on getting to the target and the pilots received a mimeographed sheet listing all the first pilot's names and where their position was in the formation.

We usually flew in "boxes" of seven planes, with each group putting up 42 planes. After our briefing, we loaded into large army trucks and were carried out onto the field to our respective planes. On takeoff (at precise times) we "joined in" on our leader who took off first and formed up. After forming, we departed our area and joined planes from other areas in an exact order and sequence. We were a very formidable force, taken all together. The greatest sight to us as we neared enemy territory was the arrival of our protective fighter planes, P-38's, P-47's and the most graceful looking of all, the P-51's.

Now back to our story of my former flight engineer. The fateful day came and we went to Austria or Germany, I forget which, but it was a tough target, a double credit. Leaving the target area after dropping our bombs, this man stood up in front of me, in the pilot's seat -he in the nose of the ship with his head up in a plexiglas bubble about six feet in front of the windshield with his steel helmet on and the widest smile ever in place. An antiaircraft shell exploded nearby causing the ship to rock and his helmet fell off his head. While he was retrieving it from his feet, another antiaircraft shell exploded nearby and shattered the plexiglas blister where his head had just been. Fate, indeed, is not always unkind.

One fine day toward the end of 1944, I was summoned to wing headquarters and into the presence of General Hugo P. Rush, our wing commander. At this point I was eligible and ready to go back to the states. General Rush asked me to come on his staff as the wing training officer with a promotion to lieutenant colonel, having by then been a major for a few months.

How do you tell a general no? I knew him; he knew me. Our field was just across the road from his headquarters and he often came over and flew with us. I greatly admired and respected him. No young officer was as lucky as I was in the commanding officers I served with. They were fair, firm, excellent officers and absolutely fearless. None of them ever turned back from a mission. I said he had offered me an opportunity I could not pass up if I were going to stay in the Air Force, but that I was going back to the family business and asked if I could decline his generous offer. He immediately said to come back the next day and see his chief of staff, who would have my orders cut to go home. When I returned the next day my orders were cut and along with them I was handed a letter written by no less than the Commanding General, Hugo P. Rush, that is today one of my most prized possessions. To say that he was generous to me in referencing my brief stint (about 13 months in his command) would be an understatement. Fate is not always cruel. I am a living proof of that as I am now into my 84th year, having been declared to be 83 last May 14.

BUILDING BRIDGES
ACROSS THE RHINE

C. Harris Ditmar

I was born in my grandmother's house in Dothan, Alabama, on January 2, 1926. The midwife who helped deliver me reportedly gave my mother two bunches of collard greens as a prize for having the first white baby of 1926.

At the time of my birth my family was en route from Harrisburg, Virginia, to Florida. My father, who had been born and raised in Fort Pierce, Florida, but had worked in Alabama and Virginia since World War I, was returning to Florida to participate in the roaring Florida land boom. He got to Florida just in time to invest his saving in land developments and see it all disappear in the great "bust" of 1926.

Later in 1926 my family moved to Gainesville, Florida, where my father supervised the construction and equipping of the Gainesville Coca-Cola bottling plant, which he thereafter managed for many years. I grew up in Gainesville with my two brothers, one older, and one younger than I. During the depression years we and all of our friends were poor, but nobody felt deprived and we had a happy childhood. I worked from the time I was 10 years old to save spending money. I sold peanuts at the baseball games of the Gainesville G-Men and the football games of the University of Florida Gators, and sold and delivered the Saturday Evening Post, Ladies Home Journal and Country Gentlemen magazines. I also delivered the Gainesville Daily Sun newspaper, worked in a grocery store on Saturdays, and started working at the Coca-Cola plant in 1941 after the grown men started going into the service.

I was educated in the Gainesville public schools. In early 1943, while I was a senior in Gainesville High School, the school was visited by a team of U.S. Army recruiters who presented a new "opportunity" to the senior boys. That opportunity was in a new program known as the Army Specialized Training Reserve Program (ASTRP.) We were told that if we would sign up and enter the army after graduation and before reaching the draftable age of 18, the army would give us a college education in a field of our choice and, before graduation from college, give us a commission as officers in the army.

After consulting with my parents, I agreed to enlist in the ASTRP. Because I had enjoyed and done well in my math and physics classes, I selected engineering as my chosen field for my college education. I signed the appropriate papers, passed a basic achievement test and a limited physical examination, and was told that I would later receive orders directing me where and when to report for duty.

I graduated on May 17, 1943, and worked full time that summer at the Coca-Cola plant. During that summer I received orders to report to North Carolina State College of Agriculture and Engineering on July 31, 1943, together with appropriate travel authorizations. Although I had been known as "Harris Dittmar" all of my life and barely knew that my first name was Charles, those orders and all subsequent papers for several years referred to me as Charles H. Dittman, my "army name."

On July 30, 1943 I left Gainesville by train dressed in my civilian suit. My family and several friends saw me off and for the first time, I realized a monumental change was occurring in my life. I was surprised to find on the train a friend, Leon Coleman, who was also going to the ASTRP at N.C. State. We had a layover in Jacksonville for a change of trains and Leon and I decided to celebrate our new freedom by going to a bar near the terminal. Being relatively uneducated about drinks we ordered Pink Ladies, a fact that still mystifies me.

When our train to Raleigh left Jacksonville, we were joined by Ted Benjamin, a Jacksonville boy who had also been ordered to N.C. State under the ASTRP. The three of us had a fairly restless night as we talked about the unknown life that lay ahead for us. I was particularly impressed by the train ride because prior to that time I had never been farther north than Atlanta. The train was crowded with military personnel and we were about the only passengers in civilian clothes.

The next morning we were met at the Raleigh terminal by Army personnel who took us to a building on the N.C. State campus. There, on July 31, 1943, we were sworn into the U.S. Army Reserve, issued O.D. uniforms, G.I. shoes, underwear, shirts, etc. and ordered to pack our civilian clothes for shipment home. We were assigned rooms in a dormitory facing a quadrangle, four to a room, where we stayed the next six months.

After depositing our belongings in our rooms, we assembled in the yard where platoons were formed according to pre-assignment and we immediately began learning rudimentary close-order drills. You can imagine what a comedy that was with totally untrained high school boys. For the next two or three days we were drilled, given limited calisthenics and subjected to cursory room inspections. That brief period was the full extent of the training in military arts, which I received in my six months at N.C. State. Thereafter, we did have reveille roll call each morning and marched in platoon formation to the cafeteria for our three meals a day.

In two or three days after arrival we received our class assignments, books and materials, and classes began. As I recall the instruction was accelerated and the classes were long. Classes included trigonometry, calculus, physics, surveying and history. My history instructor was excellent and, he instilled in me an enjoyment for history which I still have to this day. I don't recall having much spare time at N.C. State. In fact, I can only recall leaving the campus to go into Raleigh two times. N.C. State had a football team in 1943 and lost all of its games that year, none of which I saw. When I went to the University of Florida in 1946, it lost all the games played by its football team that year. Florida also lost the first two games it played in 1947. Its third game was against N.C. State and Florida won. Finally, I had supported a winning team. While at N.C. State, I did go to Chapel Hill one time to see a Gainesville friend who was there under a Navy program similar to ASTRP.

In December I saw snow for the first time in my life. I enjoyed it at first but the cold weather soon gave me a bad case of the flu. In two or three days I was so sick that I went to the college infirmary for treatment. There I was informed I needed bed care and would be taken to nearby Camp Butner for treatment in an army hospital. I was indeed carried to Camp Butner but I was seated in the bed of an open truck with snow falling on me. I figured that the Army was doing everything it could to kill me, but somehow I made it to the hospital for what was designated as bronchial pneumonia and I was soon back in school at Raleigh.

THE BROKEN PROMISE

In late January 1944 we had finished two terms of classes and I was pleased with the grades I had received. We were given furloughs to go home and were told to take all of our belongings with us because we would not be returning to the same rooms. I went home to Gainesville and soon received a letter informing me that the ASTRP program had been discontinued and that I should report to Camp Blanding on February 15 for induction into active service for further assignment. Thus the Army abandoned its promise to give me a college education and a commission and I never even thought to question its right to do so. I was of age then and eager to serve America like most every other American man was.

On February 15, 1944 I reported to Camp Blanding near Starke, Florida, where I was sworn into active service as a private in the army, issued new uniforms and clothing, and signed papers allotting a portion of my monthly pay to my mother and to National Service Life Insurance. Almost immediately I was transported to Fort Benning, Georgia for reassignment.

My few days at Fort Benning were weird. I knew no one in my barracks, there was no real organization, and the only activity consisted of people being ordered out and new people coming in. Shortly, I received my orders to report for duty with an infantry division (I can't remember the number) at Fort Bragg, North Carolina.

When I, along with a few others, reported to the proper place at Ft. Bragg, we were informed that the division was ready for combat duty overseas and would soon be leaving the states, and that we were being brought in to fill in a few "holes" in the ranks and bring the division up to full strength. I immediately realized that I was in bad trouble. I had received no basic training, had no idea how to be a fighting infantry man, and had never even held a rifle, much less fired one. Nevertheless I was soon issued my M-1 rifle and field gear and assigned a platoon.

Evidently the platoon leaders soon realized that I was not ready to be of much help in preparing for overseas combat duty and I was assigned to K.P. duty for several days. In fact, I was peeling potatoes in the mess hall when I was told to report to Company Headquarters for transfer orders. Those orders required me to report for duty with Company A, 127th Combat Engineer Battalion at Camp Chaffee, Arkansas. I will never know what a lucky stroke of fate caused someone to find me in that infantry division, pick me out and send me to the Engineers Corps. I only knew that someone was looking out for me and I was thankful for it.

I traveled to Camp Chaffee by train and on my own. When I reported to Company A, I learned that the 127th Combat Engineers was being formed for one purpose -- to build a bride across the Rhine which would have a minimum capacity of 20 tons to carry trucks and other heavy equipment across the river. This was months before D-Day and no one knew how much time we would have to prepare for our assignment. I was part of the cadre which was being assembled to train the new recruits who would be arriving in a few days and would be molded into a bridge building team.

The member of the cadre immediately got to work learning how to give Corps of Engineers Basic Training to our expected troops. This was a small group and I learned a lot from them, officers and enlisted men. It was my first close experience with real soldiers and it was an eye opener. Our first sergeant, "Rip" Coleman, was the most accomplished "swearer" I have ever known. He used expletive phrases that I had never known existed. The camaraderie was great and by the time recruits arrived I was an accomplished smoker, beer drinker and swearer myself. I was ready to be a noncom and at that time was promoted to private first class.

When our recruits arrived they were an interesting lot--45% from Brooklyn 45% Cajuns from the Louisiana Bayou, and 10% mostly from the Midwest. They were a mixture of 18 year olds and older men, some married and previously passed over, who were then being drafted as the demand for manpower increased and the war intensified. I decided I should not let these men know that I had just turned 18 so I pretended to be 20. Before long I got used to the accents and familiar with the idioms and phraseology of Brooklyn and Cajun country.

Basic training was vigorous but went fairly well. Everybody made it except for one of the older recruits, who could not make the 20-mile hike with full field gear. I included basic instruction on demolition materials and devices and their usage (which I helped teach) and the construction of footbridges. During that time I was certified as a Demolition Specialist and promoted to corporal. I was also qualified as a Sharpshooter with the M-1 rifle.

After basic training we began learning how to build the type bridge across the Rhine for which our unit was formed. About that time the D-Day Invasion of Normandy occurred and we knew there was new urgency to our job. The bridge which we would build would not be designed by architects and engineers and would not use pre-fabricated materials by the army. Rather the design and materials of the bridge would depend upon what we might find on site in a portion of Germany devastated by intense fighting and the retreat of the German forces.

Accordingly, we practiced constructing bridges out of cement, heavy bombs, steel beams and tree trunks. We learned how to build on clear sites, and on the collapsed debris of prior bridges; how to use demolitions to clear sites and debris; and how to use cranes, draglines and bulldozers. We didn't know what would ultimately be required of us but we became confident of our ability to do whatever was necessary when the time came. This was particularly true because of our confidence in the ability and leadership of our company commander, Captain William Kemp. Captain Kemp, a man in his late thirties, had been in the oil business in Texas and was able to find a solution to any construction problem. He was stern but respected by all his men.

Our construction training kept us in the field in the summer months of 1944 under the hot Arkansas sun. Shortly after it began I was certified as a construction foreman. In June I learned that the army planned to give a number of West Point appointments to soldiers in the ranks. The appointments would be given to those making the best grades in a special written test and agreeing to spend a minimum of seven years in service after receiving a commission upon graduation. This sounded like a wonderful opportunity so I took the test. After some time had passed without hearing anything from the army I figured that I had not made the cut. Then one day I received a letter telling me that I had been selected for appointment to West Point but had to accept the terms in writing by a certain date, which had already passed by the time the letter was delivered to me. Upon inquiry I was told that the letter had been misplaced by a battalion clerk who let it get hidden under other papers, that it was delivered to me as soon as it was uncovered, and that everybody was sorry but it was too late to do anything about it. The reality of the situation was a terrible disappointment to me.

That night I called my father in Gainesville and told him what had occurred. Unbeknownst to me, my father drove to Starke the next day and told our congressman, Len Green, what had happened. Rep. Green said he would see if he could help me when he returned to Washington the following day. The very next day a jeep came to the field where I was working with orders to take me to camp headquarters. When I got there I met two army doctors who said they were instructed to give me a West Point admission physical exam and that if I passed I was to be transferred to West Point.

After being examined I was told that I could not pass because I was eight pounds under the minimum weight requirement for West Point. The doctors told me that they could give me about an hour to eat bananas and drink water to see if I could get up to the required minimum weight, but they had to send their report in that day. I tried eating and drinking but I could not add sufficient weight and that was the end of my "West Point opportunity."

I was not surprised that I was under weight because I had never weighed more than 135 pounds in my life and I had lost a lot of weight that summer working in the Arkansas heat. However, I thought then, and still do, that the doctors probably had been told to find some basis to fail me so that the army could avoid changing its schedule and at the same time tell Congressman Green that they tried to do what he wanted. I always thought it was ironic that I was too light to go to West Point but heavy enough to be sent back to my unit, which was preparing to go to the combat zone overseas. Nevertheless I soon realized that the good Lord probably had his hand in the matter because I would not have enjoyed spending seven years in the army after the war was over.

GOING OVERSEAS

Soon after that we prepared for shipment overseas and moved by rail to Camp Kilmer, New Jersey, our point of embarkation. On the day of the Florida-Georgia football game in 1944, we boarded the Liberty Ship named "The Sea Lion" and sailed the next day, October 22, 1944. It was a miserable voyage for me because I stayed seasick the whole way. We were in an unescorted convoy which zigzagged across the Atlantic's rough seas, dropping depth charges at least twice on the way.

We slept in bunkers stacked four or five high, deep in the bowels of the ship. We were fed two meals a day which I promptly threw up. The only decent food was in the quarters of the Merchant Marines crew, which was guarded by U.S. Marines. A payment to the Marine guard could get you a good ham sandwich. I still have an "extra meal ticket" which I earned by carrying 100 bags from a storage hold to the galley which I could not bring myself to use.

After what seemed like an interminable voyage we finally landed in England. Before landing we were given a lecture about British manners, customs and word usages that might be strange to us. We were told that the British were more reserved and might seem aloof to us, but even before we landed I was impressed with the friendliness of the dock workers and others who greeted us. I was also soon impressed with how good it felt to once again be on solid ground.

Our battalion went to Weston-super-Mare, a seaside resort town near Bristol. The town had suffered only limited damage from German bombing, but the resort facilities were pretty well closed down by the war effort. The public baths were open however, and it was a great pleasure to visit them from time to time and enjoy hot water, white soap and heated towels.

Company A was quartered in a former school building on a hillside two or three blocks from the shore and guards were posted on the road leading from town to the school.   A limited exchange was set up nearby and we received ration cards which allowed us to buy Coca-Colas, candy, soap, shaving supplies, and even cigarettes for the overseas price of five cents a pack.

We continued to practice bridge building in the fields and hills outside Weston-super-Mare. The weather was not good; I can remember seeing a sunny sky only two days in the four and one-half months we spent there waiting for the U.S. troops to reach the Rhine.   The winter became unusually harsh with chilling rain and sleet and even some snow. In the middle of the winter we went on maneuvers in the mountains near Maidenhead, where we learned how to fire machine guns. I qualified as an expert on the 30-caliber light machine gun and also tried out on the 50-caliber air-cooled machine gun. All of this was done in bitter cold snow fields and my hands were so cold that I could not push the butterfly trigger of the 50-caliber gun with my thumbs, but had to push my hand forward from my shoulder to fire it. This was my first lesson on how debilitating severe cold can be. It was not my last that winter.

The people of Weston-super-Mare seemed glad to have us in their town and were generally friendly. The girls were lonely and happy to date G.I.s who might buy them a pint at a local pub. I became quite fond of the British "warm" beer and put away many a "half and half." I also liked the fish and chips when I could find them and afford them. Once I got a two-day pass and went to London during the Christmas season. I didn't do much sightseeing but did see some of the damage done by the German air raids and did visit Piccadilly Circus, which was teeming with soldiers, sailors and girls even though it was night and fairly well blacked out. While in London I heard a couple of buzz bombs pass over and then explode in the distance. The people would stop when that occurred but did not seem to run for shelter. I spent the night in a chair in the London U.S.O. after enjoying the entertainment and refreshments.

Between   Christmas and New Year's Day our company went from Weston-super-Mare to a port where we boarded a ship. We were told that we were going to France to help reinforce the troops engaged in the Battle of the Bulge. We did not have our machinery and toolboxes with us, and it soon became obvious that we were not going to become involved as engineers but were going to be used in some fashion as riflemen. This caused us some concern because we were ill prepared to perform that function, but it seemed that the situation in France was so dire that they were ready to use any troops they could get into the fray.

We sailed away and in less than 48 hours were in a port somewhere in France. Shortly thereafter we were informed that the tide had turned in the Battle of the Bulge and we would not be disembarking. Needless to say we were greatly relieved to receive that news. We soon sailed back to England and returned to Weston-super-Mare to resume our training.

In early March 1945 we were told that the U.S. forces were nearing the Rhine and it was time for us to go to France. We were soon on board a ship with all our machines, vehicles, tools and gear and landed at LaHavre. We drove in our vehicles from there to somewhere in France near the battlefront. From this point on I was never certain where we were. As a noncom, I was not present when officers determined destinations and was not given maps or information as to where we were. During that trip I got my first introduction to the real devastation of war. The roads were literally lined on both sides with destroyed and abandoned vehicles, tanks, artillery and carriages. Most human bodies had been removed but I was amazed at the large number of dead and bloated bodies of horses and oxen which were among the debris.

The weather was so cold that there had been no decomposition of the carcasses and little odor. Although the fighting had moved from these areas several days earlier, no effort had been made to clean up the roads or dispose of the carcasses. Almost all buildings we passed had been destroyed or damaged and evidently no effort had been made to restore sewerage, electricity or water.

The people we saw seemed to be at a loss as to what to do and whenever our convoy stopped, many would surround our trucks hoping for food or cigarettes. On one stop several of us went into the woods to relieve ourselves and came upon several German dead surrounding a German 88 mm gun. It was the first time that I had seen war dead, but I felt no sympathy for them assuming they had died trying to kill Americans.

When we got to our destination we camped out in an open field covered with snow. We dug indentations into the snow-covered ground, lined them with our shelter halves and slept in our bedrolls fully clothed. I am sure it was thought that we would be there only a day or two before being called to the Rhine. In fact, however, we stayed there for two weeks sleeping in the bitter cold and eating C rations, with nothing to do but wait. We couldn't even take a bath. One night I was on guard duty and was so cold that my hands and feet actually hurt. That night I promised God and myself that if I ever got back to Florida I would never again complain about being hot. I have kept that promise to this very date, 55 years later.

One night when we were in the field we were called to a nearby fuel dump where a fire had started. There we found thousands of tin cans filled with gas, stacked more than six feet high in blocks that were about 15 x 25 feet, separated from each other by about 12 feet in width. A large fire was raging at the end of one block with cans exploding from time to time. Our job was to remove cans from the surrounding blocks and the opposite end of the burning block. It was dangerous, hard work, but with the help of other troops we got it done without casualties so far as I know. Indeed, I kind of welcomed the work to break the monotony of waiting and welcomed the heat to ease the cold. I never heard how the fire was started.

MOVING UP
THE RHINE

Finally, the word came that the Rhine had been crossed and we were going to build the bridge for which we had trained so long. We moved up to the river, which was not as wide as I expected, but still formidable with great destruction on each side. Our officers told us that the 3rd Army, to which we were now attached, was moving so quickly that a decision had been made to have us not build our planned bridge on the Rhine but to go build another river farther up in Germany. They said another bridge was available to get heavy equipment across the Rhine. (I always have thought they were referring to the bridge at Remagen, which collapsed a few days after its capture.)

Company A was given the job of putting a Bailey bridge across that point on the Rhine before moving closer to the port. A Bailey bridge is made of pre-fabricated steel parts which are assembled sort of like an Erector set. The bridge is assembled on land and on large rollers so that it can be pushed across the river chasms. As the bridge is rolled out over the river it has to be counterbalanced by an equal length of bridge on the land side of the rollers. If the bridge were to be 300 feet you would need an equal amount of space on the land side of the rollers.

It was a simple concept for a bridge that could not carry more than a ¾-ton truck and was beneath the dignity of our company. Nevertheless we accepted the order and set out to build it. There was an electric tower blocking the space needed for the land side construction. Corporal Bernie Frankel was assigned the job of preparing the tower for demolition while the rest of us began construction of the bridge. Frankel reported that the explosives were ready for electrical detonation and construction was halted while all took cover. Frankel plunged the handle on the detonator and nothing happened. Captain Kemp immediately busted Frankel to private and figured out how we could finish the bridge without blowing the tower. It was an embarrassing start to our combat zone record.

After completing the Bailey bridge, we loaded our trucks for a nighttime trip to our next destination. A number of our squad had "liberated" a large cache of wine and we were all fairly drunk when we crossed the Rhine on a pontoon bridge somewhere down river. The next day we passed through debris and ruins of recent battles and reached the site of our first real bridge construction. It was a former bridge where the trestles, or supports, were reusable but the spans were completely destroyed. My squad was assigned the job of obtaining steel beams from the framework of nearby gutted buildings. The beams were used as stringers, which were covered with timber flooring and in a few days traffic was flowing over our bridge. When we started our work we could hear the sounds of battle on the nearby firing lines. By the time we finished, the battle sounds had moved forward beyond our hearing.

Thereafter our logistics became fairly routine. As soon as we finished one bridge, we would travel to the next site, drinking and sleeping in our trucks en route. While the officers planned what type bridge to construct, we noncoms would find housing for our men. I would take a member of my squad who spoke German and locate the burgermeister (mayor) of the nearby town to help us find homes with the least battle damage.

When we had selected houses for our use, we would immediately require the occupants to vacate the premises, taking with them only what they could carry. The burgermeister would be given the job of finding shelter for the dislocated people. Guards would be placed to guard the houses and we would begin our construction, which could take from four or five days to as much as two to three weeks. Our workday lasted from 12 to 16 hours. We usually had only C or K rations to eat, but occasionally there was a hot meal. The front lines were moving forward so quickly that we were always under pressure to get our work done and move to the next site.

We went all across a devastated Germany, building bridges with steel, concrete and even logs. We came to admire the German civilians who were mostly elderly, children under 17, or women. Even if the fighting in their own town had only been over four hours, they would be out burying the dead German soldiers and cleaning up the debris. They would soon have a system in place for the removal of sewage and the supply of water.

During the exhausting weeks of bridge construction there were only a few memorable events that I can recall. One was the morning we came off a night shift to learn that President Roosevelt had died. We were all saddened with a sense of personal loss but determined to carry on. Another was when we came upon deer in one of Hitler's private preserves and killed one for the mess sergeant. The next day we had venison for dinner, the first fresh meat we had had in several weeks. It was the best meat I could ever remember. Six days later we were still eating venison from the deer herd and I could hardly stand the taste of the stuff. To this day I still can't enjoy venison. Finally, I remember that we were building a small bridge on an autobahn on May 1 and it was snowing -- the last gasp of the longest and coldest winter Europe had experienced in anyone's memory.

When the war in Europe ended on May 8, 1945 we were building a bridge in Austria. We didn't know the war was over until some Austrian women brought us flowers and told us so. There was no real celebration, but a feeling of great relief tempered by a need to receive official word of the fact. That soon came and a short time later we were loaded up and on the road back into Germany.

We went to Frankfurt and were quartered in a former school building which was one of the few structures which had suffered no major damage. There we learned we were to assist in converting the I.G. Farbers office building into SHEAF Headquarters. Our first assignment was the clearing, leveling and paving of the streets and parking areas surrounding the building. Each morning we would take trucks to the POW camp and pick up the number of prisoners that we wanted to work that day. In general, the prisoners were not motivated but did adequate work in the simple tasks involved in clearing and paving. Later we did painting and carpentry work on the interior of the building and little prisoner labor was used in those tasks.

After several weeks without a break our work at the Farben building ended and we were looking forward to some leave time to enjoy the fruits of victory, including bartering for the favors of women with the ultimate thing of value to wit, -- American cigarettes. Instead, I was instructed to take our squad of men and some prisoners and to pave the road leading from the highway to General Eisenhower's weekend cottage near Wiestaden. I carried out the assignment but all of us involved resented giving up our free time to make General Eisenhower's free time more enjoyable. That resentment kept us from voting for Eisenhower when he ran for president in the 1980s.

After the job, we had a good deal of free time in Frankfurt. We located and liberated a 300-gallon cache of very good wine in an abandoned building near our quarters and managed to conceal it from the many other servicemen in the area. It served us well for drinking and bartering purposes. Two friends and I went to the former zoo and found a single attendant and one adult elephant. We decided to adopt the elephant and took it food from time to time until we left Frankfurt. On several occasions I rode the elephant bareback, which was an interesting experience.

One day in Frankfurt, Jim Gibson and I traded several packs of cigarettes to a German for the use of a camera and a roll of film. We took pictures of several sites throughout the city and had the rolls developed. He took the pictures and I took the negatives. In 1971 I planned a trip to Europe with my wife and two children which would include visiting a friend who was with the Armed Forces Network in Frankfurt. Before leaving I located the negatives and had my 1948 pictures printed. My friend helped us locate the sites in Frankfurt and we took new pictures to compare with the old ones. It was an interesting experience which turned out quite well.

In late July or early August we left Frankfurt and went to Marseille, France. When we got there we loaded our trucks and construction equipment on one boat and we were loaded on another. We were told we would be leaving in a few days to go to a marshalling point in the Pacific Ocean where we would be outfitted and prepared to participate in the invasion of Japan. We were informed that the invasion and conquest of Japan would probably result in one million American casualties and as many as ten million Japanese casualties including civilians who were expected to fight to the bitter end. It was not a pleasant prospect but we knew it was necessary.

Two or three days later we learned of the dropping of the atomic bomb on Hiroshima and our departure was delayed although I heard that the boat carrying our equipment had already sailed. In short order we heard of the bombing of Nagasaki and the surrender of Japan. I figured that the atomic bomb had probably saved my life and to this day I love that bomb. On V-J Day we were given leave and got uproaringly drunk in celebrating the occasion in the streets of Marseille. The French did not do any extensive celebrating that I observed.

We remained in Marseille several more days and finally set sail for the U.S.A., landing in Newport News, Virginia in early September. We were taken to Camp Patrick Henry where we were processed and given our leave papers. We were told that we would receive further orders by mail while we were on our 30-day leave. I had sufficient points for discharge under the point system which was then in effect and fully expected my next orders would tell me to report for discharge.

The orders I later received while on leave really surprised me. They informed me that I had been placed on "essential service" for at least six months and should report to the Officers Candidate School in the Harminey Church area of Fort Benning, Georgia. At OCS I was told that my service was needed as a "demolition specialist" to teach officer candidates how to handle and use all types of demolitions. And that was exactly what I did for the next six months, the period of my Army service which I considered most uninteresting.

Finally, on May 17, 1946, I received my honorable discharge in my rank of sergeant at the separation center at Fort McPherson, Georgia. It was a very happy day for me, but I will always value the time that I spent in the service of my country.

Harris Dittmar was a very successful lawyer in Jacksonville, Florida. He now lives in retirement with his lovely wife Anice.

A UNIQUE
AIR-SEA RESCUE

James Temple Doswell, II

During the spring and summer of 1945, I was a second lieutenant fighter pilot with Marine Fighter Squadron - 311 (VMF-311) on Okinawa. The squadron flew 24 F4U-1C Corsairs armed with four-20mm cannon.

Most of our missions were combat air patrols (CAP), but our division was never vectored on any enemy planes. Often, after being relieved, we would strafe enemy position on Okinawa or on the islands to the north. As the battle for Okinawa wound down and more fighters arrived, we started flying fighter sweeps and bomber escort missions over China and Japan.

On July 11, 1945 we escorted a flight of PBJ bombers (the PBJ was the Navy-Marine version of the B-25 Mitchell) on a mission to Miyazaki, Kyushu. This was my first flight to the home islands of Japan. We were at 30,000 feet with the bombers well below us. As we neared the target, big, black puffs of AA were exploding at our altitude. Suddenly I felt a jolt as my wingman and I flew through a black puff! I saw that he had a couple of holes in his flaps and he called to me that I had no prop hub and was pumping fluid overboard.

My flight leader told me to head for the ocean and then turn south. When I got over the ocean my engine started surging and I began a long glide to get as far away from Japan as I could. Several minutes and a hundred miles later my engine revved up to 6,000 rpm and then stopped. It got real quiet!

I was then at 7,000 feet and unstrapped myself to bail out. After looking at the violent ocean underneath, I decided to ditch, rather than be dragged by my chute in the water.

The wind was so strong that I decided to land into the wind rather than parallel to the swells. I hit head-on into a huge swell and sank immediately. I had a hard time getting my raft out of my chute and was about 20 feet under when I popped my Mae West. I shot to the surface and then my Mae West deflated as I had failed to screw down the oval inflation tubes. Finally, I got my raft inflated and crawled in, completely exhausted.

The next four or five hours were like being on a roller coaster. At the top of each swell I had a clear view of Amami-Oshima, ominously close, and at the bottom all I could see were mountains of water. At all times I had at least two fighters circling over me. A flight would stay about a half hour and then be relieved by another one. At last a big beautiful navy flying boat (PBM) flew over me and headed off to land in the lee of the island. Even though the fighters were still circling, I felt deserted. I could hear artillery firing. (I later learned that they were shooting at the PBM which had just landed.) Then, when I was on top of one swell, I could see the PBM on top of another and splashing in my direction. I lit a smoke flare and then another and soon the big plane was on top of me.

The crew hauled me on board and they seemed just as happy as I was for they were the only crew in that squadron that had not picked up a "wet chicken" (terminology for a downed aviator). I climbed up to the flight deck to thank the plane commander and then went down to the galley where they told me to hang on a stanchion while they made a JATO (rocked propelled) takeoff. (They were not going back to the smooth water and get shot at again). Bouncing furiously through the water, we finally got airborne when WHAM! My knees were over my head and we slammed back into the water. We kept going. The rockets fired and we were airborne!

On the way back to the seaplane tender (USS Pine Island) anchorage at Okinawa the crew took me down into the hull to show me the keel. The crash back into the water had split the keel about two inches for about a length of 20 feet. When we landed, the pilot kept the power on until we ground up on the beach. The poor bird never flew again.

I stayed in the Marine Corps after the war and flew F6F 5Ns, (Hellcat with VMF(N)-532 and F7F 3Ns (Tigercats) with VMF(N)-531. In Korea I flew night interdiction missions with VMF(N)-513. We had the Cadillac of Corsairs, the F4U-5N. I then served as a forward air controller with the 5th Marines until wounded on May 4, 1952.

After hospitalization and rehabilitation I joined VMF-334 at Cherry Point and later VMF-312 at Beaufort, South Carolina. The squadrons were equipped with FJ-2s and FJ-3s, respectively. Four years of staff duty in Japan and Quantico followed and then, in 1953 I joined MAG-32 at Cherry Point. As group operation officer, I flew the F-4 Phantom V, the F-4D Skyray and the A-4D Skyhawk, before commanding VMA-533. The highlight of that job was leading a squadron of 20 A-4s from Cherry Point to Rota, Spain, refueling from KC-130s.

Temple Doswell was born in New Orleans, Louisiana on July 1, 1924. He was raised in Jacksonville, Florida where his father was rector of St. John's Episcopal Church. He served in the U.S. Marine Corps from January 1942 until January 1968, when he retired as a lieutenant colonel with a Distinguished Flying Cross and Air Medals.

His two brothers were also Marine aviators.

As a forward air-ground attack coordinator in Korea, attached to a company of Marine infantry, Doswell stepped on a land mine and suffered shrapnel wounds to both legs, before having both his shins shattered by fire from a communist Chinese burp-gun. Doswell was knocked prone to the ground and, stunned, envisioned his life flashing before his eyes.

"I thought it was the end. I saw one enemy grenade landing less than 10 feet away from me. Miraculously, it never exploded. All the Marines in the company around me were wounded. Four were dead. Chinese soldiers were running through our position. I was waiting for the thrust of a bayonet to finish me. But Marine reinforcements arrived in time to repel the Chinese."

Doswell survived the ordeal, but his wounds kept him from flying for nearly 30 months.

Attached to VMF-513 in Korea, Doswell's squadron lost 14 aircraft in November 1951. Nightfighter qualified, Doswell participated in 60 combat missions over North Korea. Of the 14 aircraft lost during strikes at night and in bad weather, only six pilots survived as POW's. The fate of the other eight pilots remain unknown.

"ONE OF THE LUCKIER
THROTTLE JOCKS"

Jim Ferris

On 1 November 1943 at Buka Passage, Bougainville, Okie Wallen and I were happily engaged in strafing the bejesus out of a Japanese destroyer when my Hellcat was hit in the engine. I limped along for perhaps 10 minutes with intermittent surges of power followed by thunderous silences before the engine conked and I ditched. The beach was only a couple of miles off but naked panic and mounting hysteria at the thought of being captured gave in to reasoned judgment, so I paddled in circles to confuse any possible observers. Okie, sturdy soul that he is, circled me (probably until he began to be confused), and then shoved off. (I could see him shaking his head in puzzlement.)

Several hours later, having cleverly avoided detection by hiding behind my parachute pack, I was picked up by the, USS Waller, a destroyer-escort. The resident commodore, whose disdain for "flyboys" bordered on the rabid, jovially admonished me to pass the word to "all those effing zoomies on the effing flat-top to stay clear of the tin can Navy because one effing enemy was as good as any effing enemy---and don't you ever effing forget it!"

Encouraged by his warm welcome, I retreated to the nether regions where I was presented with a folding canvas cot and directed to an athwartships passageway where I could unfold it "after the movie." My appreciation for the black shoe navy continued to burgeon during the next three days an appreciation which I have held dear these past 44 years. I think it is the humor which captured my allegiance then and has enthralled me ever since. These guys are funneee!

To the intense satisfaction of all, I was dropped off at Tulagi, a few miles across the water from Guadalcanal, and made my way via whale boat and jeep to Henderson Field and the headquarters quonset hut of Commander Air, Solomons, a marine general officer. The closest I got to the general was a harassed major who listened with serene indifference as I colorfully recounted my misadventures. He smiled tolerantly when I asked for a Hellcat, rolled his eyes heavenward when I averred my intention to get back to my ship without delay, and had taken on a slightly strangled look by the time I finished my declaration. He directed me to the mess tent and choked out words to the effect he would contact me in due course. The thought occurred that he might be related to a commodore of my recent acquaintance.

I spent the next two days appealing for help from anyone who would listen and was about to throw in my jock when I came across a navy CPO who (a) wasn't all that fond of "those effing gyrenes," and (b) just happened to be in charge of the damaged aircraft pool. He told me to scrounge up some flight gear (Waller's crewmen having taken mine for souvenirs), and he'd fix me up with a Hellcat. Four hours later, after inflating tires, gassing and arming his least damaged aircraft, I took off for Munda -- sans clearance and good wishes, or bad. I did not plug in my headphone cord until I was on final at Munda. There, the twin brother of the other Marine major told me he had no parking space for me and to get my ass off his real estate and he didn't give a geedee effing you-know-what where I might sojourn for the night. This directive I hastily carried out, heading once again along the island chain toward Henderson Field, a destination the prospect of which made becoming a POW increasingly attractive. However, good judgment again prevailed and I decided to land anywhere else but Henderson Field.

From our earlier visits to the Solomons, I remembered that Jumpin' Joe's friend, Monk Russell, commanded an F6F squadron which was based between Munda and Henderson Field and I went for it, figuring I had little to lose. At least I'd be back with Navy types and avoid the clutches of blackshoes and jungle bunnies. As it developed, that decision was one of my all-time best. It turned out that Monk was still there.   His VF-33 was to supply CAP for the Saratoga group while Air Group TWELVE was striking Rabaul the next day.   I was allowed to tag along with the post-strike Combat Air Patrol and I was recovered aboard Sara in the late afternoon of 6 November. The flight leader did me the world's greatest favor by breaking radio silence and requesting a ready flight deck for Lt (jg) Jim Ferris, "one of your luckier throttle jocks."

Just 22 years later I took command of VF-33 and Captain Monk Russell, USN, was an honored guest at the ceremony.

James Ferris was born in St. Helens, Lancashire, England on November 15, 1919.   He grew up in Kearny, New Jersey.   He attended Elon College.   Jim had a very distinguished career in the Navy.   He flew over 300 combat missions in three wars.   He retired as a rear admiral and lives with his lovely wife Hazel in Alameda, California.

NAVY
SEA
STORIES

Emmet Ferguson, Jr.

I had always wanted to be a doctor or a naval officer. Upon finishing high school in 1938, I entered the University of Georgia to study pre-med. That summer my congressman asked me to take the examination for one of the service academies. I took the exam with about 300 others and I didn't do too well. My score was about 56. He said that I did better than most.

After taking the test the next year and finishing in the top ten, I received an alternate appointment. Some dropped out and I received an appointment to the US Naval Academy in the year 1940. After completing two years of pre-med at Georgia, I proceeded to enter the academy for a career in the Navy.

LIFE AT THE
ACADEMY AFTER
PEARL HARBOR DAY

Pearl Harbor was bombed December 7, 1941. On a mid-Sunday afternoon in December upon returning from a movie at Mahan Hall, we learned of the attack. Life changed drastically around the academy. Security increased, everyone stood guard duty, anxiety filled the air, and curricula were altered. President Roosevelt's Day of Infamy speech resonated through the brigade. Everyone wanted to get into combat.

Many reservists came through the academy for the ninety-day course to be commissioned as ensigns. They were the ninety-day wonders. We were all envious.

Wendell Wilkie's son was one, and he and I used to work out in the gym together.

The academic course remained the same and was not shortened. The usual three-month cruises were reduced to six weeks and confined to the Chesapeake Bay. We were the salty sailors of the Chesapeake. A wealthy ambassador gave his yacht, the Jamestown to the academy for use as a training ship. Another gave the Vamarie, a 10-ton lead keeled sailing yacht and quite a ship to sail. We got our sea legs on the "ketches" and the "knock-a-bouts." Classes were extended to Saturday mornings. Day classes were lengthened by several hours. The academy buzzed with excitement as the nation raced to war. We all looked forward to the fray. Football games took place on academy grounds. Army-Navy game sites alternated and half of the brigade rooted for the Army and the other half for the Navy. Vacations and holidays were shortened, with only a few days for Christmas. Time flew by.

AFTER GRADUATION

After graduation, we drew ship assignments. Mine was to destroyers. All non-circumcised midshipmen going to destroyers were sent to the hospital for the procedure and I was one of them. This was a cleanliness measure.

TO FLORIDA

After that, our entire class went to Jacksonville, Florida for six weeks indoctrination and flight participation in all types of naval aircraft. We dive-bombed at Cecil Field; fired machine guns at Yellow Water, flew on board PBY's out of Jacksonville and Ventura bombers out of Lake City. Many of the men rode around town on motorcycles and more that a few married Jacksonville girls. Then it was off to the fleet.

MOST BEAUTIFUL
SCENES ON EARTH

One morning about sunup we were dive-bombing at Cecil Field. As we climbed to 12,000 feet flying eastward toward the USN, we saw one of the most glorious sights I have ever seen. Bellowing, lofty, fluffy white clouds several thousand feet high and several miles wide formed a dazzling array of columns, six to eight on each side, making a corridor lane like the center aisle of a great cathedral.

At the other end of this gigantic lane, a sparkling brilliant radiation of rainbow-colored light from the brilliant rising sun pierced the fresh morning air. The glittering display flowed into the lane and into one's soul as if the Gate of Paradise had just opened. Coleridge must have experienced a similar feeling in writing Kublai Khan. I had experienced a comparable mood once before, when traveling down the Columbia River valley about four o'clock in the morning with some college fraternity brothers on the day Britain declared war on Germany.

FIRST SHIP
ASSIGNMENT AND
THE NORTH ATLANTIC

My first assignment was to the USS Livermore, DD429. I boarded her at New York. We had a shakedown cruise off the coast of Maine, shooting down unmanned drone aircraft and shelling the coast. Back in New York, we joined a convoy group taking loaded Liberty ships across the Atlantic to Casablanca. The convoys were huge, 200 to 300 ships with 12 to 16 escort destroyers.

THE NORTH
ATLANTIC
IN WINTER

The first of these convoys was through the U-boat infested wintry North Atlantic, the most hostile, foreboding place on earth. Hundred-foot waves tossed the destroyers about like toy boats in a bathtub. The propeller screws, when the ship was on top of a wave, churned, out of the water. When the ship plunged into a valley of water, a spray of freezing green water covered the forecastle and bridge. The entire fame of the ship shook and quivered as if were going to break in two.

MAN OVERBOARD

We lost a man overboard. A fellow crewman tossed a line with a grapple hook and caught the hapless sailor's life belt, luckily pulling him in, A great cheer erupted from those witnessing the event. This prompted discussion of a similar overboard incident which occurred before I joined the ship. The Livermore was cruising off Cape Hatteras, North Carolina in heavy seas when a sailor was washed overboard. The five flag was broken out. The frightened seaman washed on to the sister ship, the USS Eberly steaming in column astern of the Livermore. When the five flag appeared, the Eberly, turned broadside to, and the lucky sailor washed aboard the Eberly in nearly the same place he had washed off the Livermore. Everyone was elated over the rescue.

TOSSING
AROUND
AT SEA

In the heavy tossing seas of the vicious North Atlantic, many were seasick. Appetites were poor and when we did eat, it was necessary to latch your chair to the wardroom table with special clasp-hooks. Stanchions, placed from the deck to the ceiling, held one in place. When bunking in the small staterooms, you had to lash yourself to the bunk. One night, the ship lurched after I had failed to lash myself in. I fell out and landed on the shoulders of Monty Bradley, who slept on the bunk below. After the stormy North Atlantic, we arrived in the peaceful calm seas around Casablanca.

CASABLANCA AND
SHORE PATROL

Junior officers like me were often assigned to shore patrol duty. Two regular sailors and a junior officer comprised a shore patrol unit. One day when going into Casablanca from the harbor, we saw two sailors with two Arabs chasing them in hot pursuit. We joined the chase, up one hill and down another for about a mile of running. The two sailors ducked into a hotel. The manager of the hotel spoke French and in my broken French I asked him if the two sailors were there. He assured me they were not. The three of us in our patrol went outside to quiet the agitated Arabs. It turned out that the two sailors had swiped two bottles of wine from their cart. I asked how much the wine was worth and they said 25 cents each. I gave them a dollar. They wanted to hug and kiss me but I sought to be aloof. They sauntered off happily and we went back into the hotel.

The sheepish sailors who had been hiding there came out and wanted to reimburse me for the dollar given to the Arabs. I would not let them but ordered the men in the patrol to take them back to the ship and put them in the brig. I appeared at the next Captain's Mast and explained the situation to the captain, who confined them to the ship for a month.

Later, when going into Mer el. Kaber, one of the men responded rapidly in the engine room to a command from the bridge, saving a screw on the ship from hitting the angled walls of the French harbor. The captain pardoned him, took him off confinement and let him have liberty again.

CROSSING THE ATLANTIC

We made several convoy crossings of the Atlantic. They usually took 10 to 12 days, but some took over 20 days depending on how hard the wind was blowing. Going back to the states, the ships were empty and the high riding gunnels acted like a sail and blew the ship back. As escorts, we steamed in front of the convoy at 10 to 12 knots, zigzagging as an antisubmarine screen. The ground speed of the convoy was usually about six knots.

TAKING A ROLL AT SEA

On one of the convoy crossings, our ship was being tossed unmercifully, tilting side to side from 50 to 55 degrees so that one could put his hand out and scoop up green water when the tilt was at its zenith. It was in the middle of the mid-watch when I felt a young sailor pulling on my trousers, saying, "Mr. Ferguson, we are going to be trapped below like a bunch of rats when the ship capsizes."

I tried to reassure him that the met centric height of a destroyer was such that we could roll 65 degrees and not turn over. I told him the most we had rolled was 55 degrees at best. This gave him little comfort. Finally, I called Dr.

Rowe, who gave him a shot to put him to sleep. This same fellow later, when we were being strafed by German Fockwulf 190s at Anzio Beach Head, would go berserk. We had to place him in the bilges of the ship, passing up ammunition where he could not see what was going on.

GETTING LOST
IN THE MIDDLE
OF A CONVOY

Once about 2 a.m., while standing watch during a stormy night as a junior officer of the deck, I noticed on the radar screen that we were in the middle of the convoy. One could not see the ship next to ours. The officer of the deck told me to go and wake the captain. I told the captain that we were in the middle of the convoy.

"What! How the hell did that happen?" he exclaimed.

We ran back to the bridge. It seems that the CIC was telling the officer of the deck that we were, 9000 yards ahead of the ship astern, which was the last ship in the convoy. The officer of the deck kept taking turns off the screws thinking he was way out in front of the convoy. In actuality, we were the right distance from the front of the convoy. The captain took over the con and with fear and trepidation worked us out of a hazardous situation. Only once did we come perilously close to one of the ships in the convoy -- so close you could throw a stick to the adjacent ship.

A BIG
FUNERAL
AT SEA

Once in mid-Atlantic we were ordered to attend a burial at sea. A fellow died on one of the convoy ships, and it was one of the largest funerals I ever attended. There were 300 ships in the convoy with a squadron of destroyers for escort so I figured there were more than 35,000 people in attendance at the funeral. Life goes on even in a convoy at sea.

GET COUSIN
KARL TONIGHT

Our skipper, Eddie Siedel, was of German extraction. He and I were the only "trade schoolers" (graduates of the Naval Academy) on board. All of the rest of the officer corps were from Ivy schools like Harvard, Yale, and Dartmouth except for Luke Dargan, our chief engineer, who was a South Carolina graduate with a degree in forestry, and Bill Jones, who was a graduate of West Virginia. Captain Siedel had a cousin serving in the German navy as a U-boat commander. Every night he would sign the log, "Let's get Cousin Karl tonight."

GETTING A
CHECK CASHED

Once when we were in Rabat, a Moroccan city north of Casablanca, we were on liberty and I had ran out of money. I went into a bank and asked them to cash my check on the Farmers' Bank in Annapolis. The cashier approached a higher bank official who wanted further identification. I showed him my Naval Academy class ring, which had my name inside but he wanted still further identification. I told him my father had an "A" rating with Dun & Bradstreet. He looked it up, and since my name was the same as my father's, he readily cashed my check. A complete stranger over 3,000 miles from home got a check cashed!

TESTING DEPTH
CHARGES

Once when going into New York harbor, Mr. Bacon, the executive officer, decided to see if we could safely drop depth charges at a speed of six knots instead of the usual 10 to 12 knots. He tried it and we had to spend an extra week in port getting the screw shafts realigned. The crew enjoyed the extra liberty in New York.

A SAILOR ON
SHORE LEAVE

Another time I was officer of the day in port when two sailors came by flashing rolls of $1,000 each. They had been the successful winners of poker games at sea. The games were forbidden, but they took place none the less.

"Mr. Ferguson, we are going to leave a three-day liberty trail through New York City and everyone will know the Livermore was here," the two sailors told me.

When the shore patrol brought them back to the ship three days later, I found they had done just what they said!

ON BECOMING
COMMISSARY
OFFICER

We were leaving New York and were out past Ambrose Light when I got a call to report to the bridge on the double. The skipper said, "Ferguson, you are commissary officer."

"Yes, Sir," I said, "but what are the duties of the commissary officer?" "Whenever this ship leaves port, have fresh milk on board. I just called for a glass of milk. We are barely out of New York and there is no milk aboard. I called

Mr. McCormick and relieved him of his duties as commissary officer. Hope you can do better."

"Yes, sir."

The captain on what seemed like a whim would fire McCormick or me and make the other commissary officer. We rotated the post several times. Each time he would confine the recently relieved one to his room for several days interrupted only with duty standing watch.

You can bet your bottom dollar that when we pulled out of Norfolk before crossing the Atlantic again we had lots of fresh milk on board. Not only that, but I stocked the ship with potatoes, vegetables, fruit and everything else, so much so we had potatoes tied to depth charges all over the deck. Orders said our next voyage would be far over one month at sea.

Our group included a small aircraft carrier and several destroyers. We were to search the South Atlantic for a German Sea raider. After being at sea for 20 days or more, we received a call to strip the deck for action and prepare to engage the sea raider. Overboard went all the potatoes. We arrived a little late and found that one of the other destroyers had captured the German raider. But our potatoes were gone.

OLD MEDENA

Late one day in Casablanca, our shore patrol got the message that Mr. Blackburn and his shore patrol were overdue from a tour into Old Medena (an off limits Arab section in Casablanca). Our orders were to go in and see if we could find them. Shortly after entering the city we saw Blackburn and his three men and two others running toward the gate with a group of Arabs in hot pursuit.

All of a sudden, Blackburn stopped, turned around, pulled out his .45, and waved it toward the Arabs, telling them to get back. Blackburn was a little on the heavy side and had run out of breath. Nevertheless, he was glad to see us.

We asked what had happened. It seems that two sailors were making improper advances on an Arab girl. Her kinsmen didn't like it. The patrol tried to intervene. They were outnumbered and felt the best course was to flee, which was successful until Mr. Blackburn became winded.

FRENCH MOROCCAN
SHORE PATROL

When doing shore patrol duty we ran into the French Moroccan patrol. They were tall black Moroccan soldiers who were ruthless when it came to handling their misbehaving comrades. One day in a bar I saw a Moroccan shore patrolman break a soldier's jaw with the butt of his rifle. The French had a custom of sending the prostitutes who had been apprehended in Cannes and other French cities to Casablanca to work off their fines. The prostitutes were sent to Casablanca to practice prostitution for doing the same thing they did in France. They were usually the source of trouble in bars and caused shore patrols a great deal of trouble. The Moroccans handled the problems on the scene; we arrested them and carried the sailors back to the brig.

GIBRALTAR

Orders to leave Casablanca for duty in the Mediterranean sent us through the Straits of Gibraltar. While anchored at Gibraltar (which was under British control) we had to take great precaution to prevent sabotage to the ship. Several had received damage to the screws by divers attaching underwater explosives. To prevent this, the officer-of-the-deck used small handheld depth charges, throwing one over the side of the ship every 30 minutes at random. It was hard to get a good nights sleep, but it kept the underwater saboteurs at bay.

RAMMING
SUBMARINES

Initially we were sent to the Mediterranean to clear the eastern part of the Med. of German submarines. Our orders were to sink submarines at all cost, even if this meant ramming them on the surface. Early one morning, just at dawn, we were cruising in the Eastern Mediterranean just south of the Spanish Island of Palmer. A small blip appeared on the radar screen having all the earmarkings of a surfaced sub. The skipper called General Quarters. The captain gave the order to stand by to ram. Then had second thoughts and decided to go close aboard, illuminate the sub with the searchlight, and then ram if necessary. I was the officer in charge of the searchlight. I gave the order to illuminate, but nothing happened. Looking through the binoculars in the early light of the dawn we saw two spicules of rock piecing the ocean surface. The rocks did not appear on the navigation charts.

The captain summoned me to the bridge. "Why the hell couldn't you get the searchlight on the target?" he queried. I told him I had given the order but nothing happened. It evolved that the only sailor that knew how to turn the lights on was transferred the last time we were in the states. The captain ordered searchlight drill every watch for the next three months. Needless to say, the captain never entertained the idea of ramming without seeing again.

ON BECOMING
NAVIGATOR

Shortly after entering the Mediterranean, the captain assigned me to help Chief Madden, a 30-year navy chief, with the navigation. Mr. Bacon, the executive officer, was the navigator. Every morning, noon and night I would take a sextant reading for celestial navigation. Three sightings determined a triangle fix of location. Some triangles are large and some are small. Chief Madden's triangles were usually pinpoint in width. Mine were 10 to 25 miles wide.

One day the captain called me to the bridge and told me that he was appointing me navigator. I was elated despite my inexperience. I knew that I was a book-learned navigator and not the real thing. I always felt that I could fall back on Chief Madden if I got in trouble. That's when I learned those navy chiefs were the backbone of the navy.

WATERING THE GENERAL'S LIQUOR

We operated out of Oran, a French Algerian port. The army had a large presence here. Crisp Wilkinson, a top sergeant from my hometown of DeSoto, Georgia, was assigned as an aide to the one of the American generals and had the key to the general's liquor. Periodically when in port, several of us would go over and visit with Crisp, who was quite a popular fellow. To prevent detection we would replenish the used liquors with water. We even rationalized that we were doing the general a favor in preventing his inebriation.

SPEED RUNS

The commodore (our ship was his headquarters) received orders to test the ships in his division. Normally we carried about 140,000 gallons of fuel oil. When traveling eight to ten knots the oil would last a couple weeks. On a speed run out of Oran to Naples traveling at nearly 40 knots, we used all the fuel in four hours. At 40 knots, the ship seemed to shake apart. On that run, we refueled at sea. At

40 knots, the ship gets very poor efficiency in miles per gallon.

DEPTH CHARGING
A TURTLE

Once on a run from Oran to Naples the lookout saw a large object in the water ahead. At first, we thought it was a mine. Upon closer inspection, it turned out to be a turtle. We asked the skipper for permission to capture it for turtle soup. Pulling alongside, we threw out small handheld depth charges like the ones we had used at Gibraltar to thwart saboteurs. Then using a grapple hook, we pulled the carcass aboard. The whole crew enjoyed fresh turtle soup.

APPENDICITIS
AT SEA

The sea was rough the day one of the sailors came down with a pain in his side. Dr. Roe, the ship's doctor, diagnosed appendicitis. The doctor asked me to help him set up the wardroom table for an operation. The doctor and corpsman did the operation. We watched. Dr. Roe poured his own ether. With the patient asleep he and the corpsman rapidly removed the appendix. The patient did well. The doctor sent the patient to a hospital in Oran a few days later when we docked there.

NAPLES HARBOR

We made frequent trips between Naples and Oran with interspersing stops at Palermo, Algiers and Bezurdie. Naples has a beautiful harbor. One night while anchored in Naples bay, a storm came up. The Livermore lay at anchor near other destroyers. The wind was blowing at 25 to 30 knots and I was officer-of-the deck. Periodically I walked around the deck and I noticed we were getting closer and closer to the ship next to us. I finally notified the captain. We were dragging the anchor. The skipper called everyone to quarters. We moved the ship several hundred yards away and put out more chain on the anchor. Had we not done so, in a few minutes we would have been bagging against the destroyer next to us? A good thing to remember at sea: If the bearing on nearby structures is changing, you are moving (dragging anchor).

A SERGEANT
KICKS A LADY
IN THE BELLY

There was lots of crime taking place in Naples. When on shore patrol you were always busy trying to keep our own sailors out of trouble. One day our patrol was ambling along one of the midtown streets when we saw a big burly U.S. sergeant go out of his way to kick a poor old Italian woman in the belly without cause. We ran after him to apprehend and take him to headquarters.

There are many nooks and corners in Naples affording good places to hide and we were unable to find him. We discussed among ourselves why would a good old American fighting man do such a heinous thing. About the best we could come up with was the supposition that maybe a similar appearing lady killed his buddy as they were coming up the boot of the Italian coast. Who knows? War does strange thing to people and many become irrational.

NAPLES AND
VESUVIUS

Naples was always a great place to visit and was a favorite liberty port. One time Mt. Versuvius erupted and instantly filled the air with volcanic dust. Later, when firing the ship's guns, volcanic dust rattled through the ventilation ducts.

We often anchored the ship in the bay near the volcano. It was a favorite swimming site and frequently ship crews held swim contests in the area. We often had competitive meets with British ships anchored nearby, such as the Ajax.

Many of the crew also visited Pompeii and came back to the ship with pornographic carvings and literature common to the 70 A.D. Pompeii eruption that buried the city. Wishing for liberty on shore, but confined to the directory watch, we in the directory amused ourselves measuring the height of Vesuvius using the ships' director. From a distance of 13,000 yard (7.5 miles) Vesuvius was 3,880 feet high.

A VISIT TO THE
BRITISH SHIP

One day while in Naples the captain and several officers from our ship went over to HMS Zetland to arrange a swimming meet. We dressed up in British naval shorts, which made a hit with the Limeys. As usual, they put on the dog. They broke out the Scottish whiskey. They fed us a great lunch and we exchanged talk and tales with them.

They are funny in their way, but I suspect they think the same of us. We won the meet 37-20. We lost the water polo. Luke took them to Pompeii. Max and I joined them after arranging some duties with the ship to shore firemen. We rode the free train to Pompeii and visited the large cathedral. The altar of the cathedral had a half-million dollars worth of diamonds.

WE SINK A MINE

Once when going from Naples to Capri, we spotted a mine in our sea-lane. Using the 20's and 40's (machine guns), we blew it up at distance of 500 yards. The resulting explosion was massive. No one knew where the mine came from. We were grateful we found it before it found us.

THE ISLE OF CAPRI

The Isle of Capri guards the mouth of Naples harbor. It also was our favorite liberty port. The harbor, though beautiful, is small and difficult to enter. The mountain terrain drops abruptly into the sea. The isle is about 20 miles from the city of Naples and was an ideal favorite for R&R (rest and relaxation). Often we would fight at Anzio for two weeks and take one week off in Capri.

It was fun going ashore and using horse drawn buggies as transportation. We visited the Blue Grotto, Mussolini's summer home, and the home of Rudolph Valentino. There are many ritzy villas on Capri. They preferred blue seal dollars but we used gold seal ones. Cigarettes for barter were better than money as a medium of exchange.

THERE CAN BE
ONLY ONE CAPTAIN

Once when entering Capri harbor in a stiff onshore breeze, the captain was having a difficult time negotiating the small harbor entrance. The stern of the ship approached perilously close to the beach. The captain placed turns on the inboard screws to keep the ship off the beach.

The commodore, seeing the captain was in trouble, took the turns off and the captain didn't know about it. The ship began to surge one way and the other. It rapidly got out of control and suddenly we crashed into a small fishing craft near the bow of the ship. The commodore apologized to the captain but the damage was done.

The captain sent me over to settle with the owner of the fishing vessel. The fisherman spoke no English, but we negotiated a settlement value of $5,000. I gave him the proper papers to take to the British Admiralty, which handled such matters in the Naples area. Two weeks later when our ship came into Capri, the fisherman was there to greet us. His English had improved a bit, but he was agitated, disturbed and unhappy, and his estimate of the damage had increased three-fold to $15,000. He said it was impossible to deal with the British and he wanted us to take care of the matter. The captain sent me to the British Admiralty along with the fisherman and we came to a satisfactory resolution, or so I thought.

Every time we came into Capri after that, the fisherman was the first to greet us. After the third or fourth visit, he began to speak very good English. But he was never quite satisfied. The British assured me that they handled the matter equitably. During our last visit to Capri, he was still there.

THE ANTITHETICAL CASABA IN ALGIERS

If ever there were a city worse than Sodom and Gomorrah, the Casaba is it. Everything, every moral value, we in western society hold dear, the people of Algiers' Casaba hold the opposite view. They thrived on lying, cheating, stealing, killing, and sexual debasement. Almost all of our moral values have no place there. Thieves, murders and fornicators were the backbone of the society. We would tell our crew not to go into the Casaba and inevitably, not a day went by that we did not have to rescue one of them. When doing patrol work in the Casaba, we doubled the group from three to six and it was still not enough.

Emmet F. Ferguson, Jr. was born in DeSoto, Georgia on March 28, 1921. He received his M.D. from the University of Georgia and he had a very successful medical career in Jacksonville. He is the author of three books. He and his loving wife Jerry reside in one of Jacksonville's historic homes.

"THOSE KIDS
ARE ON
THEIR WAY"

David W. Foerster

A Jacksonville native, I was in my freshman year at Washington & Lee University on December 7, 1941.

My introduction to wartime on that date led me, along with four other students from the five corners of America, to make a midnight drive to Washington, D.C., hopefully to witness President Roosevelt, in a joint session of Congress, asking for a declaration of war. Even in our teenage naiveté, we realized that it would be a momentous occasion.

As we drove into and around the City of Washington at 2o'clock in the morning, we observed every government building, including the White House and the Capitol, ablaze with lights with a multitude of armed military personnel carrying guns and fixed bayonets, patrolling the bridges, streets and buildings.

The next morning, the five of us stood, somewhat isolated from the crowds in front of the Capitol, to watch the President in his motorcade move into the Capitol. As his limousine came abreast of us, some 20 yards away, the car slowed perceptibly, a rear window was lowered and the President leaned out and waived at the five of us. We, of course, waved back and I am confident that he may have silently observed -- "Those kids are on their way."

We returned to the campus and, indeed, within a few months, we were all "on our way to one part of the military or another." I chose naval aviation and received my wings at Pensacola as a "brown shoe" ensign.

Our squadron, assigned to multi-entire land-based PB4Y-2's, spent the remaining months of the European war searching at night, by radar and huge wing lights, for

German submarines in the North Atlantic as they surfaced to recharge their batteries. Toward the very end of the war, one plane in our squadron was actually credited, in a unique occurrence, with "capturing" a sub by directing allied surface sips in the vicinity to the sub. Our greatest hazard was being shot down by allied ships at night as a result of poor radio communication.

With the war in Europe ending, we were sent to the Caribbean to learn the "art" of hurricane patrol which, in those days, was in its infancy. Spotting hurricanes, flying at low levels to visually observe the wind velocity, was an experience, particularly when 125 mile per hour winds were churning the sea.

Returning to civilian life, I finished my undergraduate work, then went to law school. After that I practiced for over 50 years, handling eminent domain trial work in Jacksonville and elsewhere in the State of Florida.

I shall forever value and remain proud of my Navy Wings of Gold.

David W. Foerster was born in Jacksonville, Florida on July 22, 1923.

104

Eugene Martin Frame

I was born in a small railroad town in West Virginia by the name of Gassaway. My birthdate was May 27, 1915.

I grew up in this small town and didn't leave until after high school. I graduated from West Virginia Tech in 1936 with a B.S. degree and a major in chemistry. I worked for Union Carbide in a research laboratory for two years, after which I attended West Virginia University Medical School. I graduated from Temple University Medical School with an M.D. degree in 1942.

I immediately joined the navy and was commissioned Lt. (jg) in the Medical Corps. I served an internship at the U.S. Naval Hospital in Portsmouth, Virginia, and then I was ordered to Kearny, New Jersey, where I participated in the fitting out and commissioning of the destroyer Allen M. Sumner. I served on the Sumner until McArthur and the Japanese emissaries signed the peace treaty on September 2, 1945.

I will attempt to list some of the important events that occurred while I served as medical officer aboard this destroyer. This listing is purely from memory. I am sure that there could be some inconsistencies, since I have to trust my memory.

HAZARDS IN
THE DARK

This occurred in late 1944 or early 1945. We were anchored in Leyte Gulf in the Philippines and one morning a motor whaleboat, from the commandant, came alongside.

The mission was to remove all our "publications," which were highly classified tactical battle plans. The reason for this was an order we received for an after-dark operation that was very hazardous, and the task force commander didn't want these plans to fall into enemy hands.

We proceeded leading three other destroyers in column, after-dark, through the Surigao Straits. It was in the dark of the moon and the navigation problem was very hazardous. However, our exec guided us through the straits without incident.

We proceeded to Ormoc Bay, where reconnaissance had spotted the Japs unloading supplies on the shore. We had orders to circle the shoreline and destroy all the targets we could locate.

We had just entered the bay when an apparent shore-based torpedo struck the last destroyer in the column. It struck midship, and the ship practically broke in half and sank in 45 seconds. The men topside all floated off, and everybody below was lost.

We proceeded as ordered and found many targets on the shorelines, including ammunition dumps. The Japs ordered air strikes and we were credited with shooting more than one plane out of the sky by radar gun control. In the process we were hit by an antipersonnel fragmentation bomb. There were several injuries, but no fatalities. There was one serious injury, but we were able to transfer him to a hospital ship the next day. As far as I know, he recovered.

After circling the shoreline with constant bombardment, we left the bay and steamed past the men who had floated off the sunken destroyer. We were steaming at flank speed, and the division commander thought that if we stopped to attempt to rescue the men, the three remaining destroyers in all likelihood would be lost. At daybreak, a PBY amphibious plane came and rescued all the men floating in the area of their lost ship. The PBY had P38 fighter coverage.

ESCORT DUTY

We spent a fairly long period escorting the large carriers north of the Philippines. At dusk the task force would steam north and during the night the small escorting vessels would be refueled by the carriers. At daybreak we would steam toward Manila and air strikes would be launched.

The big carriers would steam at flank speed, and we had a terrible time keeping up with them, especially in a high sea. We encountered a typhoon one night, and our captain received orders to pump ballast and prepare for refueling. The sea was so high and treacherous at the time that he refused the order to pump ballast, fearful of the loss of stability. Another destroyer in our squadron pumped ballast, the ship capsized and practically all hands were lost.

RESCUE SERVICE

We were part of a large task force assigned to the bombardment of the shore in Lingayen Gulf, three days before the arrival of McArthur and the troops preparing to land on Luzon and more on to Manila. While in the gulf bombarding the shore, we were provided with navy air cover. The carriers were operating in the South China Sea and the cover was provided by these carriers.

A Jap pilot broke through the circle of U.S. planes providing the cover, and a U.S. pilot took off in pursuit. Practically the whole task force focused its attention on the Jap plane with antiaircraft fire. In the process both the Jap and U.S. planes were shot out of the sky.

The U.S. pilot was floating near our ship and we rescued him out of the water. In bailing out, he had struck the tail assembly with his thigh and received a nasty fracture. When we got him aboard, he asked "What kind of a ship is this?" He was told it was a destroyer and he said, "Oh, for God's sake get me off this thing!"

107

He had a terrible fracture of the mid-thigh (femur) and the fragments were almost at right angles. We could control his pain, but could not possibly reduce the fracture. In a short space of time we transferred him by breeches buoy to a battleship.

SOMETHING TO REMEMBER

Late in the war, we were ordered from the war zone back to Pearl Harbor for the purpose of minor repairs. It was to be a short interlude, but it was enjoyed by all hands. I was ashore in the officers' club and had about two hours before we were to get under way and rejoin the fleet.

I was having a beer with another young doctor who was attached to a destroyer in another squadron. He was a graduate of Harvard and an interesting man to talk with. However, he said that he certainly did not like his destroyer duty and hoped he would soon be transferred. He said the captain didn't know his job. He couldn't get along with the crew and the morale was terrible. He added, "You know, you might get killed on that thing."

KAMIKAZE ATTACK

We continued the shore bombardment and in the p.m. of the day before the arrival of the troops, a kamikaze plane hit our destroyer. The modis operandi of the kamikaze pilot was to hit the bridge of the target ship. This, of course, would destroy the center of combat control and would really be disabling if successful.

The kamikaze pilot took dead aim at our bridge, but overshot the bridge and came down in the middle of the after deck house. This was the battle station of my chief petty officer and, of course, he was killed instantly. We had, as I remember, 35 fatalities and many serious injuries. I was in the wardroom, which is just below the bridge, and luckily escaped without a scratch.

I had two medical corpsmen left and we worked feverishly to treat shock and relieve pain. This went on until after dark, at which time we transferred the wounded by breeches buoy to a battleship (I don't recall which one).

Our ship was badly damaged, but seaworthy, and we were ordered to leave Lingayen Gulf and proceed unescorted to San Francisco. It was a long, long, very slow trip due to the ship's disabilities, but we had no problems and never came under attack after leaving Luzon.

We were ordered to Hunters Point in San Francisco and the ship was in dry dock about eight or ten weeks. At this point the crew enjoyed a lot of leave, and San Francisco was quite a relief.

After a long repair period we were ordered back to the Pacific and joined a small task force comprised of about eight or ten destroyers, and as I remember, about three to five cruisers. We had orders to arrive very close to Wake Island (occupied by the Japs and heavily fortified) and conduct a shore bombardment at close range. We were not looking forward to this due to the heavy artillery present and operating on the island.

If my dates are correct, we arrived in the area on August 14, 1945. The cease-fire was ordered for Aug 15. We did a 180-degree about face, and that ended all of our action in World War II.

We were ordered to proceed to Tokyo Bay, where we anchored just off the bow of the Missouri. With binoculars we had a good vision of McArthur and the emperor's representatives signing the Peace Treaty.

At this point I was relieved of my duty aboard the Allen M. Sumner and ordered back to the states. Of course, I had a multitude of "points" to get out of the navy, but they wouldn't accept them because I was Regular Navy. I was told by the bureau that I could have my choice of duty. I chose duty "under instruction" in the field of pathology. I was assigned to study under some internationally known pathologist and I was delighted. However, at this point the navy almost ran out of doctors because practically all the reserve doctors went back home.

My training was cut short after nine months and I was ordered to the Naval Hospital at NAS Jacksonville, as chief of the Laboratory Services and Pathology. I served in this capacity with my meager training until July 1947, at which time they finally accepted my resignation. Following this I completed training in pediatrics at the University of Virginia, and then returned to Jacksonville to open practice in the field of pediatrics. I retired in 1982.

DIXIE, CHAPPIE,
RED DOG AND THE
SACK AND SOCIAL

Rollin Ellsworth Gray

The membership qualifications for the Sack and Social never were formulated explicitly. I don't suppose anyone ever thought about them at all. The severe exclusiveness was not due to any kind of snobbery but to limitations of the physical facility and, although no one knows how many members there were at any particular time, it never had more than three inhabitants -- Dixie, Chappie, and me, the Red Dog.

The physical facility was a sheet-iron cube about nine feet on each side and it showed on the blueprints of the U.S.S. Saratoga as living compartment No. 112. It had been assembled with a large locker, a bunk space with drawers below, a dresser with fold-down desk, and a washstand and medicine cabinet, all of sheet metal and firmly affixed by bolts or rivets. Across from the original bunk, two more had been added, with flat cot springs and frames of iron pipe hinged at one side to the sheetiron bulkhead and suspended at the inner sides by a chain. The built-in bunk had coil springs -- a strangely mixed blessing in heavy weather because when the ship's bow rose and fell, hugely and ponderously, the bunk's occupant levitated or sank on its springs in miniature mimicry. We drew lots to decide which of us would get the good bunk, then from time to time, we rotated places, like the Mad Teaparty. Across from the door, on top of the desk, was what seemed to be a large suitcase, on its side, with one end facing into the room. It was ivory in color, padded and covered in imitation leather, and when various latches, lids, and panels were opened, strange complex mechanisms could be seen inside.

It contained a radio receiver for both regular and short-wave frequencies but most of it was an automatic record-player that had been custom-made for some world traveler in the recent past when it was both safe and stylish to be a world traveler. It ran on either AC or DC current and could be switched to accept a range of voltages from 100 to 250 so that if electricity was available, it operated. The automatic record-changer was very well made but unusual in concept. The records to be played, 10 or 12-inch, were stacked on the turntable in advance and, as each one finished playing, the machine would peel it off the top of the stack and eject it, like a Frisbee, through a narrow, piano-hinged trap door in the side. If some kind of arrangements had been made to catch the records, it did them very little harm. There was an exceptional eight-inch speaker in the face end and the whole padded, ported enclosure acted to provide an unexpected additional octave of full clearly defined bass. If "hi-fi" had been thought of in those days, the label would have fit nicely.

I had come across it during an exploration of Hollywood. A handful of us had climbed aboard a bus in San Diego to see for ourselves the magic homeland of the Stars. The homeland included a large radio repair shop and there I found it, with a matching carrying case for about a hundred records. It was for sale, and I handed out most of my Hollywood funds for it -- over $60 -- and learned immediately that it had been made for someone who didn't carry his own luggage. It was heavy. But it was not immovable and I lugged it with me almost everywhere from then on. It flew on and off of aircraft carriers and Pacific islands in the belly of an F6F, tied to a ledge behind the armor plate. It made a natural centerpiece for the Sack and Social.

In these days, in this country, few people do without music for very long. Wildly excited vocal artists sing their hearts out, ceaselessly, about underarm deodorants, baby diapers, or hot, steamy feet. Joggers wear their stereo earphones and, afterwards, there is a special waterproof radio that plays in the shower. For most everyone out in the Pacific, in the early 1940s, it was very different. Music seldom was encountered and rarely was obtainable. Weeks or months without music were commonplace -- part of the general dreariness of war. And the dreary part was the good part.

Anyway, wherever the ivory jukebox went, it drew people. All kinds. From everywhere. On Maui, sunrise in the valley was accompanied by the Light Cavalry Overture. Psychologists had reported that it had a rousing effect on human beings. There was some initial grumping by those less human than the rest of us, but in a little while the eggheads were proved right. On sun-bleached, semi-inhabited atolls, the sounds of the 7th Symphony in A-Major would bring strangers running up, waving their arms and shouting, "My God! Beethoven!" In Ceylon (Sri Lanka) on the fringe of the ancient jungle, the apes in the trees bobbed and grimaced to Benny Goodman while the snakes pursued the rats across the rafters of our open hut.

Before we had reached the West Coast and joined VF-12, we had been required to prove that we could land modified SNJ training planes aboard a paddle-wheel aircraft carrier (U.S.S. Wolverine) in Lake Michigan -- an undertaking that gave us an occasional opportunity to slip away into Chicago and catch Woody Herman or Alvino Rey at the College Inn. One such night, we slipped into the old Garrick Stage Bar. I didn't know anything about Billie Holiday. Female vocalists were not in short supply. Helen O'Connell, from Libby High School in Toledo, showing lots of promise with Benny Goodman. Ella Fitzgerald already was busy being Ella, and I couldn't ask for anything more, so I just hadn't paid any attention to Billie. After that night, I did.

Entertainers are expected to be nice, and this woman was trying. She was black when Chicago wasn't much, had a good gig, and needed the bread. But when she sang, the truth came through and not all of that was nice. I didn't know much about it, but it was clear that she did, and she was trying to tell me, if I knew enough to listen. I missed most of it, I suppose. I wasn't looking for truth, I was looking for more nice hype, and it troubled me to realize that. Months later, out in Pearl Harbor, I was in the submarine base ship's service store when they opened a new shipment of records from back home. I picked out all of the Billie Holiday records I could find.

Back out on the Sara, under the tropical sun, breathing was made possible below decks by blowing outside air in through great labyrinths of sheet metal ductwork. A single four-incher emptied into the Sack and Social. The incoming air was warmed, when necessary. Electric fans were the greatest luxury available and ours worked endlessly to keep the warm, moist, used air in motion. In the living quarters, most people lived in their skivvies and tried not to move unnecessarily, while the ship, a valiant old veteran, hummed and churned and roasted and rusted around them. The ship usually was not going anywhere special, just staying out of trouble, doing zigzag patterns to avoid being torpedoed -- an aim we all supported, fervently.

We all agreed, outwardly, that our side was going to win the war, of course, like in the movies. But already we had lost enough pilots to notice that it didn't seem to make much difference who you were. It could, and did, happen to the good guys, too, purely by chance. Even during the dull periods, no one could be certain that if he passed up a chance to hear Artie Shaw play Stardust again, he ever would get another. So, when the sounds of the big dance bands echoed down the old dark metal passageways, a shuffling of feet followed -- not the feet of the dancers back home with some sweet young thing in their arms, but the variously shod, feet of the faithful homing in on the Sack and Social.

Inside we had one chair, which didn't help much, and people simply fit themselves in as best they could or clustered around the door. When the music was merely background, or was stilled for a while, we talked. We talked with each other or with anybody else, anytime, about anything at all. No taboos. And when we needed an expert, we sent out. With so many reserves on board, it would not have been surprising to send for an Egyptologist, a zither-maker, a bookie, or a lion-tamer, and get one.

At one time, we held all-out, fully frank rap sessions with three black steward's mates who had been lured, perhaps by Billie Holiday, perhaps by the aroma of Australian gin, into thinking it might be possible to talk with us and be understood. It was. And it was very educational, too much so even for here and now, so I'll leave out the important parts. They thought that if we would teach them some ground school subjects like aerial navigation, it would make them specially qualified and help them to get transferred to the Army Air Corps, which they had heard was desperate for pilots to fly P-40s in North Africa and was recruiting black men for that purpose. We lucky ones already had the opportunity to fight it out with the enemy, up in the sky, man-to-man, and would recognize, somehow, kindred spirits who wanted to do it, too. Otherwise, if we all lived through the war, they faced a whole lifetime of standard career choices ranging from waiting on tables to nothing.

Nowadays, there are men, and women, who are professionally black and are making careers of that. It just brings back what we learned in the Sack and Social: Everybody has trouble telling the good guys from the bad guys and skin color won't do it for you.

Even when there were only three of us, the talk went on, as usual. Once, it began with a casual observation that almost all of the old veterans we had encountered looked back on their wartime service, with the old outfit, as a high point in their lives and tended to get all maudlin about it. There was a presumption that some sort of senility factor that clouded men's minds was at work and we took a couple of minutes of silence to look around us and evaluate where we were and what we were doing. We were thousands of miles from home, in a dim, crowded metal box, sweating in our skivvies, unable to remember the last time our hides had been dry. We were supposedly fighting a war, remembering the guys we had lost, and forgetting, if we could, that our own futures were hardly under our own control. We had a whole ready-room full of guys whom we could trust with our lives, but it was not exactly the same thing as trusting them with your girlfriend. When it all had sunk in, we made a solemn pledge that never, ever would we succumb to the fud factor and look back with fond longings and sentimental reminiscences on what we were going through.

I think I've kept that pledge pretty well. The human facility for retroactive censorship is a mainstay in making life livable and it's tempting to remember only the good parts. But if I do, the days in VF-12 become the playing out of a scenario, a pre-ordained valiant victory interspersed with fun and games along the way. As I remember, they were mostly grim and deadly times with a constant pervasive possibility that there would be no tomorrow. Through it all, though, I can still hear Billie Holiday "Travelin' Light" along those sheet-metal corridors, and the footsteps converging on the Sack and Social Society, and I'm aware once more that even when it was bad, it wasn't all bad. I'm glad, now, that we shared those experiences. I just wouldn't want to do it all again.

RED DOG AS OTHERS
KNEW HIM – No. 1

RABAUL HARBOR (5 Nov. 1943)- His division's mission was to cover TBF's. During retreat from the target area several Zekes attempted to attack these bombers. He shot down the first one and in the ensuing dogfights became separated from his division. He was attacked by 8-10 Zekes. During the following 20 minutes, combat ranged from 200 to 1,500 feet above the water. He destroyed two Zekes, probably destroyed another, and damaged at least two more. His own plane was damaged by 7.7 and 20 mm gunfire. As more Zekes joined the fight, he managed to break away and outspeed his attackers low over the water.

RED DOG AS OTHERS
KNEW HIM - No. 2

Red Dog Gray -- Boy Wonder. Red had a creative and inquiring mind and I never knew what he would come up with next. For instance, on a boring mid-altitude CAP over the carrier I glanced over at Red Dog just as a stream of fire shot out of his mouth. It scared the hell out of me! Well, it seems Red, making full use of idle time, had figured out if you first lit a cigarette and held it aside while you filled your lungs with oxygen, then put the cigarette to your mouth and exhaled, you would give the appearance of a flame thrower as the cigarette was instantly consumed. Thank goodness I had not called for an emergency landing! By: Lt. Pearly Gates, USNR

Rollin E Gray was born on July 7, 1921 in Toledo, Ohio. He attended the University of Toledo. Commander Gray retired from the regular Navy and lives in Memphis, Tennessee.

COMBAT
PILOT
DOCTOR

Donald Richard Hagel, M.D.

    I was born in Methodist Hospital, Omaha, Nebraska, on Feb 18, 1924. The M.D. portion of my name was not bestowed on me by my parents but by the University Of Nebraska College Of Medicine some 27 years later. Shortly after birth, my family moved to a small town in northwest Nebraska, Rushville, from which my parents originated. At that time Rushville was so small that traffic on U.S. 20 had to slow down or it was missed. There was not a traffic light in town, not even on the corner that separated the Sioux Indian ingress from the 18-wheeler traffic on U.S. 20.

    I attended grade and high school in Rushville, graduating in time to prepare myself for winning WWII. I was a short fella with a strong Napoleonic which led to many black eyes and bloody noses. It also led (the complex) to participation in all high school sports, i.e., football, basketball, track and baseball. Football was my favorite sport and was also my best. I received All State Honors from some of the big city newspapers (Omaha and Lincoln) to be a large star at the University of Nebraska at Lincoln. Finances and WWII came along to thwart my aspirations.

    I graduated from high school in the spring of 1942 and entered the University of Nebraska that fall. I joined the Army Air Force Reserve on Dec. 13, 1942 and was called to active duty on Feb. 22, 1943.

    Joining the AAF Reserve was a ploy to stay in school, stay out of the war and become a football hero. However, with the call to active duty six weeks later, my ploy became an earlier opportunity to serve Uncle Sugar than if I had waited to be drafted. The University of Nebraska AAF ROTC contingent was called in its entirety and sent to St. Louis, Missouri for Air Force basic training. When we arrived in the dead of winter with 10 degrees below zero temperatures and lots of snow and wind and no Air Force uniforms, we marched all day in the clothes we brought.

I thought my years of growing up in Rushville would "steel" me from the cold but not so! I suppose getting the measles after about three weeks of training saved my life but I wasn't certain after four weeks in the station hospital. After approximately seven days of hospitalization I developed meningitis.

However, I did recover and returned to find my squadron shipped out (AAF term) to pre-flight school. I couldn't even find my uniforms which had been issued to me while being hospitalized. I sat on my butt for over a week getting a re-issue of uniforms, plus a second go at all of my inoculations and orders to California. All of my pals went to Texas.

Pre-flight school was located at Santa Ana, not far from Los Angeles and Long Beach. I have only two significant memories -- one was having Joe DiMaggio as a P-T instructor and the other was a re-call to the psychiatrist. This M.D. recall presented the possibility of having flunked the "masturbation or first sexual encounter" questions. This was not the case, however, as I had filled out the Pilot Only square in the Pilot, Navigator and Bombardier choices section of the questionnaire.

From preflight to primary, basic and advanced flight training followed. All went well except for basic training in single engine BT-13 and BT-15 aircraft. While taking my final instrument check ride with a Bryant Instrument School graduate lieutenant, he allowed me to fly into a flock of flying geese. The reader needs to understand that Aviation Cadet Hagel is in the rear seat, flying beneath a hood that prevented any view outside the cockpit. To make a long story short, the instructor bailed out. Old Don in the rear seat is pretty much unaware of conditions outside but is aware of the erratic flight of the plane and the whistling wind.

With the removal of the hood and a view of the prevailing conditions, my only choice appeared to be a forced landing, with the canopy broken, the prop wind milling and geese in the forward wing sections. The plane responded to control to a degree and I landed in a rice patty in northern California. With the fixed gear BT15, I very quickly nosed up, gathered my thoughts, controlled my fear and climbed out. Local folks saw the accident and were soon at the site for my rescue. They were kind and returned me to Chico Army Air Force Base where I had a routine hospital admission and checkup. No broken bones or major lacerations. But I had flunked my final test ride since I had flown through a flight of Canadian geese. This flunked test normally washes one out of cadet training. But after an interview and flight test by the commanding officer, I was passed and allowed to continue in flight training.

During this interval my class graduated and moved on to advanced flight training while I spent a second tour in basic. Advanced flight training was in twin-engine planes, AT-17 and AT-22, and was essentially uneventful. I was chosen cadet colonel as an upper classman and enjoyed the RHIP (rank has its privileges).

In December 1943 I finished pilot training and was promoted from cadet to second Lieutenant in the USAAF. The next few months were spent in B-17 transition, acquiring a crew of nine men and being shipped to England via HMS Aquatania, a sister ship of the Lusitania. Our orders were as a replacement crew and not an intact squadron or group.

Bomber losses were very high at this junction of the war and we were assigned to the 360th Squadron of the 452nd Group-heavy bombers. We were finally into the war in a very personal way. The 360th Squadron was down to seven crews with a normal contingent of 15. The 452nd Group was made up of four squadrons with a normal complement of 60 crews, and was down to 31 crews. The future didn't look too bright from my point of view. Our crews consisted of four officers, (two pilots, one bombardier, and one navigator) and five enlisted men. The crew chief, radio operator, ball turret operator, tail and waist gunners constituted the enlisted crew. The ball turret gunner and I were the junior crew in age and the crew chief was the senior in age. It was a super crew. They all knew their jobs, were literally cool under fire and never shirked their duties. During my tour of duty the crews were changed but the first one is the one you remember.

We began flying bombing missions soon after arrival at Dephon Green airdrome in East Anglia, England. Our first five missions gave us all a false sense of security; ack-ack was minimal and there were no German fighters. The tough missions began on Feb 4, 1944 and included raids on Hamburg, Swinemunde (a plant producing heavy water in the effort to gain atomic energy weapons), and several missions to Berlin, a tough target with flak so thick you could walk on it and ME 109 and FW 190 fighter planes filling the skies. Our losses up to this point were heavy but the job was not yet completed.

On my last Berlin mission we had been briefed for a 70 mph wind from the west while we were on our bomb run, which was north to south. We had a 100 percent under cast so that bombs had to be dropped by radar sighting. Radar in aircraft in 1944 was not too accurate at best. The wind on the bomb run had increased to 130 mph from the west and resulted in the bomber stream being several miles east of target. The wing commander flying the lead plane dropped his bombs on time, with the remainder of the bomber stream dropping on his signal. The resulting target now included Russian troops moving on Berlin from the east, and the Russians shot back!

In March 1944 I flew 12 more missions, most over by Germany, including two trips to Kiel, trying to sink a pocket battleship (the Admiral Shear, as I remember) that had slipped in for repairs. The weather was horrible on both missions. We missed the ship but did destroy the fuel dumps for all of northern Germany. The RAF followed the next night and sunk the ship.

Our toughest mission was a Nurnberg trip. It was a 12-hour mission with favorable winds and the limit in miles for the B-17. We had to lower our munitions and increase our fuel with bomb bay tanks. Our air speed was 155 mph to the target and 150 mph coming back. It was a long trip under any circumstance. On the way back, just when we all thought we had it made, we were too close to an ack-ackgun (probably on a railroad car) and the explosive force blew away most of the plexiglass nose of the aircraft. B-17's don't fly too well with 150 mph winds coming through the plane. The bombardier was not in the nose at the time of explosion but the navigator was.

We couldn't maintain our lead of the squadron and had to drop down and back. We had picked up P-51 escorts earlier and two dropped down for our escort. When we finally crossed the English Channel at 128 miles/mph. and 280 feet of altitude, we were nearly out of fuel. We made it to the emergency field in eastern England and all survived. The navigator was in better shape than we could have imagined and returned to the U.S.A. in a few weeks.

We flew two missions to Royan (in southeastern France) to knock out a stranded German tank group that the French couldn't handle. On both missions our plane carried napalm hardware. On the first mission we hit the tanks from 18,000 feet, but on the second trip the first bomb didn't clear the release coupling and hung up. We dropped down to 12,000 feet and kicked the bombs out over the target tanks. We took a lot of small arms fire but none hurt and there was no major plane damage.

On a mission to Plauen, Germany, our group was attacked by ME 262 jet fighter planes. It was our first exposure to jet aircraft and a harrowing experience. They were much faster than our P-47s and P-51s (fighters) but the P-47s could out-dive them when they ran out of fuel or started down.

We also had two missions, during which ME 253 rocket aircraft hit our group, firing only twice - once going up and once going down. On both occasions the ME 263 damaged only two planes, both of which were able to limp home.

My last mission was directed at Dresden, Germany's marshaling yards. We later learned the city was packed with German refugees and I am certain the body count was high.

The squadron and the troops had green lights until VE Day. At 4 a.m., on the day following VE Day, the crews were awakened for a 5 a.m., breakfast, 6 a.m. briefing and a 7 a.m. takeoff. The mission was to fly 452nd Group ground-pounders on a low-level flight over Germany so they could see the results of their labors. We flew at 200 feet, which precludes a smooth ride in most areas. Airsickness was rampant among our passengers but they all made it back to Merry Old England. A few days after VE Day, the group was still intact and we were assigned a mission to Lentz, Austria, to pick up French POWs and return them to France. The POWs were in good physical shape when we reached them and were very jolly at eating K rations on the flight to Orlean, France.

After leaving the French at Orlean, we started back to England. The weather was terrible and we had no weather station to contact. Over the English Channel, while flying on instruments, we ran into the roll of a cumulo nimbus cloud. We hit the updraft side first, with a resulting rate of climb greater than our climb indicator could record. In a few minutes, in near level flight in severe lightning and hail, we hit the downdraft side, and went down as fast as we went up. Engine power did not affect the winds in either direction, up or down!

We controlled our descent just as we neared the water and we were able to re-establish normal flight altitudes and get to England. The aircraft had been buffeted so badly that it never flew again.

Some portions of the war are vivid in my memory but important experiences are not. I have partial recall of a cemetery crash landing but fail to recall any details. With the war ending in Europe, the war in the Pacific was still going and there was talk that our talents, might be needed to help out. The Air Force Command had worked out a points plan, based on time in service, number of missions flown, decorations received and total flying time in combat, for order of separation from the Air Force. Most of us far exceeded the required points for separation and had no fear of Pacific War participation.

We flew our B-17 back to the U.S. and left it at Bradley Field, Connecticut. My last assignment was at Galveston Air Force Base in Texas. On the base we had a new P-47 group on its way to the Pacific. The pilots were all on leave when Galveston was hit by a hurricane. Many new aircraft with no pilots presented a true dilemma. We could not find the pilots for a flyaway so we flew the ones we could to San Antonio and tied down the rest. The story is not complete but better that way.

I was separated from the AAF at Fort Leavenworth, Kansas, and returned to Lincoln, and the University of Nebraska. Somewhere, during the war, I decided on medicine over engineering as a career.

Just before going overseas, in August 1944, I had married my high School sweetheart. Bette had graduated from the University of Nebraska College of Pharmacy and was working, so with her help and the GI bill I could go to college full time. I finished my undergraduate education in the spring of 1947 and started medical school in the fall. I graduated from medical school in 1951 and then started my OB-GYN training. I stayed on active reserve status throughout medical school with regular military flying as a routine at Offutt Air Force Base, Nebraska.

This was a demanding time, fulfilling my military obligations as well as being a full time student at the University of Nebraska College of Medicine. It was at this period of my life that I met General Curtis LeMay, SAC Commander and superior human being. General LeMay was always complementing me for being "a combat pilot doctor." We flew together on many occasions and he touted me constantly for a Regular Air Force commission with Air Force Surgeon General as my goal. (Note: the Air Force became a separate military entity in 1946 with both regular and reserve commissions. I could not concur with the full-time military in peacetime and did not accept the regular AF commission.)

During the summer between my junior and senior years of medical school, I was requested by General LeMay to re-enter the AF on active duty on the medical staff of the station hospital at Offutt AFB. Offutt Strategic Air Command headquarters and a busy place. The "cold war" was a prominent new item at the time and the Korean War was in progress. Most of the station hospital staff had been transferred to the Korean conflict and the station hospital needed staff.

With the general's guarantee of release from active duty to return to school in the fall, I accepted the re-call and, as a consequence, have had Korean War duty as well as WWII duty. My duty was that of a physician, not a pilot, although I maintained my initial MOS. I had many hours flying that summer as well as hospital duty and had the opportunity to fly many different types of aircraft. As I remember I flew a B-25, A-26, B-36 and B-47. In my reserve group we had C-46, C-47 and C-54 transport aircraft and AT-6 and P-51 single engine aircraft. This was an amazing summer for the country boy from Rushville.

After more than six years of marriage, Bette and I had our first of three children, in 1950. After one year of postgraduate training we moved to Jacksonville, Florida for continued medical training in OB-GYN and to leave the ice and snow behind.

On completing my OB-GYN medical training I joined another physician in practice for 17 years and enjoyed a successful OB-GYN practice. The original partner retired with a practice too large for one man and after about one year, a younger physician joined me and we practiced together until my retirement in 1989. But I found I wasn't quite ready for retirement, so I went to work for the County Health Department for the next eight years. Now I am retired! 1997.

Lieutenant Don Hagel was awarded the Air Medal with three Oak Leaf Clusters for meritorious achievement in England with the Eighth Air Force.

"FLYING WAS
DANGEROUS AND
SEX WAS SAFE"

Stanley David Hall

It's strange that I can't remember what I had for dinner last night, but still have vivid memories of some incidents in my life that occurred 50 years ago. Let me share some of them with you.

In February 1941, 22 bright and eager men in their early 20s descended on Lowry Air Corps Base in Denver, all of us applying to be flying cadets in the old U.S. Army Air Corps. None of us had entertained the possibility of ever being involved in a real fighting war.

Of the 22 hopefuls, only one was accepted. I was rejected because my two front teeth were too long, thus making me "unable to hold an oxygen pipe-stem" in my mouth. (I never saw a pipe-stem in use.) The next morning a Denver dentist agreed to drill back and forth until the two culprit teeth were even with the others. Late that afternoon I was accepted into the ranks of flying cadets.

In those years, very few people saw a need to rapidly expand the corps. Consequently, the Air Corps was very selective. After all the physicals, each applicant was interviewed by the flight surgeon. During my interview, he was briefly called out of the office and I had a quick glance at one of the pages to guide him in assessing an applicant. For example: "Are his finger nails clean?" "Would you invite him home for dinner tonight?" "Would you allow him to date your daughter?" I assume that was part of the old "Officer and Gentleman" standards.

At last we two new flying cadets joined 62 others at Thunderbird Field outside of Phoenix for primary flying and ground school. Of the 64 students, all were washed out except 14 of us. One of the 14 was Dick Bong, a very quiet, shy fellow that some of us thought would never survive the training. As we all know, he became America's Ace of Aces in the Pacific.

Basic training lasted three months at Taft, California and was mostly smooth sailing. Our final stage of training was at Mather Field near Sacramento, where we flew AT-6's -- SNJ's to you navy guys.

Eight of us newly commissioned graduates were sent to Albuquerque, which was the only school for bombardiers at the time. One of the pilots we saw there at the O-Club was Lt. James Stewart. We were too shy to invite him to join us and he was too shy to invite himself, so he usually sat alone at the bar.

We eight classmates stayed at Albuquerque for three months while we were getting acclimated to the procedures of a bombardier school. We were then transferred to Victorville, California where a new bombardier school had recently been opened.

I can still vividly remember the state of panic that engulfed the citizens and officials in California. There were weekly scares and rumors that a Japanese task force was steaming toward California. Thousands of Japanese-Americans were rounded up and moved to detention camps in Colorado and elsewhere. Now we know how wrong that was and how much of an injustice it was to many loyal American-Japanese. However, at that time it seemed to be the prudent thing to do.

During my first week at Victorville, I was named Officer of the Day for one 24 hour stretch. Among my duties was approval and signing of the flight plans of anyone passing through. One civilian pilot under contract to ferry planes was a young fellow whose last name was Corrigan. I've forgotten his first name but the world knew him as "Wrong Way". When signing his flight plan I desperately tried to think of some comments I could make about compass headings. Everything I thought about seemed to be in the nature of a wisecrack so I kept my big mouth shut.

One month after reporting for duty at Victorville, the small group of pilots that opened the school was transferred. We eight classmates were then the oldest and most experienced pilots on the field. Three were named squadron C.O.'s; three were deputy squadron C.O.'s; one was deputy director of flying and I was named director of flying. To this day I firmly believe that our names were picked out of a box.

By this time the Air Corps was expanding so fast that there was no other choice than to assign us "kids" to the jobs. If the magnitude of that responsibility were thrust upon us when we were older and more experienced, we probably would have fainted in fear of what we faced. But I am proud of the way we "kids" did the duty. During the year we exceeded all of the goals that had been set -- and without a single crash or fatality. During the war years, "Being Transferred" was the name of the game. After a little more than a year, we eight classmates were transferred to Hobbs, New Mexico. where we checked out in the B-17 Flying Fortress -- in my opinion the finest aircraft ever built.

After a couple of short assignments, I was transferred to MacDill Field in Tampa to be C.O. of one of the four squadrons. Wishing to keep good personnel morale, the Air Corps programmed a boxing match tour that included Sgt. Joe Louis, Sgt. Sugar Ray Robinson and an assortment of trainers, etc. After they completed their "show," I was told to fly them to Orlando for their next appearance. Joe Louis was an enthusiastic small plane pilot, so I invited him up front and let him play co-pilot. He took control and made a few short easy turns. Joe was a quiet and polite man and later told me that it was a thrill for him to fly a B-17.

One day the group commander called me to his office and asked if I would "volunteer" for an unusual assignment. I would be working with the Office of Strategic Services (O.S.S.) on a project they called "Joshua". I could pick my own B-17 and crew and fly to Bolling Air Force Base in Washington, D.C.

While O.S.S. had many agents behind enemy lines, the only method of getting their information back to London was by radio. The radios being used were so large that they had to be enclosed in suitcases. When the agents were transmitting, the Germans in radio vans were able to vector and locate the area. Usually the agents had to discard the radios to avoid being captured.

Project Joshua was devised to combat that problem. Lt. Colonel Shore, a radio scientist with RCA, had invented a new communication system. It consisted of a tiny, pocket-size transmitter with a telescoping antenna and a very large receiver and tape recorder. The receiver was almost the size of an office desk and this required a large aircraft to carry it. The plan was to establish appointment days and times for an aircraft to fly over an agent and receive his information in four-letter code. The reception area was similar to the old cone of silence -- the higher the aircraft, the longer the time to receive. That time was usually about three minutes.

We flew some simulated missions in the states to test the equipment and train some agents. The B-17 was not the desired aircraft for the project but it had to be used because of the size of the receiver and recorder.

I remember what happened to wounded and slow bombers that fell behind their protective bomber formations. They were easy prey for German fighters. I designed my flight plans to avoid radar as long as possible. I flew at treetop level until approaching the agent's location, where I climbed to 10-12,000 feet. At first I would fly to a nearby town,making one circle to make my tormenting adversaries assume that I was flying over my target. Then I would fly to the agent's spot and pass him by without any turning, circling or doing anything to make one think that town was of any interest to me. The agent usually started transmitting a couple of minutes prior to scheduled talk time. We were at higher altitude only a short time before descending once more to treetop level for our trip home.

I never once was sighted or attacked by fighter planes. Occasionally we saw a few puffs of ack-ack. I don't know if this was what I thought was a genius flight plan,

God's will, the beginning of a serious shortage of Luftwaffle planes and pilots, or just plain good luck.

Near the end of the war, Colonel Shore was able to greatly reduce the size of the receiver, which enabled us to borrow three Mosquitoes from the Royal Air Force. That aircraft was a much better match for that work than the B-17.

Project Joshua was the predecessor of the post-war project that Gary Powers flew. By that time, O.S.S. had changed its name to Central Intelligence Agency (C.I.A.). In comparison to Gary Powers U-2 operation, you can say that Project Joshua was clumsy and amateurish. But we did do some good and from my selfish point of view, we were Not Shot Down.

O.S.S. was a very tight-lipped organization. People involved with the project knew and were told only what was necessary to do their part. I never saw or heard the tapes we brought back. I never once was advised of the information they contained. And by the same rules, nobody knew any details of the missions we flew. In order to give us freedom to operate as we needed, O.S.S. prevailed on General Hap Arnold to sign my orders. Otherwise, any group commander I landed with could appropriate my aircraft and crew.

During the last few months before V.E. day, I had occasion to see much of Germany. We, as sightseers, circled both Cologne and Frankfurt and could see the results of the bombing by day, by the Eight Air Force, and by night, by the Royal Air Force. There was nothing left of the downtown areas except the untouched cathedrals in the center. That was the result not of the skill of the bombardiers, but of the will of God.

There were times I flew over detention areas used to control German prisoners. Because the surrenders were coming in mass numbers, the Allies were able only to provide tall barbed-wire enclosures. The camps reminded me of the stockyards in Chicago, Kansas City and Denver. They were completely filled to standing room only.

One day I landed at Frankfurt to refuel. I called for a staff car to take my co-pilot, navigator and me to the Post

Exchange for a quick launch. The car waited for us and when we were ready to return, an older man in coveralls asked if he could have a ride. As a cocky and patronizing Air Force major, I told him he could sit up front with my driver. He politely accepted. When we arrived at the flight line, he got into an AT-6 and took off. I asked and was told that he was General Quesada! Later, back in Washington, I was seated near him at a hotel dinner. He did not seem to recognize me and I tried to make myself invisible.

Near the end of the war, I landed at Halle, Germany -- some 40 miles southwest of Berlin. It had been captured the day before and like other German fields had no runways -- only a large grass area. As I flared out for touchdown, I saw many stakes with white clothes. I was afraid they were mud holes. After I taxied to the flight line, I learned they were mines which had been located but not yet disarmed. God again was looking out for Stan Hall and crew.

We then went to a nearby German radio technical facility wondering if the Germans knew the frequencies used in our mission. It was next door to Nordhausen concentration camp. The camp supplied the labor to build the factory that built the German V-2 rocket -- the rocket that killed so many civilians and soldiers in London. The camp had been liberated the day before. The U.S. soldiers had pushed the German civilians from their homes and installed the camp survivors with new lodging and food. I saw bodies and skeletons in large pits. I saw, and smelled, the ovens. I saw evidence of the German cruelty and torture methods. I saw with my own eyes the things we heard about in the states and wondered if it was just propaganda.

After the war was over, I flew for Pan American World Airways. It was three months before I stopped worrying about German fighters behind each cloud.

Oh well, it is old guys like us that say, "When I was in aviation, flying was dangerous and sex was safe." And now I guess it is time for this old guy to take his afternoon nap.

Stanley David Hall was born in Trinidad, Colorado on Nov. 23, 1919. After the war he was a pilot with Pan Am. He later entered the life insurance business. He is retired and has a home in Cypress Village, Jacksonville, Florida.

CHIEF PETTY OFFICERS
IN THE NAVY

Marvin Burnette Harper

Chief petty officers play a unique and very important role in the United States Navy. I think of them as the link between the officers and the enlisted men. One incident involving a C.P.O. and me had a lasting effect on my life. In 1944, after two tours in the fleet as a fighter pilot aboard the Saratoga, I began to believe how great we fighter pilots were. This was bolstered when soon after I was promoted to lieutenant.

My first duty ashore was as a fighter instructor at NAS. Daytona Beach. We flew F6-F Hell Cats and F4-F Wild Cats.

Once after a gunnery flight we landed for re-arming at our satellite field at New Smyrna. I reported to the radioman that my radio was erratic and that I could not communicate with the students. He told me to take the spare airplane and that he had just checked out the radio.

Well! The radio in that airplane didn't work either. Another wasted hop. When we landed, the seven students and I went into the hangar for a coke. And there I saw the radioman. In front of the students and the enlisted men I blasted him with every ugly thing I could come up with. When I got through there was utter silence. Then the door to the office of the chief opened and he said nothing but beckoned me to come in. He closed the door and his first words were, "That was the damnedest exhibition by a navy officer I have ever seen or heard." That was the nicest thing he said. Then he really let me have it. He wound up saying; "Now get your ass out there and apologize to that man." That is just what I did.

The students and men had heard every word the chief had laid on me behind the closed door. I was sure that my dignity and all respect for me would be absolutely destroyed. Then an amazing reaction occurred. I didn't understand it then and neither do I now, almost 60 years later. The students and the men seemed to treat me with enhanced dignity and respect. Thereafter, when we landed at the base they obviously gave us their best service. My lesson…I have tried to never again berate anyone, and if I needed to discuss a mistake, to do so in private.

THANKS CHIEF

While stationed at NAS Daytona another C.P.O. was a great help to me. One night I had tower duty as night flying officer. I had flown a lot at night but knew nothing about tower operations. The chief in charge soon picked up on that and treated me with respect, but also coached my every decision.

After the airplanes had been in the air for an hour or so he came to me and said, "Sir, the dew point is __," He gave me a number.

I didn't even know what the dew point meant. I said, "Chief, what do you advise?" He said to bring the airplanes in closer to the field as we might get fog. I said, "Chief, would you please bring the airplanes in closer to the field?" He replied, "Aye, aye, sir."

Shortly he came back and said, "Sir, the dew point continues to drop." My quick answer was to ask what he would advise. He said, "I would land the airplanes immediately." My reply, "Chief, would you please land the airplanes." His reply, "Aye, Aye, Sir." That is not all the Chief did that watch. One of the airplanes landed wheels up.

We were flying F4-F's, the Wild Cat, and the landing gear was lowered by a hand crank with a bicycle-like chain. The pilot had not locked the crank in the down position thus when he landed his wheels came up and he made a belly landing. I rushed down to the runway thinking that, as duty

135

officer, it was my job to direct the removal of the damaged airplane and get the landings resumed.

In a nice way the chief informed me that the airplane was leaking gasoline and that gasoline would cause the tar in the runway to soften and he didn't have time for any distraction. I got the word and went back up to the tower where I tried to look important; I didn't have much to do.

The chief wasn't through yet. It was reported to me that the pilot of the damaged airplane was Lt. John Wesly. John and I had been boyhood friends in Chattanooga. When I was a cadet at Pensacola, John was a Lt (j.g.) there. He called on me in my room in the cadet barracks and told me that if I needed him or needed to borrow his car to call him.

Now he was in trouble. Apparently he had not locked his landing gear down and he would be charged with pilot error. When I told the chief that John was a good friend of mine and a fine navy officer and that I was sorry to see the trouble he was in, the chief replied, "Sir, why is Mr. Wesly in trouble because the chain broke in his landing gear mechanism?"

John Wesly never met the chief.

COFFEE

When the Saratoga was serving in the British fleet we were based in Colombo, Ceylon. The fleet had British, U.S., French, Dutch and Indian vessels. Each Sunday a detail of officers from one ship would visit another ship for a meal.

I was detailed to a Dutch land-based PBY squadron and enjoyed it so much that I would visit there every Sunday. They were very hospitable.

I asked the Dutch C.O. if there was anything I could bring to his mess. Without hesitation he said yes, coffee. They had plenty of liquor and everything I could think of but coffee did not occur to me.

When the Saratoga was under way I played poker with the senior supply corps officer so I did not think getting coffee would be a problem. However, when I asked him he said no; it wasn't his job to furnish food to other messes.

Later that day I was down in the photo lab and happened to tell the Chief about the coffee episode. His reply was, "When did you want the coffee?" I told him I was going ashore to visit the Dutch Squadron at noon on Sunday.

He said, "Sir, there will be 10 pounds of coffee waiting for you on the quarterdeck. I will have beans roasted and ground that morning." It was.

The Chief did with no fanfare what a lieutenant commander wouldn't do.

Marvin Harper was born in Chattanooga, Tennessee on Oct. 5, 1918. He graduated from the University of Chattanooga in 1941. He was called to active duty in the navy in November 1941 and was released in August 1946. He was a naval aviator. He and his wife Kathryn reside in Jacksonville, Florida.

Edward A. Hawks, Jr.

During the latter months of WWII, I was a 21-year-old junior Ensign, USNR, flying the SB2C-4 with VB-6 from an Essex class carrier, the USS John Hancock (CV-19), with the Third Fleet bombing Japan.

The SB2C-4 was an underpowered "beast". On a combat mission we usually carried a radar bulb plus a 100-gallon drop-wing tank plus a 1,000-pound bomb plus 2 HVAR rockets plus ammo for two 20mm cannon plus a rear seat gunner with twin 50-caliber machine guns and APS-1 radar.

The "beast" that I flew had a large drum on the right hand side of the cockpit with a handle on it for the landing gear. After takeoff we had to switch the stick to the left hand and with the right hand push a button on the drum handle and then pull the handle backward to retract the landing gear. This maneuver by itself could make takeoffs a bit hairy.

Quite often during a combat deck-run takeoff, the underpowered "beast" would sink from sight after we left the deck. Having to switch hands to retract the wheels did not make things any easier. (A friend of mine in the squadron went in the drink twice on takeoff; the second time he did not get out.)

This "beast" had a large, lighted bomb/gun sight, which we stowed in tracks on the floor on the right side of the cockpit. After takeoff we would move the sight from the floor and lock it into tracks at the top of the instrument panel, where it stuck out in your face. Prior to landing, we would move it back to the tracks on the floor.

Much of what happened is so long ago that my memory is somewhat hazy. My logbook shows that on Aug.

13, 1945 we bombed an aircraft plant near Tokyo. (It may have been Mitsubishi.)

Rumors about the war being over were rampant but with no final word Admiral Halsey directed the Third Fleet carriers on Aug. 15, 1945 (Aug. 14th back in the states) to launch a maximum effort, early morning strike against the Japanese homeland. I think that some of the earlier fighter sweeps may have actually completed their attacks.

About halfway to the target we were ordered to "return to base." Although no one actually said so, we knew the war was over! Holy Toledo! Talk about a madhouse! Because the carriers would not take us back aboard with armament, tons of bombs (mostly armed) were dropped in the open sea, wiping out who knows how many fish! Rockets were fired off in every direction! Later I heard that whole divisions of F6Fs were doing slow rolls!

We returned to the Hancock and started landing aboard. I was coming up the groove with my wheels and flaps down when the engine "quit." We were so close to the end of the carrier that my gunner thought I had taken a cut to land aboard.

I guess that most of the time when you landed in the water, the wheels would hit first and flip the plane over on its back.

For some reason -- through luck, sheer terror and/or superb flying -- I was horsed back on the stick and the tail hit first and the wheels second. It was like running into a brick wall but at least we did not flip over.

I have no recollection of getting out of the cockpit. The first thing I remember was standing on the wing calmly peeling my gloves off finger by finger. With all the excitement about the war ending I had forgotten to take out the bomb sight and stow it on the cockpit floor so my head hit the sight hard enough to knock me out for a bit and to gash my forehead. Mac, my 19-year-old gunner from Brooklyn, had gashed his head also but was able to get out the life raft and inflate it near the trailing edge of the wing.

The plane was starting to sink so I calmly stepped off the wing, into six-foot ocean swells instead of into the raft.

We finally got into the life raft but were so exhausted that when the destroyer (USS Collett, DD 730) came along side, with a cargo net over the side crew members had to climb down to help us up.

The people on that ship treated us royally! They washed and dried our clothes and had them back in short order. As the MD was stitching our foreheads, he mentioned he was short of morphine so I gave him the small first aid kit we carried which had morphine syrettes. An ordnance man brought back my .38 all cleaned and oiled. He admired it so much that I told him to keep it (after all the war was over so who needed a gun?).

Later, I had some cause to regret my generosity. Later, lying on a bunk, I can vaguely remember Admiral Halsey announcing over TBS that the war was over.

The people on that ship treated us royally, but with a price! That evening they transferred us back to the Hancock by breeches buoy line but NOT before they got a number of gallons of ice cream from the Hancock plus movies and mail.

For years I argued that the engine had "quit," through no fault of my own. It wasn't until recently that I checked my logbook and faced the probable truth. I ran out of gas! We would take off on the main fuselage tank and switch to the wing tank and then back to the main tank during combat and landing. Most strike flights lasted 4-5 hours. This flight lasted 2.8 hours. With all the excitement I simply forgot to switch back to the main tank.

What a way to end a war!

Edward Hawks is from Concord, Massachusetts. After the Korean War he remained in Jacksonville, Florida. He was a very successful pension plan consultant.

MOTHER WAS
ALWAYS RIGHT

Caldwell (Chick) Haynes, Jr.

On December 7, 1941, I was shocked to learn of the Japanese sneak attack on the U.S. Fleet at Pearl Harbor, and I ultimately thought, "What should I do?"

My wife and I had just moved into our new home, our first born was just a few weeks old, and I was making a modest living as a local insurance agent.

Would I be drafted? I had a high draft number and there were several other reasons why the draft board might defer me.

My mother, who lived in New York, called to ask what I planned to do. In a few days, she arrived by train and one of her first questions was, "What are you going to do for the war effort? What are you going to tell your children you did, when they grow up?"

Was my mother asking me to enlist or volunteer for service in the armed forces? She was my mentor and, yes, she was suggesting just that. My only qualification was ROTC at the University of Florida, from which I had graduated in 1938. At that time, no service upon graduation was required.

It didn't take long for me to apply for a commission in the Navy. But insurance types were not much in demand, and I was turned down not once, but two or three times.

One evening, in the men's room at the Florida Yacht Club, Commander Archie Freels, USN, told me he had heard of my rejection by the navy and of my application to go to OCS. He wanted to know if I really, really wanted to get in the navy. I told him, "Yes and, incidentally, my mother is also anxious that I serve my country!"

Before too long, I was on my way to Fort Schyler in New York. After basic training and 30 days of destroyer school, I reported to the USS Shaw DD373 at Mare Island, California. The chief who logged me on greeted me with, "The Shaw has been whammed again." She had first been whammed in dry dock at Pearl Harbor when the Japs attacked. She had received a direct hit in the forward magazine compartment and her entire bow was blown off.

It wasn't long before we joined a convoy as an escort heading west across the Pacific. Our first action was in the Mariannas. When the islands were secured we headed west again. We were on a "watch in three" (two off and one on,) General Headquarters an hour before sunrise and an hour after sunset. "All night in" meant five hours of sleep and "Liberty" meant a whaleboat trip to an atoll with two cans of hot beer.

In time, we reached the Philippines and shot down several Jap planes during their surprise attacks.

Some protection was afforded the ships at anchor in the harbor by putting down a fairly dense fog at sunrise and sunset. When the fog oil, which was needed to do this, gave out, our ship was assigned to go to New Guinea and bring back a deck load of fog oil. We made it to New Guinea and loaded the oil, but on the way back north we received a communication stating that the second battle of the Philippines was in progress. The Jap fleet was headed south.

We were heading north to deliver the fog oil and it seemed we would inevitably meet the Jap fleet. Fortunately, they turned west and we were spared the task of having to take the fleet on single-handedly.

Our first real liberty was when we went south to Biak, where there was a navy hospital. You can't believe what a few hours with some broads can do for morale.

When we went back to the Philippines, we had some excitement while looking for some stray Japs among the islands. A group of Kamikazes surprised us, with the first one attacking our ship. The Jap pilot was lacking in marksmanship, and missed us entirely. His bomb was a dud, too. Hence, I'm still here to write this yarn.

I'm a little hazy about our last venture in the Philippines. I think we were looking for Jap stragglers in poorly charted waters when we ran aground and badly damaged one of our propellers. The crew started yelling "stateside" as we dragged along the bottom. We made our way back to a floating dry dock. The damaged prop was removed and we headed back to the states. We were able to maintain speed with our remaining prop by adding just a few more r.p.m.'s.

The war was soon over. We went through the Panama Canal and up the east coast to the Brooklyn Navy Yard, where The Shaw ended up as scrap metal.

When the Korean War started, a "friend" talked me into joining the active reserve as an ordnance officer in a patrol squadron. The weekend pay came in handy, but I soon was transferred to a fighter squadron, VF742 at NAS Jax, and was then recalled to active duty for two years.

We ended up again in the South Pacific with some more excitement. We engaged an enemy destroyer on the darkest of nights. I don't know what happened to the enemy ship, but all of a sudden it stopped returning fire and we "claimed" another enemy ship. We then went back to the U.S.A. when the war was over.

My son, Hank, was active in the Air Force ROTC at the University of the South at Sewanee in 1963. He applied for a change to Navy ROTC and, after learning some navy lingo, was on a destroyer headed for Viet Nam.

When I was asked to write this story about my military duty, I thought it would be interesting to tell the story of a mother who encouraged her only son to do his duty in time of war, something for which her son has been, and will be, eternally grateful.

"Chick" Haynes was born in Jacksonville, Florida on Aug. 30, 1916. He was president of Haynes Peters and Bond, a bond, insurance agency, which was founded in 1877. The original partnership name was Foster Marvin and

Haynes. The Barnett Bank was founded in the same year. His company is probably the oldest continual operating company in Florida. Chick Haynes died on Aug. 13, 2002.

LEARNING A LESSON
OF LIFE
THE HARD WAY

Caldwell Leyden (Hank) Haynes

The year was 1963 and the United States was getting more involved in the Viet Nam conflict. My friends and classmates were very concerned about the draft and constantly discussing the best ways to avoid being forced into military duty, usually the U.S. Army. Most were opting for graduate school, primarily medical school or law school, and today most of my friends are doctors and lawyers.

My dad has always been my hero. Even though he was away in the Korean War during three of my most formative years and his best friend and my godfather, Dr. Champ Taylor, filled in as my hunting and fishing buddy, Dad has always been the man I admired most. He served with great pride and distinction in the Pacific Theatre during WWII. I am so grateful that some of the Japanese Kamikaze pilots weren't on target or my dad may not have come home alive.

As a student at the University of the South, Sewanee, Tennessee, I was a cadet in the Air Force ROTC program and about to be commissioned a 2nd lieutenant. One night I lay awake thinking of my future and suddenly realized that I wanted to serve my country in the navy, like my father, and not in the air force. Also, I grew up on the St. Johns River, had a small boat all my life and loved the water. The air force was not very receptive to my change of mind and only after some assistance from my friend, Congressman Charlie Bennett, did the air force release me from my commitment and only after I promised to serve at least three years on active duty in the navy. I immediately made application to Naval Officer's Candidate School in Newport, Rhode Island. I was accepted and reported for duty in September 1963.

I enjoyed my six months in Newport. Snow was still a novelty to me and I saw plenty of it from September to February. One of my most vivid memories of this first phase of my naval career was in November 1963. I had been chosen "section leader" of Charlie Company, Section 3 and was drilling the troops in the snow on the parade grounds when an E-6 chief petty officer ran up to me and yelled, "Haynes, get these men into the barracks! The President has been shot!"

We "double timed" to our barracks and all gathered around one small transistor radio and listened to the news being broadcast. Rumors started everywhere. One was that the Russians had assassinated President Kennedy and they were about to attack the U.S., a nation in total chaos. We would all be commissioned ensigns immediately and would report to various ships about the country.

Of course, this didn't happen. Vice President Johnson became President and the Viet Nam War intensified. I was fortunate to graduate in the top 10 percent of my class. I was then asked what type of ship and which port I would like to be stationed. I responded that since I'd spent my entire life in Jacksonville, on the east coast; I desired a newer, smaller ship on the west coast. Shortly thereafter, I received orders to the USS Bridget (DE-1024), a destroyer escort home-ported in San Diego. I was shown the boatswain's locker, relieved the first lieutenant, and three days later, we left for Viet Nam, first stopping at Guantanamo Bay, Cuba where we spent six weeks training with three other destroyer escorts, four destroyers and the USS Yorktown, an aircraft carrier.

Sometimes during the evening activities at the Officer's Club, I would hear pilots from the Yorktown telling of their exciting flying experiences and I would wish that I had chosen to fly. I was surprised to see how quickly the entire "carrier group" learned to work together and support each other. Whether we were conducting flight ops, underway refueling, antisubmarine exercises, or just trading movies, each ship would do all it could to support the other.

Bridget's primary duty was plane guarding. We would position ourselves 1,000 feet astern of the aircraft carrier and pick up pilots who did not make it on take-offs or landings. Fortunately, we had only one rescue in my three years. A helicopter tail rotor stopped, the helicopter crashed into the ocean and sank in a matter of seconds, but the pilots were rescued. When not plane guarding, we were providing anti-submarine services for the fleet.

The morale of my ship and the navy in general was excellent. A hint of disappointment would surface only after our task force had planned and trained for a major offensive against the North Vietnamese and the day before action was to commence, we would get word from Washington, D.C. that we could not carry out portions of the plan, which usually made the mission less effective. The "political" aspects of the war were difficult to deal with.

Plans were being made to bomb some heavy industrial areas and the oil storage tanks near Hanoi. The night of the attack, Bridget was assigned air early warning duty in the northern part of the South China Sea. If the North Vietnamese Air Force was ever going to attack ships off its coast, intelligence indicated it would be that night. Bridget would be "combat ready" all night long.

About 2 a.m., as we were watching the glow in the sky originating from bombing attacks that resulted in flames, radar men picked up an unidentified aircraft about 200 miles away, approaching Bridget. We began the various procedures to determine if this aircraft was "friend or foe." With no success on the various radars and radio frequencies and the aircraft approximately 50 miles away, Captain Rorie ordered the gunners to "load hoppers."

As officer of the deck, I was the one primarily responsible for making sure the captain's orders were immediately executed. The aircraft was now only several miles away with its red and green lights visible on the tip of each wing. The captain then ordered the crew of our 3"/50 antiaircraft gun to "Stand by." The only order still to be given was, "commence fire."

The captain suddenly turned to me and instructed me to challenge this aircraft with the two-letter code from the SECRET operations manual. This code was sent out via flashing light by the signalmen and the two letters changed each hour according to the time zone we were in. I'm embarrassed to say I was not prepared for this. Before I could look up the proper two-letter challenge, the captain went to the wing of the bridge and as the aircraft passed overhead, he hollered, "O God! I hope they're friendly!" He did not fire because he felt an enemy aircraft would be completely darkened and not have its wing tip lights on.

The aircraft turned out to be friendly, but the captain wasn't. He explained that my unpreparedness could have cost the lives of 224 men and our ship and he ordered me off the bridge and to my stateroom.

Knowing my navy career was over and a dishonorable discharge imminent, I sat in my stateroom and wept. After an hour, which seemed like days, a messenger indicated the captain wanted to see me on the bridge. My darkest hour brightened when the captain explained that the "on the job training" I had just experienced made me the most qualified person to run the ship and told me to "reassume my watch."

The incident was never mentioned again and Captain Rorie's giving me a second chance has remained one of my most memorable "lessons in life." I never went "on watch" again without mentally picturing every possible incident that could happen and being prepared for it.

I had many memorable and proud times while serving on active duty. I was officially the antisubmarine officer, but also had several other collateral duties. As the ships lay chaplain, I performed church services when at sea and a chaplain was not available. After one of my "sermons," the captain called me into his stateroom to assure himself that I would be able to fire torpedoes when commanded by him to do so and not hesitate due to my concern of killing Vietnamese submariners. I convinced him I was more concerned about American husbands and fathers that might be killed if I did not fire the torpedoes. I was privileged to conduct several funerals for retired navy persons who desired to be buried at sea.

I was also our "People to People" officer whose primary duty was to improve U.S. relationships with local citizens in the foreign ports we visited. We replaced hurricane-damaged windows, painted elementary schools, welded broken basketball hoops and backboards, and performed many other projects that made life better for many communities of our allies.

One of the best things that happened to me while in the navy was meeting my future wife, Billie. Billie and I had known each other in Jacksonville, and had attended high school together. She became a stewardess for National Airlines and had been dating one of my best friends. I was putting a friend on a plane at San Diego International Airport and ran into her while she was on a Miami-Los Angeles-San Diego flight. We chatted a few minutes before she had to reboard her plane. I called her a few weeks later to see if she was scheduled to be in San Diego the night of our squadron party. She was and made a big hit with the Bridget wardroom. I was very proud to have her as my date.

A few weeks later, on Christmas Day 1965, I had the duty and was sitting in the wardroom feeling sorry for myself. The messenger entered to tell me I had a visitor on the quarterdeck. I have never been so surprised to see Billie. She had Christmas Day off and had flown to San Diego from Miami, talked her way onto the naval base, found the USS Bridget and brought me a Christmas present. She could only visit a minute because her flight back to Miami was leaving shortly. To this day, that was one of the nicest things anyone has ever done for me.

Serving in the U.S. Navy is one of the proudest accomplishments of my life. I learned much more about the Viet Nam conflict on public TV after I got out of the navy than I knew during my two tours in that country. I was ordered overseas and never thought twice about going and have never regretted that decision. My Viet Nam Campaign medals hang proudly in my office today. I feel that everyone who has not put on a uniform and served in the armed forces of the United States has missed an unbelievable opportunity and blessing. My dad feels the same way.

Hank Haynes was born in Jacksonville, Florida on June 12, 1941. After leaving the Navy in 1968, he entered the family insurance business. The firm, Haynes, Peters and Bond Co. is the oldest insurance agency in Florida. Hank resides in Jacksonville.

LIFE IN THE NAVY
WITH "THE WORLD'S
GREATEST AVIATOR"

Rogers Baldwin (Tiger) Holmes

What follows is very hard for someone who was not alive during World War II to comprehend. The emotions of the times made people do very patriotic things.

My name is Rogers B. (Tiger) Holmes, born November 13, 1921, in Jacksonville, Florida where I have resided most of my life.

Upset by Hitler's sweep through Europe in 1939-40, I left home in the summer of 1940 with the idea of joining the Royal Canadian Air Force. I hitchhiked to Macon, Georgia, where my brother, John L. Holmes, Jr. was stationed as a U.S. Navy recruiter. Somehow he persuaded me to return home and try later to U.S. Navy flight training. Damn, I wanted to get at Hitler like all Americans but it had to wait.

When Pearl Harbor happened, I left the University of Florida and applied for U.S. Navy flight training. First, I had to pass a physical examination in Atlanta, Georgia. Unfortunately for me, they detected a deviated septum and flunked me out. I returned to Jacksonville, had the operation to correct the deviation, then decided the U.S. Army Air Force was more to my liking. I passed my physical in Nashville, Tennessee and headed to San Antonio, Texas to start my training to become the world's greatest aviator.

There were a few bumps on that path. Primary training at Bonham, Texas was a nightmare. The first six flights in the open-air cockpit PT19 saw the world's greatest aviator puke six for six. Really, it was bad. The poor instructor pilot could not wash me out because he had to officially log eight hours of total flying time with me first, and we would only be up a few minutes before I would let loose. However, I did get better with each flight but when the eight hours of required flying time were up, ol' Pop, the instructor told me to taxi back to the ramp -- it was all over. He did say that I was nice guy, but that I just was not suited for flying.

At that moment, I jammed on the brakes and told him the only way he was going to get me out of that cockpit was to cut me out with an axe. I wanted one more try. After a few minutes and a lot of "no's," he reluctantly agreed to one more flight. Things worked out and I was on my way to a flying career. Ol' Pop Simpler, the primary flight instructor, gave a little party at his home on our last day at Bonham after we had graduated from primary flight school. I asked him then about our confrontation and why he had relented, giving me that last chance. He said, "Holmes, you wanted to fly more than anyone I've ever taught, and I know you'll serve our country well; I was right in staying with you."

Basic flight school at Greenville, Texas was a breeze with RAF Instructor Pilot Officer Moore, who taught me more about acrobatic flying. I ate it up. I could just see myself shooting down those lousy Krauts or those slant-eyed son-of-a-bitches. What a disappointment it was that, after graduating from basic flight training at Greenville, they sent me to twin-engine advance training at Ellington Field at Galveston, Texas. That meant I would not get to fly those beautiful single engine fighter planes that were rolling off the production lines.

The explanation was that I was too tall to get into the cockpit of the fighter planes. What a blow! What was worse, after graduating from Ellington, they cut orders for me to report to Selman Field, Monroe, Louisiana to fly and train navigation cadets -- the real pits. Didn't those jerks in the War Department know they were clipping the wings of the world's greatest hot pilot by sending me to that armchair flying job that required hours and hours of straight and level, truly boring work?

This was something that did not fit my personality and it showed. To liven up the program, I drank excessively and did some stupid things, hoping the senior officers would recognize a real screw up and transfer me to a combat role. One such stunt was to try and outrun the local highway patrol. That landed me in the Monroe city jail for the night. After that I turned that same Packard automobile over, trying to make a turn going way too fast.

One unplanned stunt involved an airplane crash in which I sat helplessly in the copilot seat of a twin engine AT-7 and let the pilot cartwheel me down an embankment. Luckily no one was hurt but it ended that pilot's career after a flight examination review.

Seven months after coming to Monroe, I finally got my orders. This time I was delighted to get a chance to fly a really hot combat aircraft -- the B-26 Marauder, which was also dubbed the "Baltimore whore" because the wings were thought to be too small to support the large fuselage and provided "no visible means of support." The air base was located at Del Rio, Texas on the Mexican border.

The day I arrived the base sirens sounded twice, each time signaling a major aircraft accident. This aircraft had big problems inasmuch as the electrically controlled pitch of the propellers occasionally malfunctioned at inopportune times. When this occurred on takeoff, before single engine speed had been reached, it meant big trouble. The "runaway props" seemed to occur too many times on takeoff and it caused some tense moments at airspeeds between 110 mph and 165 mph as you were clearing the fence at the end of the runway.

Sure enough, my time came on takeoff after only 10 hours in the "whore." I circled the field at 150 feet till the tower cleared me for a straight-in landing on a taxiway. I was extremely lucky and extremely peed off at the poor maintenance on these aircraft.

After two months at DelRio, it was a pleasure to go to Barksdale Field in Shreveport, Lousiana. There I was to meet my crew of six copilot, navigator-bombardier, crew chief, and three gunners. We were to train for nine weeks, get combat ready, then head for Europe to join units of either the 8th, 9th, or 12th Air Forces.

Senator Harry Truman and his Senate Investigation Committee toured Barksdale after a series of accidents that caused 65 deaths in the Marauder in a short period of time. His committee decided the aircraft was unusually unsafe and cancelled the entire B-26 program. The first pilots were singled out with the crew chiefs of each crew and sent to Florence, South Carolina to train in the new Douglas A-26 program. This was a smaller, faster light attack plane that was a delight to fly.

After months of intense training, low altitude skip bombing and gunnery, we were ready to go. The war in Europe was winding down and attention shifted to the Pacific, to finishing off those slant-eyed bastards that had kicked our butts and caused so much pain and suffering.

I rode a troop train for five days to Salinas, California to pick up my aircraft. After some maintenance delays, I was briefed at 2 a.m. for an over-water flight to Hickiam Field on Oahu Island in Hawaii. Ten and a half hours later, I was there. I happened to have the phone number of my brother's father-in-law, Lt. Cmdr. Moody Clarkson, a dear friend and a wonderful guy. He picked me up in his jeep that had a bar in the rear. He gave me a wonderful welcome and after a couple of hours, I was flying high again.

The next day, I flew to the island of Kauai and landed at a replacement camp called Barking Sands. I was assigned as a replacement pilot for the 3rd Bomber Group. We were to be the front-runners for the invasion of Japan. It was while I was at Barking Sands that we heard the news that a B-29 had dropped a new bomb, called the "atom bomb," on Hiroshima, Japan. Then, another similar bomb was dropped on Nagasaki. Soon Japan called for surrender and the war was over.

New orders put me on a troop ship going to TacLoban Airfield in the Philippine Islands, and from there to Manila. I joined my new unit in Okinawa just before the great typhoon of 1945 set in. I hid underneath a truck on the side of a hill for most of the night. Our ground crews did a great job saving most of our aircraft and equipment.

Soon after the typhoon, we stored what was left and I flew to my new home at Atsugi airfield near Yokohama, Japan. As we were some of the first troops to set foot in Japan, we didn't really know what to expect from the Japs. They were told by their emperor to lay down their arms and comply obediently, which they did. There was no trouble.

The base at Atsugi had once been the proud home of Japan's finest navy pilots. The Japanese had built miles of tunnels underground to assemble their small, one-man suicide Kamikaze planes. Rocket powered, no instruments, just stick and rudder, with the pilot riding the bomb. A one-way ride with 800 pounds of high explosive material sitting under their butt.

My new job as squadron operations officer was simple. We were to buzz most of the towns on the island to remind the people that we were there and in charge. One day, we got word that our commanding general, Douglas McArthur was to visit our base to greet the new Army Chief of Staff, General Dwight Eisenhower who was flying in for a visit. This was to be the first time the two had seen each other in many years -- since McArthur had been the commanding general of the Far East and Lt. Col. Eisenhower had been his aide.

General McArthur was a great general, but also very pompous, and he considered it a great indignity that he must now greet his former aide as his superior officer. I was on the ramp with my buddy "Gutbucket" Gutzler when a Cadillac pulled up in front of us with General McArthur and General Eikleburger in the rear seat.

Ike and his C-54 were to arrive shortly and park on the ramp in front of us. There was a crowd gathering around so "Gutbucket" and I moved in closer to the Cadillac. I was standing close to the rear window next to McArthur when he wheeled in my direction, eyeballed me straight in the eyes and immediately rolled up the window.

"Gutbucket" remarked that it nearly caught my nose. What a stare from the Almighty!

When Ike arrived they rolled out the platform stairs, opened the door and this great smiling hero came out with arms in a great "V" and the crowd roared. McArthur was waiting and they saluted. It was a moment in history.

Later, Eisenhower was asked about his relationship with McArthur in the Philippines when serving as his aide. He remarked that he had spent five years in dramatics under McArthur. Then McArthur, when asked about his relationship with Ike, replied that he was one of the best clerks he had ever had.

As Operations Officer of the 89th Squadron, 3rd Bomber Group, I had the privilege of flying all the aircraft assigned to our Group -- several B-24 Pathfinders, a couple of old C-47's and of course the A-26's. We were short on mechanical parts for the aircraft and short on alcoholic beverages for our new "O" club. I assigned myself a C-47 to fly to Manila to remedy the situation, but also to see my father who was commander of a Jap P.O.W. camp outside Manila.

Dad had re-upped (re-enlisted) since both his sons were in the service and by damn he just couldn't stay out. He had been a captain in the infantry in World War I, serving with distinction in the European theatre. The Army gave him his rank back and he wanted to do his part. I couldn't wait to see him.

I landed in Manila and caught a ride down to the P.O.W. camp. When I arrived, I was told that Dad was sick with malaria and was in a tent on a far row. I arrived at his tent and unceremoniously made a Japanese phrase greeting and opened the tent door, whereupon I nearly got my ass killed as Dad stuck his .45 right at my forehead. He hated Japs and I nearly paid for it.

Luckily, I had brought six bottles of Old Suntory Jap Scotch whiskey to enhance the reunion and spent the night with the greatest dad a man ever had. We were American soldiers and damn proud of it. We had played just a small part in what we thought was the war to end all wars. We were blessed to be alive and couldn't wait to get home and enjoy the wonderful country we represented.

Roger (Tiger) Holmes was born in Jacksonville, Florida on November 13, 1921. After release from the Army Air Force he returned to Jacksonville and founded the Holmes Timber Company. He was one of Jacksonville's leading businessmen.

He has been active as a swimmer since college days when he was captain of the University of Florida swimming team. He won the national and world championship in his age group. Tiger and Jacqueline live in Orange Park, Florida where he has a vineyard.

REMEMBERING
A MIRACULOUS
MISSION

John Hughes

There are many happenings I remember while with VF-12 in San Diego, at Maui and in the South Pacific. I suppose they will remain in my mind most of the rest of my life. Certain memories I know will never leave me as long as I am of rational mind to understand and remember.

I remember my first acquaintance with the Corsair and my captain Jumpin' Joe's chewing out after I blew out a tire while making field carrier landings on my first hop after checkout in the plane. I remember the race between Jumpin' Joe in a Corsair and a leiutenant from the 1st Squadron flying Hellcats to determine their relative performance. I also remember the flight out to the U.S.S. Core for our first landing on a carrier with the Corsair, and how choppy and heavy the sea was. Never will I forget the black pre-dawn takeoff in Maui when we lost Bayless and his division. There are many more occasions too numerous to mention here.

The flight I will remember the longest, though, is the one at Nauru Island while I was on loan to VF-23 on the Princeton. The number of strikes made that day I am not sure of, but we were to neutralize Nauru as a support base for Tarawa during the marine's invasion of that island. During the earlier strikes there had been no sighting of enemy fighters in the sky. We were going on the last strike of the day and I was leading a single section, flying rear high cover. My regular wingman had engine trouble on takeoff and a spare pilot was flying my wing. Unfortunately, he was a new replacement with the squadron, having joined us just before the carriers started back to the states.

Everything went smoothly until we reached the target area and the bombers, followed by the fighters, entered their dive on the target. I dipped my wings, indicating that it was our turn, and started my dive. I looked over my shoulder, expecting to see my wingman following, but instead saw him climbing toward what appeared to be about three division of Zeroes flying overhead.

Cussing him for doing such a stupid thing, I pulled out of my dive and climbed after him. By the time I had climbed to his altitude he was sitting there fat, dumb and "unhappy," I suppose, smoke trailing behind him while the Zekes were attacking him as if making practice runs on a target. I yelled on the radio at my wingman to dive and head out to sea and, at the same time, I turned into the attacking planes as they came down from both sides in the rear, firing at them and trying to divert them from their attack on my wingman. I continued sweeping back and forth firing at the attack planes and yelling on the radio at my wingman, "Get the hell out of here!!!"

The tracers were flying past me on both sides from Zekes on my tail. After what seemed then to be an extremely long time, my wingman did make a dive and headed in a southeasterly direction away from the island. I waited what I considered to be sufficient time for him to get a good head start and then took off after him. After a while I caught him since he apparently did not have much power. We scissored once, hoping to get the two Zekes closest behind us, but they were so close we couldn't get a good sight on them. Then we flew into a bank of clouds above us and that was the last I saw of the wingman until later aboard the Princeton.

When I came out of the clouds, there were no planes in sight. In fact there was nothing to be seen in any direction. After flying in circles for awhile, searching for planes in the air, or signs of wreckage in the sea, I headed back to the carrier. After landing and talking to Captain Richardson (I believe) on the bridge, and some time later my wingman landed. Immediately after his landing his engine stopped, having run out of fuel.

When I talked to my wingman later, he explained what happened. The clouds we had entered were larger and extended all the way back to Nauru and beyond. I came out on one side of the clouds and he went out the other side. The Zekes were on his side of the clouds, and every time he poked his nose out of the clouds, they chased him back in. They drove him all the way back to Nauru and beyond.

Apparently figuring he would crash anyway from lack of fuel or malfunction of the plane because of the hits it had received, they abandoned him and returned to the island. He was later found by Jumpin' Joe's division, which happened to be on combat air patrol and had been directed to investigate a blip on the radar screen by CIC. When he landed, my wingman's cockpit was filled with oil and his flight suit was completely soaked. He got out of the cockpit, knelt and kissed the flight deck.

One last comment on the incident. The next morning after breakfast, while I was walking on the hangar deck, my plane captain came up and said, "Come here. I want to show you something."

He led me to my plane and pointed to my left aileron cable. I saw where a shell had pierced the cable and it was holding together by what appeared to be only two or three strands. The shell had to have pierced the cable during the heat of battle. Why it did not snap immediately after the shell pierced it, only God knows. One thing is certain. If the strands of the cable had snapped, I would not be here now. I have thanked God ever since for our miraculous return to the carrier.

John L Hughes was born December 11, 1919 in Sullivan, Wisconsin. He grew up in Washington, Iowa. After the war he graduated from law school. He retired as judge in the 19th Judicial Circuit of Illinois. He lived and died in Waukegan, Illinois.

TWO WARS
TWO DIFFERENT
KINDS OF DUTY

Mark Hulsey, Jr.

An LST is 325 feet long by 50 feet wide (longer than a football field). It draws 9 feet forward and 13 feet aft. It has 40 mm with 20mm and 50 caliber machine guns with both a bow and stern anchor. Naturally it is flat bottomed to allow it to beach -- like Jax Beach. It can pitch, roll and shimmy simultaneously, wide open at 12 knots. I lived on one for two years.

Our Captain Ray Willett made Captain Queeg look like a sissy. I was the communication officer with radio, signal (light) and quarter masters (steer and asst. navigation. They wore undress whites (not dungarees) and worked in officer's country. The Captain called me Miss Hulsey and her radio girls.)

Capt. Willett was a mustang warrant officer - had been promoted to Lt. (2 stripes) - having joined the Navy when he was 16. He put me in my room several times.

INVASION

In early January 1944, I went to England on LST 56 (carried LCT on deck) in convoy, (300) Halifax to Clyde, Scotland, down to Falmouth, Fowey and Plymouth (Daphne De Maurer wrote Rebecca at Fowey.)

LST (Landing Strip Tank) also Large Slow Target (12 kts.) 22 officers, 150 men (Group Flag Ship). Cdr. Sam Purdy Commodore (1 star) (War Time).

Prepared for Operation Overlord (code name for Normandy landing). Left from Plymouth June 4 for invasion. Weather forced recall to Plymouth. Left again

June 5 fully loaded: 1 battery of 105 Howitzers - 1 company of MP's for beach traffic. Weather: rough sea, raining. There are five invasion beaches - 2 British: Sword and Juno, 1 Canadian: Gold, and 2 US: Omaha and Utah.

Arrived Omaha - Dog - Red, 7-8 AM June 6 (site of "Longest Day" movie). High tide - ships in sight from North, East and West - giant armada. Battleships, LSI, LCT, LST, AKA destroyers, DE's, Corvettes, cruisers every make and model. (Approx. 4,000)

Army Air Corps had bombed landing area. Unfortunately started five miles inland. Most beach defenses intact, i.e., mines, barricades, famous German 88 mm. Guns in cliff and above cliffs.

We had worn gas protective clothing from Plymouth - got too hot - so we decided poison gas was better than heat prostration. The tide was high. The beach was a mess (Dante's Inferno - fire, explosions, tank traps), soldiers, tanks, trucks, guns, etc., all headed for a slope between an opening in the cliffs; became a deadly bottleneck [way behind schedule].

Offshore, approximately ½ mile, we waited for further orders. Signal light - "standoff; await orders; signalman refused to take light, I did, Capt. put signalman in brig, threatened court martial and execution). Anchored by stern anchor. Explosions continued amidst the American forces on shore - seemed unable to move. Saw tanks drop in tank traps - first one in - second on top - third went across; terrible personnel casualties.

Destroyers called in to help break logjam. Director fire by their 5 inch 38 guns at German tanks on the top of cliffs and gun emplacements within. Saw bodies and guns, etc. Slowly mass began to move up slope (after several hours) and progress made.

While anchored, a German shell from German 88 on top of small church (later saw) inland, landed between the shore and us. Second shell let us know we were intended target. Got underway. We began hoisting the stern anchor, which pulled us toward (not away) beach. Next shell went over us but exploded in air close to ship. Shrapnel showered our main deck causing soldier casualties (4 or 5 killed, 10-15 wounded). As OD i.e. Officer of Deck - found MP hit hole size of quarter in front - rolled into stretcher (hole size of basketball; died quickly). Later church gun silenced by battleships. Their shells coming over us sounded like fast freight trains; the bang sounded like a sledgehammer hitting a metal wall six inches from your ears although the battleships were several miles away.

We launched our 6 LCVP's (Landing Craft Vehicle Personnel). All were lost but the safe crews later found us in England. Our passengers and equipment made it ashore on rhino barges (floating roadways) from the LST ramp to the beach.

Eventually we were loaded with wounded rangers who had scaled the cliffs and silenced the big German guns there.

During the day, we began seeing increasing numbers of bodies floating in the water upside down. Unfortunately, these soldiers were wearing full battle packs with a single lifeboat around their waists. As they jumped form the LCVP's to go ashore, sometimes the water was too deep and they would turn upside down and drown. It was very depressing to see hundreds of bodies floating around upside down. We pulled men from the water, but they were all dead.

After the first day, we took wounded back to Netley Hospital in South Hampton, England, loaded up and brought supplies back to Omaha or Utah beaches - from June 6, 1944 to March 1945.

EXCERPTS FROM
LETTERS HOME
(MOTHER SAVED)

6/9/44

I was there D-Day and saw much and learned more-someday I'll be able to tell you about it. I have been pretty busy these last few weeks particularly this one. I never thought I'd leave my clothes on so long without change - but time is very scarce. Someday I'll take a hot shower every night - put on pajamas and sleep late. We've anchored awaiting further orders now.

6/24/44

Back and forth across the channel. After I left New Orleans, then New York, Davisville, R.I., Boston, Halifax, over to Clyde, Scotland, then to Southwestern England and have been here since except for our trips to Normandy, France. Stay awfully busy night and day and probably will until the French situation is well along. It is pretty cold here and some days I still wear my long underwear.

7/4/44

Today has been another day to us and we don't know what day of the week it is. Everyday is the same, we never realize whether it is Sunday or Thursday - just another 24 hours and you're glad to see them roll around. Message [signal light], which came in from two British LST's on the beach with us at dawn and until high tide "Thank God there was a Declaration of Independence." It's still raining here (off and on) and not too warm - we still wear jackets, etc. Guess you know more about the war than I do.

7/11/44

We are in for brief rest 48 hours to have a little work done on our bow doors - an LCT hit one of the doors loading casualties one dark, rough night and it has been 'acting up' ever since. Our crew gave up their beds for the wounded. We have crossed the channel 20 times now, have carried a lot of stuff over and evacuated quite a few wounded and prisoners. They're a surly lot (the Nazis) - some are 14 or 15, others 55 or so - these seem to be the defense troops (coastal - and are rather shabby). Their uniforms are warm though they are well equipped - their guns and ammo are of good quality too. These jerries are smart military men - we have and will learn a lot from them. We saw Italians, Poles, Mongols, Russians among the P.O.W.'s. They were told to fight or die so they decided on the former. We are all enjoying the brief rest - the monotony of these trips one after another gets you. The shuttle goes on - the robot bombs still fall and it still rains every day. Miserable weather - cold most the time - good old Florida for me.

MISCELLANEOUS

It was strange to get used to the 30-foot tides. At low tide, we were high and dry on the beach and could no-see the water over the horizon.

On either our first or second trip to Utah Beach, we were taking on wounded. LST 1066 passed us going toward the beach; it was about 50 yards away when it hit a mine. It exploded in sight and of the approximately 700 people aboard, we picked up 4 survivors. One was a truck driver who had been sitting on tank deck in his driver's seat awaiting the landing. He still had the comic book in his hand when we picked him up out of the water.

One of the most vivid recollections is going back to Omaha Beach within a week of the initial landing and seeing a dead French girl tied to an apple tree. She had been the spotter for the 88 gun in the church that hit us and had been executed by some of our troops.

OTHER RECOLLECTIONS

- Capt. Willett: "You are nothing but an asset to the U.S. Navy."
- The jeep disappears at Utah.
- Plymouth Harbor - smoke maker - preparation aborted start on June 5, left on June 6.
- MP Company. 105 Howitzers. Convert to hospital ship: 3 docs, 15 corpsmen. Carried wounded on tank deck. (Rangers - Point duHoc).
- Ens. Hulsey - Thompson submachine gun (Prisoners).
- Show book and Times Union (Photo with LST 56).

Although 57 years have passed I remember these events vividly.

COMMENTS ON THE
KOREAN WAR: PART II

After discharge from the Navy in September 1946 and enrolling in the University of Florida Law School, I joined a naval reserve squadron, VP (ML56 - later VP-741) at NAS Jax in March. 1947 as an IFGO (Ignorant f------ Ground Officer). Actually I was an ersatz navigator and administrative officer. I remained with VP-741 until December 31, 1952.

VP-741 was an antisubmarine warfare (ASW) squadron (with mine laying, patrol and reconnaissance qualifications). We had nine P2V airplanes, which were the predecessors to the P-3 Orions you now see every day over Jacksonville.

Our reserves duties required drills one weekend per month with two weeks active duty each year. We were called to active duty in January 1951 during the Korean War. We were returned to inactive duty on December 31, 1952. During that time we were stationed at NAS Jax except for one six-month duty period at Malta in the Mediterranean Sea to carry out our missions and participate in exercises with the Sixth Fleet. The Navy has continued ever since those six-month deployments for the Sixth Fleet.

Malta is an island (19 x 7 miles) located south of Sicily and North of Libya. St. Paul was shipwrecked there (New Testament -- "Acts") en route from Jerusalem to Rome. It is almost a pure theocracy (98% Catholic) with many religious holidays, bars and churches. The Knights of Malta came there in 800 AD after being defeated during the Crusades by Suleiman at Rhodes.

A recitation of my activities during that period would be exhausting and difficult. Here are a few examples:

During our inactive period, we flew ASW and reconnaissance hops from Argentina, Newfoundland to Port-au-Prince, and Trinidad. Needless to say, my wife was not convinced that these flights were necessary. While on active duty, in August 1951, we lost one plane at Fleming Island, Florida. I was designated "Crash Liaison Officer."

THE CRASH

Our squadron executive officer, Lt. Cmdr. L.B. Worley was the P2V2 pilot on a routine training mission from NAS JAX to West Palm Beach. On the return flight to NAS, smoke was detected and the "crash bar" was hit, turning off all electricity in the plane. L.B. decided to land at the Fleming Island field used in WWII. Cows on the runway prevented this, so he "went around" to try again. He pushed the propellers to full power but with the crash bar on, the Hamilton electrical activated props did not change the pitch. He slowly climbed out until the port wing hit one tall pine tree and cart wheeled the plane into the ground.

Seven of the nine crew were killed instantly including L.B. Lt (jg.) Ralph Jones was severely burned out survived. Airman Apprentice George Barnett was thrown out of the tail gunner's seat into the tops of pine trees and was unhurt except for a few scratches and bruises. I interviewed him fairly soon after his arrival at NAS hospital and many times thereafter until he left the squadron a year later. He remembers putting on his parachute harness before they left the squadron area but had no memory of anything else until he was being examined for injury at the hospital. My duties included being the Navy Liaison Officer for all families of the dead crewmen. It was a very difficult time.

We left for Malta on March 10, 1952, with overnights at Bermuda, Azores and Port Lyauty, Morocco.

We were stationed with the Royal Air Force (RAF) there. We lived in Quonset huts. Flies were everywhere. Reconnaissance flights covered the entire Mediterranean including visits to Nicosia, Cyprus; Athens, Greece; Nice, France, Gibraltar, Madrid, and other places. We visited Naples and the Isle of Capri near Naples many times.

We were stationed at LUQA, an RAF field still flying Lancasters. as in WWII.

Our mission was to mine the Dardanelles from Istanbul to Crete to prevent the Russian fleet from leaving the Black Sea and thus start World War III. We were the first reserve squadron in the Sixth Fleet on six months turnaround. We were in approximately four exercises with the fleet. All of our pilots were WWII types and the new fighter jets with ensign pilots were no match for them. Their performance during the exercises got our commanding officer, Cmdr. Chuck Rogers, a fitness report guaranteeing his appointment as Chief of Naval Operations (CNO), one admiral said. The USN squadrons before us would send three to four planes. All nine of our planes were there for each exercise. They dropped water filled condoms on the carrier (the Essex) deck, lowered flaps, slowed down and faked an apparent attempt to land on the carrier. The Sixth Fleet Commander, Admiral Cassidy was impressed.

We covered the Mediterranean Sea from east to west, Nicosia, Cyprus to Madrid, Spain. We also reluctantly toured various tourist and historic places such as Gibraltar, Munich, Nice, Pompeii, etc.

The RAF could not have been nicer. On our arrival, RAF Group Captain Ogbert gave us a welcoming reception, and we reciprocated when we left. Admiral Lord Louie Mountbatten was senior naval officer in the area, aboard the flagship cruiser Halifax. Ed Rood (wife Dorothy), American Consul at Malta, had regular parties honoring Lord Louie and his wife Edwina, who were very charming.

We performed our duties well and my life was changed because of my Korean War experience.

OTHER EVENTS

VP-741 awarded "Noel Davis" Trophy -- Most Outstanding Patrol Squadron -- U.S. Navy.

I was selected as a member of the Royal Navy Sailing Association at Valetta, Malta. We sailed "Star" boats liberated by England from the Germans in Bremen, Germany during WWII.

Mark Hulsey, Jr. was born in Jacksonville, Florida on September 25, 1922. He had the unusual experiences of serving in two different branches of the Navy in two wars. In WWII he served aboard an LST and during the Korean War he served in an aviation squadron. He is a graduate of the University of Florida Law School and is in the practice of law in Jacksonville. Mr. Hulsey has been a prominent member of the Jacksonville Port Authority.

THE EMBARRASSMENT
OF LANDING AT
THE WRONG BASE

Noah Jenerette

Each squadron had a Landing Signal Officer and of course the ship had an L.S.O. VC-20 was scheduled out of Pearl about 60 days after the bomb dropped so we did not deploy. We would have been the only squadron aboard the jeep carrier. I can't say for sure, but a jeep squadron flew about 15 fighters and 10 torpedo bombers.

AN INTERESTING
EVENING

We were finishing up training in SNV's (Vultee Vibrators) at Saifley Field in Pensacola before going into SNJ's. We had to have a dual bounce drill at night and if an "up," immediately shoot some solo landings. The weather was unbelievably bad -- snowing, some ice on the runways, etc. The cadet flew in front with the instructor way back and totally blocked from any view. At Dallas we flew Yellow Perils and used flare pots with no great problem. Here we had flare pots but we also had to turn on our landing light which, on the surface, would seem to make for even easier landings. Not so in my case.

Four times we went around and four times I made a full stall landing at least 100 feet in the air and fighting the fall with everything I had. Each time the plane jumped entirely out of the portion of the runway illuminated by the pots. The poor ensign had to be terrified. He directed me to go to the line and crawled out on the wing.

"JENERETTE, YOU'RE GOING TO KILL YOURSELF BUT I'M NOT GOING TO BE WITH YOU."

Why would he do this? If he had given me a "down" he would have had to have flown with me the following night. Fortunately, I did fine for the rest of the evening.

AN EMBARRASSING MOMENT

VC 20 prepared for its second deployment at a base in Kings City, California. This was a small town and the base, which was originally Army Air Force, would only accommodate one jeep squadron. In the middle of the lovely Salinas Valley we had it made. I was the squadron LSO. Having gotten all of 30 minutes in a TBF and seeking some big town recreation on a Friday, I checked one out and accompanied by three or four of a like mind, I took off for Alameda NAS. Never having been to the Bay Area and no great shakes as a navigator and flying a big handful of an airplane, something was sure to go wrong and it did.

Thinking I was approaching my target, I radioed for clearance, received it and was told the appropriate runway. In a few minutes it appeared and armed guards came roaring up with emergency lights flashing. Of course, I had screwed up and landed at an Army base 50 miles south of Alameda. The tower ate me out but obviously enjoyed the stupid Navy pilot and let me turn around and take off. My passengers and squadron mates never let me forget it.

Noah Jenerette was born on June 11, 1923 in Jacksonville, Florida and grew up there. He served in the U.S. Navy from August 1942 until October 1945. He was the Landing Signal Officer for VC-20. His squadron was scheduled to go aboard a Jeep carrier when the A-bomb was dropped. He is retired from a very successful law practice.

"KLONDIKE, OLD BOY, YOU'RE ONFIRE"

Dale Christian Klahn

Being shot down by the enemy is no heroic event. The purpose of warfare is to reduce the personnel and material resources of the enemy until he no longer has the desire to proceed.

If the enemy inflicts damage to you, you have lost valuable assets of your country, and endangered the lives of your shipmates (strafing while I was in the water), and the lives and material of your allies (the British sub and its crew.)

If an enemy fighter had shot me down, I would have really been embarrassed, but being shot down by AA takes some of the sting out of the incident.

The fact that this rescue received so much attention is that it was a joint effort and the British sub actually entered an enemy harbor and succeeded. While strafing at low altitude in the harbor at Sabang, Sumatra, I heard a loud explosion on the starboard side of my aircraft. Simultaneously I noted that my right wing was on fire. I could see the strength members in the wing and knew I had to exit immediately or lose the wing and "spin in."

I heard the "Babe," Lt. Charles Winterroud, say "Klondike, old boy, you're on fire." I pulled the radio cord loose, placed my hands on the port gunnels of the cockpit, stood in the seat, and went out headfirst. I must have pulled the ripcord by instinct; there was no count to 10, clear the tail and pull the cord. My feet hit the water and as I settled into the bay, I released my chute.

Next I remember my emergency pack bobbing along behind as I inflated my Mae West. I opened it and inflated my rubber raft and tried to salvage as many of the enclosed "goodies" as I could. At this point I saw or heard something.

Almost immediately there was firing from the beach, either 3" or 5". I had not entered my rubber raft but did so quickly since the concussion of the explosives was uncomfortable. As quickly as it started, the firing shifted from me to another target. This was my first glimpse of HMS Tactician. The sub was approaching at good speed and overshot me. This was the first time I could identify the vessel. Heretofore, I didn't know whether it was a friend or foe.

I started to swim toward the sub, but towing my raft slowed me so I cut it loose. The crewman on the fantail threw me a line, which fell short. Two crewmen dived into the water carrying a line. We finally made contact and were unceremoniously hauled aboard. The crewmen herded me up the deck toward the bridge as fast as I could move in a wet flight suit, Mae West, et al.

I learned then the meaning of "down the hatch." The captain was in no mood for conversation! He shoved me "down the hole," the crew had already left the bridge, and I was half sitting, half lying on the deck. I heard the hatch close and glanced up to see the captain descending the ladder. He was wearing a wraparound loincloth, or whatever they are called in the Far East. It was a great sight! This was my first glimpse of Captain Collett. He would have done well in Piccadilly Circus.

After we had settled on the bottom of the harbor, the captain sent for me. We exchanged greetings; I thanked him many times over, and asked to see the crewmen who went over the side to rescue me. My request was granted and they were summoned to the wardroom, which was about the size of a phone booth.

The quarters assigned to me were the bench along the bulkhead adjacent to the wardroom table. There I settled into a world of sleep all day; tinned mutton; hard, so-called biscuits, and warm tea. The air aboard the sub during the day was terrible. Piled garbage sat along the passageways and there were bodies that had not seen soap for a long time. A native coast watcher who had been removed from one of the islands put lime in his hair to keep out the insects. Still I was contented!

The first several nights I was not asked to the bridge. We surfaced each night to get some air and charge batteries. Finally, after three or four nights, the captain sent the messenger, who repeated exactly, "Ask the Yank if he would come on the bridge." I did not frequent the quarterdeck until I was asked; therefore, I had no knowledge of our position.

After he had set the watch topside, the captain showed me our position and informed me we were on a 30-day patrol in the Andaman Islands. Joy! He also asked if I played cribbage, to which I responded in the affirmative. He explained that none of his officers could count fast enough to play crib. They played solitaire at the wardroom table with cards that were old enough to be retired. Captain called this "mental masturbation."

Almost every night the captain and I played crib in his cabin until just about dawn, when he went topside to relieve the watch and take the sub below. The thing I liked about the crib games was that the captain had several bottles of scotch. He allotted each of us one drink while we played crib. I did not mind that there was no ice.

We finally entered the harbor at Trinco, Ceylon. The sub hoisted the "Jolly Roger" with a life preserver sewn thereon at the foremast. I suppose this is a British tradition. The welcome home party from the Sara brought ice cream for the entire crew of Tactician.

Home again, halfway around the world from home. Which proves that "home is where you hang your hat!" Two ships met in the mist, hailed each other and passed on.

Klondike was shot down on May 19, 1943. He was in VF-12 flying an F6-F and was wingman for the air group commander. Air Group 12 was on SARATOGA-CV-3 and was operating with the British fleet in the Indian Ocean. After a distinguished career, Captain Dale C. Klahn, U.S.N., retired June 30, 1966.

IT IS NOT
WHAT YOU
HAVE "DUN"...

Col. Joseph Bland Love

It is not what you have "dun," but what you have "dun" lately... When cavalry Capt. John Wayne retired his watch, he said, "One day every face is turned toward ya. The next, they don't know your name."

My story is set when The Republic of Viet-Nam was alive. When half a million Americans were there doing the noble thing. Before Cronkite told us we had lost. Before McNamara revealed his fears. Before Lyndon quit. Before the 94th Congress tarnished their honor.

On 17 December 1967, in Phu My District, Binh Dinh Province, the 2nd Battalion, 5th Cavalry, First Cavalry Division, is patrolling with four companies. It is Sunday, hot and dry, before the wet monsoon. The riflemen of Company A, about 100 strong under Capt Clay Pratt, are strung along the hamlets of the village of Tan Phung by the South China Sea. Apache Company is searching for North Vietnamese recruits, newly infiltrated by water and en route to the 3rd NVA Division.

The habit of the North's soldiers is to hide among the rocks and caves of the beach area or to seek shelter in the hootches and bunkers of the VC populace. So far the U.S. soldiers have met with only a few shots, one child-thrown grenade, and the flat, unwavering look of hatred from the youngest to the old. Pratt, with his usually firm control, has prevented any retaliation. He, his interpreters, and SVN police have found no overt enemy soldiers. No female nurses, no orators, no supply caches---only the people of a fishing village.

Back at 2nd Brigade Headquarters, on Landing Zone Up Lift, 10 miles to the northwest and near Phu My, a light lunch is over. A visitor has dropped in to get the score. He is Lt. Gen. Bill Rossen, CG, IFFV (our corps), a wise, hard, popular soldier. In the briefing tent all partake of the deliciously cold Jp-4 (our purple-blue cool-aid drink named after the lifeblood helicopter fuel of the Cav). Colonel Joe McDonough and his S3 are briefing Gen. Rossen in front of an eight-foot high map of our area. Four others are there, because my battalion is active and close by. A sergeant from S2 comes from the back, a small sheet of paper in his hand, and gives it to McDonough. Joe glances at it and hands the paper to me with the words "go get 'em." A mission-type order.

Out of the tent I read the note. A simple set of coordinates. The location of an enemy radio transmitter used only minutes before. Not routine. Seldom intercepted in the day. Always in code. Short. Meaningful and a key to start the great engine of the First Team's swift power. A break for us.

Major Bill Murphy, Bn S3, is close by. We check his always ready map. The point is just a few hundred yards NE of Pratt's column in Tan Phung. As we found later, the pressure of Apache on the North's soldiers was growing and the NVA leader had sent a warning to his own chain of command. Murphy alerts our Charley-Charley command ships and Pratt. We decide to lift the entire Company D, deployed 10 miles inland, to the ocean about three miles N of Pratt and on the concave side of the beach and rock formations. The Huey (HU1-B) support is requested -- we are first in line -- and Captain Joe Carpenter's men will be picked up in 20 minutes. It is now 1330; the lead men of Co. D, Navajo, will be on the ground, deployed, blocking, ready to tackle in half an hour.

Back home the NFL games will be kicking off in a few hours. Bart Starr of the Packers will be throwing his bombs for Vince Lombardi.

Companies B and C-Bravo (Capt. Bob Carroll and Comanche/Capt. Jim Estep) are alerted but with no change in mission. We don't know how big the hornet's nest might be.

Brigade issues me a pink team of aerial scouts -- a white OH-6 chopper and a red gun ship with heavy guns. The white pilot is Lt. Bruce Mauldin, a favorite of mine because he is fast, bold and deadly, perhaps trying to overcome the WWII rep of his antiwar father Bill. The scouts are at the beach within minutes, looking for movement and firing at likely hole-covering rocks, literally anything that casts a live shadow.

Carpenter is now on the ground marching with his first platoon. The 22 troopers are deployed across 300 meters, in three squads of two and three-man fire teams. Their mission is to block any escape or attack to the north of the enemy force -- a force of unknown number from 2 to 100. This place is near the site of caves in which 67 NVA replacements were trapped in September when McDonough had commanded the battalion and Pratt was first leading Company A. The team still meshes well, practiced, confident and with no undue pressure. A few shots from either side, from both north and south. Pratt presses north. It is 1430. Carpenter's boys hold while another of his platoons is put on the beach.

There -- motion in the shadows! A break from the rocks. The pink team darts in -- the white bird dancing over the outcropping, and seconds later the red flyer in the HU-1 engages with its heavy machine guns thumping and rock chips and sand escalating into the air. From the air command post, through the glasses, it all looks too bright or dim, slow motion, and only the radio voices from the company net bring sense. Dark sacks are on the sand.

One of D Company has been seriously wounded. The Charley-Charley is low on fuel so the "Ready Bird" lands, drops Murphy to watch over at the beach, while Arizona Six stays with the higher radio nets, makes the med-evac, and gets the JP-4. Twenty-five minutes later, 1515 hours, Ready Bird is back. Murphy is in the saddle again. Carpenter has moved cautiously forward to check the kill area. Pratt's boys have scored one enemy KIA. Things are on pause. The scouts, having refueled, are back, snooping about. To listen, to hear well, the birds are ordered to orbit over other terrain features 2,000 meters away. This entire Brigade is told.

The coast seems clear and Navajo is ordered to police the area. This is high alert work – the caves, rocks and hills are many. Every sense, every intuition of the soldier is now working at maximum. This is what the rifleman gets paid for, and he gets very low pay. Later, his reward will be at dusk and he may hear his buddies mutter "Today Ben had his guts -- he did his job." The accolade of the infantryman.

This day there will be no more U.S. 5th Cavalry blood shed. Carpenter's men find seven NVA dead, zero wounded, three weapons, and a bundle of waterproofed papers. Later, we find the papers are 60 days of radio traffic, with many complaints of the difficulty of moving in daylight under the Americans' helicopter watch and foot patrols. This is encouraging for doubters have often called our efforts "walks in the sun." One enemy officer is killed: Major Van Ha, Political Officer, 2d VC Regiment, 3d NVA Divison.

Pratt's men find one enemy KIA, without weapon. No uniform but black pajamas, trying to run from area, and having the youthful age that every army must have. Apache killed no women and children and though sorely provoked caused only a few deep bruises to the larger "children" and very capable looking women. There are no American casualties.

It is now 1700 and 60 minutes to dark. Company A, Apache, is airlifted inland to the edge of the deep jungle. There is a hot supper. Plans for the patrol next day will be made. The troopers will sleep in soft beds of jungle leaves under ponchos, and have the warm, full feeling of duty well done. Company D, Navajo, is pulled back from the rocks 500 yards and sets up a perimeter, well aware that they could be easily mortared. Deep foxholes are dug along the place of preferment for their ponchos. In Navajo Company there is some elation. They had a visible win. There had been exciting flight and march to success. The moon shines over the South China Sea. They are America's heroes, and going to win. Like General MacArthur they believe…

THERE IS NO SUBSTITUTE FOR VICTORY

The scouts lift birds, and the Charley-Charley team all fly back to their tents and hot food at LZ Uplift. They feel "up". A clean win, small, but neat and at almost no price.  The soldier will recover from a serious leg wound and it won't hurt his fatherhood prospects. Major Murphy, a bit miffed from being left in what turned out to be a minefield, recovers his good humor and makes his nightly scheme for watching over comrades in the field. Arizona Six is quietly happy. It had gone well from the first moment, there are two letters from home, and the First Team is winning.

Two days later, Captain Carpenter gave Arizona Six the pistol of Major Van Ha over a supper of hot C rations on the beach near Tan Phung.

The pistol is on the wall now, 33 years later, a piece of the coonskin LBJ sent us to get.

Captain Wayne understands.

Colonel Joseph Bland Love was born on March 30, 1925 and served in the United States Army from 1943-1975. He was Commanding Officer, 1st Corps Support Command, Fort Bragg, North Carolina, 1973-1975. He is now retired.

THE GREAT WAVE:
A TALE OF
KOREAN WAR TIMES

William N. Morgan

(Recalled by William N. Morgan who was born in Jacksonville, Florida on Dec. 14, 1930, attended Harvard College 1948-52 on a Naval ROTC scholarship, and served in the Pacific Far East from June 1952 to August 1955.)

Guam's bright tropical sun was a welcomed relief for the severely cold winter I left behind in North Korea. Off Chongjin in December 1954, I disembarked from the destroyer I had served aboard for some 19 months, the U.S.S. Bausell (DD-845), leaving the ship to resume its seemingly endless coastal patrol.

Being stationed on a tropical island presented new opportunities undreamed of at sea. After the daily routine of the admiral's staff, I donned the appropriate attire and joined in the evening routine of the B.O.Q., notably drinking heavily and lying mightily.

A few weeks later my commanding officer, Rear Admiral Marion E. Murphy, called me in, closed the door, and verified that I was a good swimmer and familiar with secret code decryption procedures. He then assigned me to assist a group of scientists who would arrive on Guam shortly on a mission about which absolutely no questions were to be asked. The admiral gave me a code word no one else was to know; he said that I would know what to do when I decoded the word MAYFLOWER. This all seemed very curious: Do what? When?

The chairman of the Department of Physical Oceanography at Scripps Institution, Dr. William G. Van Dorn, arrived on Guam in the company of a dozen Ph.D. candidates who looked like olympic swimmers. They brought with them a dozen or so plywood instrument cases marked "fragile", overnight bags and little else. After spreading their gear out on the B.O.Q. lawn, Dr. Van Dorn gave me a short list of his group's needs: Several hundreds of feet of garden variety plastic hose and many dozens of large flashlight batteries.

None of the materials was available within a thousand miles of Guam. One message later, and within a matter of hours, a navy transport landed at NAS Agana with more hose and batteries than we had requested.

Every morning the oceanographers quietly disappeared in jeeps, and every evening they reappeared in time for the evening meal in the Officers' Mess. One day Van Dorn asked if I would like to join them. I couldn't wait.

The former ship channel near Cocos Island was one of two sites where the oceanographers were working, free diving off the end of the long coral jetty into some of the deepest water on earth. They were taking a section of hose down perhaps 40 feet below the surface of the sea, and then rolling the biggest boulders they could manage over the end of the hose to hold it in a fixed position without pinching the hose. A second hose was fixed in relatively shallow water. Both hoses were connected to the instrument case, which also contained a battery, and instruments that I was not supposed to see and had no interest in seeing.

After swimming, diving and working arduously for several hours, the day's routine shifted to surfing, scuba diving, drinking beer, and sun bathing or snoozing until the time arrived to return to the B.O.Q.

The following day I accompanied the group to a secluded cove about 20 miles north of Cocos Island. The cove site also faced due east, and was on the shore edge where the bottom dropped precipitously to unknown depths. The installation of hoses here was to be similar to the installation of the day before: One hose anchored at a depth of around 40 feet, and the other hose stabilized in shallow water. Diving on the reef was exceptionally dangerous: The powerful waves crashed into the base of the cliff, receded across the reef and plunged down into the sea, creating a powerful current down to an undetermined depth. If a hapless diver were caught in the current he would be plunged below the surface for an indefinite time, and perhaps returned to the surface half a mile or so offshore in a current bound for the open sea.

The relentless waves crashed over the reef in a deafening roar as the diver assigned to secure the deeper hose was bound in an improvised rope harness and lowered into the sea. The rope extended across the reef for a hundred feet or more, held by a dozen oceanographers braced to raise or lower the diver according to Van Dorn's signals. The arduous task of securing the deeper hose finally was completed. Just as the signal was given to retrieve the diver, a set of exceptionally powerful waves began to thunder over the reef, knocking several of the rope handlers off their feet and disorienting the others. Their footings on the reef top began to loose traction. One by one, as the wave pounded in, the line handlers slid helplessly across the reef, each releasing his grip on the lifeline as he neared the reef edge.

At the last moment the end rope handler looped the dwindling end of the rope around a coral outcropping. The rope held. The tumultuous wave set began to relent, and the oceanographers scrambled to regain their grips on the rope. Together they won their tug of war with the out-rushing current, and the diver finally reappeared over the jagged reef edge, half drowned but as relieved to be back from the deep as his fellow oceanographers were to retrieve him.

Within a few days all of the oceanographers except Van Dorn packed their gear and departed for a dozen different islands stretching to the south in an arc more than a thousand miles long, from the Mariana Islands almost down to the north coast of New Guinea. Each man set up an oceanographic station similar to the ones on Guam, and each continuously maintained radio contact with the admiral's communication center.

Days stretched into weeks, my tennis game improved (but then it couldn't get worse), my tolerance for alcohol became prodigious, and my ability to prevaricate became legendary. All was quiet on the island stations.

Then an emergency message from one of the stations interrupted the calm: One of the oceanographers had broken his leg and required medical evacuation. Van Dorn summoned me to his room in the B.O.Q. where he was packing hurriedly in preparation to leave for the injured man's station. I would have to take over the two stations on Guam in Van Dorn's absence. He explained hastily what I would need to know, which is what the admiral had said I would not need to know. The oceanographic recorders we had installed were designed to exclude such short frequency waves as those caused by wind, and also to exclude such long frequency waves as those associated with high and low tides. The recorders were designed to record only tsunami, or medium frequency waves commonly known as tidal waves, such as those caused by earthquakes, geological plate shifts or similar phenomena.

Van Dorn continued: A coded message will arrive at any time giving only an hour and minute. The message time must be transmitted immediately to each station. I then will drive to the stations, verify the ink level for the continuously moving stylus, check the instruments, confirm that the hoses are functioning, and wait. I asked what I would wait for? Van Dorn said he was not sure, maybe for nothing, or for very little, or maybe something quite noticeable. But make sure both stations are working flawlessly. When it's over, remove the record rolls from the instrument cases and leave with them on a waiting plane. Then forget that any of this has happened, and never mention anything about it to anyone.

The days after Van Dorn left stretched into weeks without event. Transport planes droned in and out of Anderson Air Force Base on their missions to resupply the French garrisons in Indochina, and something about the Chinese Nationalists was rumored to be going on at Saipan. Tedium reigned.

As luck would have it I was well into my evening routine at the Officers Club bar about 2 a.m. when, in the midst of another tall and improbable tale, a marine orderly appeared with an urgent summons to the Communications Center. I sobered up fast. The encoded dispatch yielded line after line of random letter groups until the word MAYFLOWER appeared followed by numbers representing a time about three hours later. Within minutes messages transmitted the time to the twelve oceanographic stations in Van Dorn's group.

Borrowing the orderly's jeep I rushed to the B.O.Q., grabbed my bathing suit and a flashlight, and made it to the north cove station in record time. Marine guards watched the cove from the cliffs above. Somehow the jeep made it down the rugged cliffside trail in one piece and stopped at the lagoon's edge. Clutching my flashlight I swam across the lagoon to the inlet where the instrument case was ticking away confidently. I refilled the ink reservoir, checked the battery, hoses and instruments, closed the case securely, carefully wrapped the case in a waterproof membrane, and wedged a large rock against the case so upsetting it would be all but impossible.

By the time I reached the Cocos Island jetty, less than two hours remained until the code time would occur. Years before the Japanese had blasted a channel across the reef enclosing a placid lagoon in order to establish optimum conditions for a submarine base in the middle of the Pacific Ocean. The coral debris was deposited on the north side of the channel to protect vessels traversing it from mid ocean winds and currents. The resulting jetty measured several hundred yards in length.

Leaving the jeep at the base of the cliffs I made my way in badly torn tennis shoes along the rugged, uneven coral jetty leading into the darkness of the sea. The instrument and hoses were functioning properly. I decided to wait there for the appropriate hour because the instrument case was in an exposed location; it might be overturned if rough seas developed.

The longer I waited, the colder I got. Musing as I waited, it dawned on me that all of the oceanographic stations were in an arc focusing on islands in the vicinity of Eniwetok or Bikini. I had read about ongoing tests of atomic bombs in Time and Newsweek magazines. My guess was that my activity was part of the A-bomb business, and that something unusual was about to happen. The scheduled hour, about 5o'clock local time, came and went. Sitting on the reef in my bathing suit, I was shivering. Van Dorn had said maybe nothing perceptible would occur. A warm blanket lay under the driver's seat of my jeep; I waited. Around 6:30 or so I decided to return to the jeep for the blanket. First light now showed the outline of the jetty, the reef, lagoon, and the cliffs ashore several hundred yards away. I began to pick my way along the coral jetty, proceeding toward the shore.

Possibly halfway back to the jeep, I began to hear an unusual slurping sound that I had never heard before. I looked down at the lagoon and the water was gone. The slurping sound was like thunder.

Turning to see where the lagoon's water had gone, I saw looming up from the sea a terrifying mountain of water that blotted out the horizon, a tidal wave of unbelievable immensity heading straight for me. I followed my instinct to return the instrument case in order to keep it upright.

Grasping the case I took the deepest breath I could manage while the seawater rose over me. The higher the water about me, the greater the pressure on my ears, and the less breath I had remaining. Strangely I sensed almost no turbulence, just increasing pressure, decreasing oxygen and growing terror.

Finally I released my hold on the case and bolted for the surface with all my remaining energy. An eternity later I reached the wave top, only to realize that I was dropping down the receding slope of the wave as it crashed into the shore.

Falling back on the jetty, I landed a few feet from the still upright case. Gulping air, I grasped the case again and suddenly realized that a second wave, as big as the first, was bearing down on me relentlessly. Again the water rose quickly over the case and me, and the pressure increased until it was almost unbearable, but the sense of panic gave way to the realization that this wave, too, would pass. For perhaps the next half hour tidal waves of diminishing size rolled over the case and me until the waves returned to the size of large swells, and then to normal.

Removing the record roll from the instrument case, I stumbled back across the jetty to the shore. My drowned jeep finally started, permitting a fast trip to the north cove station, which fortunately had survived the tidal waves intact. Returning to the B.O.Q. for a dry uniform, I spread the record rolls across my bedroom to view my triumph.

Unfortunately, the rolls were blank except for a few vertical lines at very broad intervals. I guessed that the styli must have been jarred as the tidal waves struck them, and that their records were lost. Then I noticed that at the ends of both record rolls the ink lines returned to normal wave configurations at proper intervals. The vertical lines at broad intervals traced the true magnitude of a wave caused by an energy release of unimaginable proportions. The record rolls left NAS Agana within the hour. No mention ever was made to me of the tidal waves or their origin.

Two years later I was discharged from active duty and visited Dr. Van Dorn at his research Laboratory in La Jolla, California. He showed me the records of all 14 stations and confirmed their significance. We had measured accurately the energy released by the detonation of one of the world's first hydrogen bombs in a lagoon more than 1,500 miles east of Guam, the first such record in history.

William Morgan FAIA received a masters' degree from Harvard and was a Fulbright Scholar. He is a renowned architect and is the author of four books. The Morgans reside in Atlantic Beach, Florida.

AN UNFRIENDLY
RESPONSE TO AN
UNSCHEDULED LANDING

F. Ray McIntyre, Jr.

Under a lovely blue Italian sky, I left early from Naples for Rome in my L-4C, cruising nicely at 95 mph with a full tank of gasoline -- all 12 gallons of it. In September 1945, the air traffic was minimal, and from 1,000 feet of altitude, with a wind from the southeast, the trip was too short. My business in Rome was done quickly and the return to Naples was undertaken without refueling but it was slower going than the morning journey.

Entering the Naples area, I was struck as usual by the gentle curve of the bay shoreline, and I found a new visitor anchored less than half a mile from the docking area -- one of our small flat-tops. The best view had to be from sea level, so I dove on the carrier, leveling off at 25 feet above the water, at the breakneck speed of 120 mph.

There seemed to be no personnel on deck and it was nearly empty of navy planes, and then it hit me that the uncrowded deck could accommodate my little plane with room to spare. The time spent at Ft. Sill, Oklahoma learning short-field landings and obstacle landings, crosswind landings could be demonstrated here although the reception would likely be very cool. To hell with it. The navy should recall we are on the same side and perhaps they would appreciate a skillful landing by a first lieutenant, Field Artillery, later of the 34th Division. I was now assigned as pilot to the Peninsular Base Section, General R. M. Oxx, commanding. The general had grown weary of taking a navy crash boat from Naples to Capri for R and R, since it required 45 minutes of his time, and somebody told him that liaison pilots could land anywhere and the air trip would be less than 10 minutes. I had been sent to reconnoiter a landing area on Capri and spent two weeks at the Quisisana Hotel, reporting back that there was not 100 yards of level field on the island, all of which irritated the brigadier general and he had not ever been persuaded to fly with me.

The ship was anchored with the bow pointing southeast, so acting on impulse I made a tight turn and approached the stern from the northwest, nose high, nearly full right rudder, and right wing high. The plane fell into a 20-degree descent, an attitude we spent hours learning at Ft. Sill with constant practice, and it had been useful over obstacles into short fields during the war sometimes with wounded aboard. The airspeed of the little Piper was only a mile or two above stalling, but the interesting part was yet to come. If the liaison pilot kicks the tail straight, holding the stick fully back, and if the heel brakes are fully depressed and then relaxed somewhat, the plane can be stopped in no more than three lengths. All this was done, but some guy came running down the deck, waving his arms and when I lowered the window of the Cub, I did not expect such a rude welcome.

His collar insignia I recognized as a lieutenant commander and he shouted that I had 30 seconds to get off "his deck." I decided that departure was preferred to lingering, but I wanted to bring him greetings from General Oxx and also hoped that he would offer a refueling and perhaps refreshment. It was not to be. I told him that if he got out of the way and gave me another 100 feet of "his deck," I could make a course reversal and leave, which I did.

It seemed important now to demonstrate a short-field takeoff and leave this unfriendly environment. If the brakes are held firmly, it is routine to raise the tail to cruise attitude with full throttle and when the brakes are released the little plane nearly leaps into the air. Although downwind on the takeoff, I decided to make a quick turn and fly alongside the ship.

The same commander appeared, waving his arms again. Not a friendly place, but I did not mention the incident to General Oxx. Some idiot on the ship took note of the numbers on the plane and complained to base section but nothing came of it. It is my opinion that they were not willing to believe it.

The matter is better forgotten, but it would have been a nice intraservice gesture if they had filled my tank at the very least.

Ray McIntyre, Jr. was born in Jacksonville Florida on September 11, 1921. He served in the Army Air Corps from June 1943 until September 1949. He was a very successful stock broker. He and his lovely wife Jeanne live in Jacksonville.

"DANGEROUS DUTY"
IN EUROPE IN THE
QUARTERMASTER CORPS

Henry G. Motes, Jr.

My first job was with Equitable Life Insurance Company. In 1941 President F. D. Roosevelt got worried about Hitler and instituted a one year draft for all eligible young men and I was so fortunate as to come up with the no. 3 draft number. I was off and running in early 1941 to Camp Blanding, Florida to learn to be a fighting infantry soldier in Uncle Sam's United States Army.

I lasted just three days because they quickly decided that I couldn't see well enough to see the enemy, much less shoot him. All the employees in the Equitable Office threw a big going away party for their future hero, who was on his way to war. They showered me with gifts and when I returned they wanted the gifts back. I said, "No way, I am a war veteran."

In June 1942 one post card from Uncle Sam changed me from 4F to 1A. I was sent to Fort McClellan, Alabama for 90 days training, again to become a fighting soldier in the U.S. Infantry. This time the war was on.

After the 90 days the infantry captain, the 1st sergeant and the platoon leader decided, if America was to win this war they needed to get me out of the infantry. Off to school I was sent to become a second lieutenant in the United States Quartermaster Corps. I found out that an officer in the Army got $30 more per month if you were married, so on the March 21, 1942, just two days after I was commissioned a second lieutenant we tied the knot.

My first assignment was 90 days special training at the Harvard Graduate School of Business Administration in Cambridge, Mass. My new bride, Marguerite Sherouse Motes spent her honeymoon at Harvard seeing me from 6 p.m. Fridays to 5 p.m. Sundays for those three months. In February 1943 I was off to Europe assigned to Major General Littlejohn's quartermaster headquarters, responsible for all the clothing, food, vehicles and miscellaneous items for almost two million troops stationed in the European Theater of Operations.

I arrived in Paris on September 1, 1944 just two days after it was liberated. When the Germans took Paris they took over all the buildings, hotels, etc. and when the Americans threw the Germans out, we had access to all that property. Major General Littlejohn summoned me to his office for a special mission. I am sure that out of almost 200 officers under the general's command, they had searched and found the most expendable candidate for the mission and it was I.

There was just the pilot, me and all those helmets on that rainy winter evening in France headed for the real war. We were flying real low and visibility was very limited. We were following the river and the pilot was studying the map and I asked him if he knew where he was going and he said "not really; if it gets too cloudy or dark that I can't see the river we will be in trouble." The helmets were delivered on time and that was as close as I ever got to the war except for the few times I heard the put, put bombs Hitler dropped in London the few times I was there.

The war ended in August 1945 and I arrived in America on March 21, 1946 exactly three years after our wedding date and 26 months overseas. I was awarded the Bronze Star medal for my contribution to the war effort. I tell my friends that the Quartermaster Corps is a dangerous branch of service -- We lost a man in WWII----A sack of sugar fell on him. (Joke) I also tell them when they question my war effort, "Someone had to do it."

Henry G. Motes, Jr., was born in Palatka, Florida on July 17, 1918 where he grew up. He graduated from the University of Florida in 1940 and enlisted in the Army July 1943.

After the war he was employed by E.H. Thompson, a restaurant equipment business, as a salesman. When he retired he was the sole owner. Henry and his lovely wife, Marguerite, live in Jacksonville, Florida.

WHAT A DIFFERENCE
50 YEARS MAKES

Claude L. Mullis

In 1995 I was invited to spend a few days aboard the Aircraft Carrier U.S.S. John F. Kennedy as VIP representative of the community to observe actual training flights. That invitation opened up a floodgate of memories going back to my days aboard the carriers U.S.S. Franklin, U.S.S. Wasp, U.S.S. Essex, and U.S.S. Ticonderoga.

The most beautiful sight of my life occurred over 50 years ago while I was standing on the flight deck of the Ticonderoga as she passed under the Golden Gate Bridge in San Francisco returning from Tokyo Bay after the peace treaty had been signed aboard the U.S.S. Missouri. Our decks were lined with several hundred sailors, as proud and happy as me, to be returning from the war.

I had shipped out for war in February of 1945 from Alameda Naval Air Base aboard the ill-fated U.S.S. Franklin. As we passed under the Golden Gate Bridge going out, I thought that I would never see the bridge again.

I did live to see it again, despite being involved in the greatest U.S. Naval disaster of WWII, which occurred when the U.S.S. Franklin was sunk losing 832 men and suffering 270 wounded.

Without a second thought, I accepted the invitation to go aboard the Kennedy because I had long desired to go aboard one of the newer carriers. When the day arrived, we (myself and other representatives of the community) were flown out to the ship aboard a C2 aircraft. On board to escort us were both men and women of the Navy. Yes, what a difference 50 years makes.

While flying over the water, en-route to the Kennedy, my thoughts raced back fifty years to the U.S.S. Franklin when we were bombed while 60 miles off the coast of Japan.

We were fighting fires and throwing ammunition overboard until explosions forced us to jump form the ship only seconds before the part of the carrier I was on exploded. I was in the cold water for a little over five hours before being picked up by a destroyer. Several destroyers had made a V formation to try and rescue the 800 or so men who were in the water. Some were never rescued. I remember Carl Castle men, an eighteen year old who was on the fantail when we were told to jump. I never saw him again. After the war, I mailed his family some photos of us taken in Hawaii. His father came from Nashville, Tennessee to visit me.

The flight to the Kennedy took about 45 minutes, and as we approached the carrier I got very concerned about the landing because of the dangers involved, and because we had women aboard. I had been raised with the philosophy that women should not fight in wars and that they should be protected in case of danger. Here we were about to enter the most dangerous phase of our flight. To say that I was very nervous is an understatement. However, the calm demeanor of the Navy women accompanying us on the flight put me at ease. I am sure that if we had gone down, these women would have been in the water helping to rescue me. Henceforth, women in the military will have my respect and admiration.

We landed safely aboard the Kennedy and were greeted by Chief J.D. McNally of Public Affairs and immediately treated like royalty. I was almost speechless. Here I was, the son of a Georgia sharecropper, being hosted to a VIP stay aboard the U.S.S. John F. Kennedy, all meals included. We were also greeted by a female yeoman who posed us for a group picture standing beside a plane similar to the one that had flown us to the carrier. Looking around, I noticed several other women, African-Americans, and other mixed nationalities working side by side in peace and harmony. I thought this must be the type of harmony our forefathers had envisioned for America. What a long way we've come in just 50 years.

Fifty years ago, it was the Navy that changed my life by giving me a way out of Bacon County, Georgia where illiteracy was high and opportunities scarce. One of the most ominous threats to society is ignorance and my Navy experience lifted that veil of ignorance for me. The modern Navy has made tremendous progress in the integration of races and sexes and is a kinder, gentler one than what I served in 50 years ago.

After the group picture was taken, we were escorted to the Chief's mess hall for lunch because the chiefs had the best food on the ship. This was no different from 50 years ago, except for the presence of women.

Later, with pleasantly full bellies, we went up to the bridge to observe flight training. We watched F18s, F14s, C2s and EZs take off and land on a flight deck that was somewhat longer that the decks of the CV9 class carriers. The flight deck was a busy, noisy, and seemingly chaotic place. In reality though, the flight training was a well-choreographed activity thanks to the efficiency of the young men and women working side by side, while carrying out their critical assignments.

Chief McNally then took some of us on a mini tour of the carrier, which has 17 decks and the population of a small city. We ended up in the chapel, where we were greeted by a female Chaplain. This brought back memories (which I shared with the group) of Chaplain Joseph T. O'Callahan, a Catholic Priest who was on the Franklin with me. He was described by the skipper of the Franklin as "The bravest man I ever saw." Chaplain O'Callahan was the first Chaplain to receive the Congressional Medal of Honor, which is the highest award given for heroism.

After hearing of my experiences aboard the Franklin, Chief McNally asked if I would consent to an interview, to which I agreed. The interviewer was a fine young man named Antwine who, it turned out, came from the background similar to mine. He plans on furthering his education after he leaves the Navy, just as I had done. One difference, however, is that he is African-American, and I am Caucasian. All of us, however, have red blood and I sincerely think I can now judge people by their character and the way they treat me rather than by the color of their skin. As the song goes, There's no good and bad, there's just you and me." And we must get along.

What a difference 50 years has made for me.

Claude L. Mullis was born near Alma, Georgia on November 12, 1923. He is a graduate of Stetson Law College. His practice of law was representing municipal governments throughout Florida. Claude and his lovely wife Mary reside in Jacksonville.

47 BOMBING MISSIONS:
A LOT OF LUCK
AND A BIT OF SKILL

Russell B. Newton, Jr.

I joined the U.S. Army Air Corps in March 1943. I was 18 and had completed one year and seven months at the Virginia Military Institute in Lexington, VA. This, added to my experiences in high school ROTC and as an Eagle Scout in Columbus, Ga., plus one summer at Culver Military Academy, made me an immediate success in the early stages of Air Corps Cadet training. I had a saber in hand and was shouting commands at all formations - that is, until flying instruction began, when I was reduced to the same beginner status as everyone else.

Sixty days at Maxwell Field, Montgomery, Al., covered the indoctrination and preflight work. Quarters, food, and curriculum, as I remember them, were excellent. Then to Orangeburg, S.C. for Primary, where we flew approximately 60 hours in silver Stearmans. Cy Rich, my instructor, was a civilian employee of Bevo Howard, the famous stunt pilot from Charleston, who contracted to build and operate several primary flight schools for the Air Corps. Ours at Orangeburg in June of 1943 was luxurious and efficiently beautiful: white, two-story dormitory buildings with screens extending from the ground to the second floor, double-deck bunks on both floors, good baths, fans and foot lockers. There was a white, one-story administration building and a similar mess hall, plus a library - classroom. All the buildings were set in a semi-circle around a flagpole and grass parade ground. The open end of the circle faced the dirt field and hangars where the PT 17s (Stearmans) were lined up.

Several things stick in my mind about Primary. My first ride. Unbeknownst to me, Cy Rich was notorious for making every student sick the first time up by demonstrating the entire 60-day course in about 30 minutes. He made no exception for me. Then there was Bevo Howard's once-per-month visit. He came in a plane similar to a Pitts Special and wrung it out at 10 feet off the ground for 30 or 40 minutes. Just watching him made us all try harder. He was inspirational. I'll also never forget the one person - a first-rate man - who had to leave simply because he could not get over his airsickness. Another who had to leave was the first person to damage a plane - even though it was only a slight taxiing accident. There was no forgiving careless plane damage in the Air Corps. Another memory is of my first visit to the Cadet Club in Orangeburg - an old southern mansion with tall, white columns set among magnificent magnolias. A few of the local girls came (they were told we were officer candidates and that always attracted southern girls). There were no hard drinks, which fit in just fine with the constant Air Corps lectures about mixing drinking with flying, so we drank "Co-colas" with the girls in white dresses. The girls were untouchable, of course, but I understood because I was a native and my mother had already drilled into me how to act with southern ladies. Even so, I don't remember any complaints, nor any efforts to go 200 miles to Atlanta for possible higher levels of sophistication.

Late in August 1943, we finished Primary and went up the road to Basic at Sumter, S.C. It was back to a real military base - and a good one. It had white concrete runways in several directions, a large parking ramp where numerous BT 13s (Consolidated Vultee Vibrators) were lined up in front of a row of impressive metal hangars and administration buildings. The barracks, mess hall, cadet recreational facilities, classrooms and parade grounds were all neatly placed among pine trees behind the field. The town of Sumter was like Orangeburg - hot as Hades in August, with little or no entertainment to be had. We stayed on base, flew or went to classes day and night and played sports. Perhaps to take our minds off the lack of anything else to do, we held a two-month long, 21-event decathlon. Scoring was based on cumulative points awarded for placing in each event. I never won a single event, so I was stunned when, at the final mess hall, I was named the winner. I still have that trophy.

Without the personal touches of Cy Rich, flying was a lot tougher. My instructor here was a teed-off first lieutenant who hated his job and us, too. Despite that, we learned instruments navigation, night flying (remember leveling off 10 feet up?), aerobatics and formation flying. Many more cadets washed out at this point. A few left after damaging planes, and one, I remember, was killed. Nevertheless, those who remained felt a strong sense of comradeship. Late in October or early November, we went to George Field, Ill., near Vincennes, Ind., on the Wabash River. This was my first real shock in the Army. The weather was cold. Every building was made of tarpaper and rough lumber, with cracks in the floors and walls. The only heat came from the pot-bellied stoves, which had to be fed coal constantly, so a new set of "stove maintenance duties" was introduced to us. George Field was multi-engine training, which meant that we could request what we wanted to fly. I figured that every 19 year-old in the country wanted to fly a P51 - which made my chances of getting one slim. So I requested the biggest plane in the Army, thinking at least I would get what I asked for, as well as a better shot at being in command, instead of a mere co-pilot. This is exactly was happened.

My memories of advanced (twin-engine) are hazy. Throughout the weeks until January 7, 1944, we swept a lot of snow from wings at 5 a.m., flew in a lot of bad weather, took many instrument flight checks with surly Army check pilots, did lots of cross-country. No one was killed, that I remember, but a lot more cadets washed out for inability to fly instruments. There was a little drinking and no fun on the base and one trip to Vincennes in search of it was plenty. Have you ever been to Vincennes? Fortunately, there was little leisure time, so I guess we didn't think we were missing much.   The most exciting day was when the uniform salesman came through. We were "fitted," as you were, with poorly cut but magnificent "pinks," "greens," and a crush hat with no grommet, a "beaver" short overcoat and all the paraphernalia of a new officer.

On January 7, 1944, we were graduated as 2nd Lieutenants and were given 10 days leave, the first of my Air Corps career. I caught a train for Danville, Va., where my family now lived, picked up my girlfriend at Randolph-Macon Women's College on the way, and had about six days at home without ever taking off my uniform. My father was a vice-president of manufacturing in one of the biggest textile companies in the country, employing 20,000 people. He proudly showed me off in this non-military community as if I were already a hero. I am still convinced that walking through the vast textile mill with my father introducing me to mill hands at every step, day after day, raised productivity in that company as they cranked out uniform fabrics and other war-related products.

I reported to Maxwell, Al., in mid-January. The base had been converted to B24 transitional training and though we lived alongside the pre-flight cadets, we had different administration buildings, mess halls, athletic facilities and classrooms. It only took a short time to get checked out in B24's, and then we got down to the serious study of the plane and its capabilities. After landings and takeoffs, we went to instruments.   When those tests were complete, we did formation flying, long-distance navigation, overnight trips, high-altitude (30,000 feet) flying. We were allowed to make one or two overnight, cross-country trips and the favorite destination was always Des Moines, the center of WAC training. The stories about those trips were always far better than the realities. We chased all night, but wound up in the transient BOQ at 2 or 3 in the morning, with departure scheduled for 5.

B24 training was just plain fun. No more parades, no more inspections, no more doubt about becoming an officer. Montgomery was pleasant enough for a small Alabama town just emerging from the Depression, but, as usual, between flying and classes we had little time to sample its meager offerings.

At the end of the 60-day training period, we were given 5 days to travel to the next assignment where we would take final training with a permanent crew of 10 men. My roommate, John Garrett of Baltimore (a Princeton man, class of '46, with his freshman year only partially complete), announced that his family chauffeur was being sent to drive him back to Baltimore, a good lift toward Westover Field, Mass., the next base assignment. John invited me along to Danville. A Ford convertible, complete with liveried chauffeur and enough gas coupons to make the trip, appeared on the day of departure. So two 2nd Lieutenants, wearing grease-covered, 50-mission hats, left Montgomery in great style, with the top down, wishing devoutly for more cars on the sparsely traveled highway to witness our glory. Once more, I was hailed at home like a hero, though my mother was already racked with anxiety over her eldest son. I believe that the intense worry she felt throughout this period affected her for the rest of her life. She is now 89 and in fair health, but suffers from a high level of anxiety over everything. But then, at age 19 and in high spirits about my adventures, I was hardly sensitive enough to find ways to allay her fears for my safety.

As new bomber commanders, we received a real ego massage from the first few days at Westover. Shortly after arrival, all the enlisted and officer air crewmen were ordered to assemble in a large theater. I saw my name and all the other commanders' names posted in large letters all around the room. A captain welcomed us and then asked each commander to stand up for applause from the audience. Then came the business of assigning our crews. The captain told each tail gunner, ball-turret gunner, waist gunner, navigator, bombardier, and co-pilot his commander's name, after which a mob scene ensued as all the men shuffled and shoved to get to the sign with the appropriate name on it.

This was my big moment. I assumed the best air of command a 19-year-old could possibly muster, shook hands firmly with each man, and declared that this was going to be the best crew on the base. To seal the deal, I gladly accepted my first-ever cigarette, offered me by my tough, Chicago-born, 24-year-old engineer-sergeant. As I tried to stifle my coughing, I noticed that Osborn, the 26-year-old co-pilot, was the only man not even faking a smile. Tall, red-headed and from Amarillo, Osborn had fancied himself a P51 pilot, and the humiliation of going to work as a co-pilot for a 19-year-old bomber commander was almost too much to bear. Besides him and the navigator, a sissy from Long Island, everyone else was perfect.

Our first task was a required check ride, with full crew in tow. I quickly realized that I was on stage. The entire crew was checking me out as severely as the stern check rider, a major who gave me complicated orders for various maneuvers while carefully marking his pad with my grades. After an hour, we began the return to the base and the moment of truth-the landing. I had to make a greased landing if I wanted to impress the crew, not to mention the major, with my flying abilities. I will forever remember that moment. The landing was so smooth they never knew they were on the ground. What luck! On top of that, the major gave me a straight A in a loud voice right in front of my men. This set the tone for my entire career as a bomber pilot. My crew was confident and I was in complete command.

The next order of business was to teach my co-pilot how to fly the B24, while carrying out the daily schedule of training at the same time. He was not good at it, but he was smart and understood electrical, hydraulic and mechanical systems very well, so between the two of us, we were a good balance. After the first few days, we actually began to get along pretty well, too.

We practiced bombing missions, both simulated and actual (with practice bombs), formation flying at altitude, emergency procedures, repairs, night flying and the usual ground school. One evening in May of 1944, we were ordered on a simulated mission to bomb Philadelphia. My roommate, John Garret, took off just ahead of me. I proceeded down the Connecticut River toward Long Island and finally over water toward Atlantic City. But because my radio fouled up, I didn't find out that the mission was recalled because of weather over the target area. I continued until I ran into the worst thunderstorm I have ever encountered in 40 years of flying. Over the center of Philadelphia, the storm tossed us upside down. Gear flew in every direction. We rapidly fell 5,000 feet. After an everlasting struggle, we finally managed to right the plane. The radios were gone, so I bet my hunch and headed north at right angles to the front, figuring I would come into the clear somewhere in New York State. Fortunately, there was still enough fuel left for three or four more hours of flying.

The plan worked. We broke out of the rain in about an hour. I called my navigator for sextant positions so we could find our way back to Westover, but he was useless. Not only was he sick with fear, he had forgotten his instrument. Contact navigation was our only hope, and it took us another 30 or 40 minutes to spot an identifiable town from which to get our bearings. Finally, we made a heading for Westover, some four hours overdue. Just then, after the crisis was pretty well over, the radios came back on. "Where the hell have you been?" came the response from the tower when we called in. The Colonel was relieved at our answer-there had already been one casualty in the storm. John Garret had crashed just 30 minutes out of Westover. It seems two engines went out on one side and, though he managed to bring the plane down smoothly on one of those grass fields surrounded by parked Piper Cubs, the runway was too short. The big bomber's nose dropped into a ditch at the end of the field, bent to the left, and crushed the pilot in his seat. No one else was hurt.

Although I had known others who had been killed in training, this was the first time I had lost a friend. I was the one who prepared his belongings to be shipped home. I was the one who wrote to his mother and father. I still remember how gracious they were to me through the mail, in the midst of their terrible grief. (They were much older than my parents, since John was the youngest of six boys. All the boys, and Mr. Garret as well, were Princeton men and I finally met John's father in 1946 or '47 at alumni day ceremonies.)

We finished our tour at Westover in about 60 days and instead of going straight overseas, as we had expected, we were ordered to Langley Field, Va. This was somewhat mysterious. My crew and I reported there immediately and were assigned to fly with radar navigators and bombardiers. This meant I exchanged my navigator, who was no good, for one of the most delightful and effective men I was to know in the war. His name was John Dillon, he was from Pittsburgh, about 28 years old, and prematurely gray, so of course he became known as "Pop". After about 14 weeks of radar training and whatever crew adjustments were necessary, we were ordered overseas in a new Ford B24 from Dearborn, Mich. It looked like a Ford.

We departed in September for Bangor, Maine, where we spent the night. The next morning, we received sealed orders, along with stern instructions not to open them until one hour after takeoff on a northeasterly heading out of Bangor. I had come up through the honor system at VMI, so of course, I held the orders in my pocket for the requisite hour. My crew was badgering me to open them up, but I went by the book. I must have been impossible. Finally, I tore them open and we saw we were headed for Italy, via the Azores, Marrakech, and Tunis to the replacement depot at Goia, Italy, a village in the southeastern part of the country. We spent the night at each stop, had new briefings for the next leg, and had a leisurely trip-with only one near disaster.

Our plane was new and the manuals were not quite up to date. While the engineer was transferring fuel on the leg from Gander to the Azores, he followed the procedure he was used to - and shut down all four engines. We were at 15,000 feet, halfway across the ocean. I shouted at him to put the valves back where they had been, and luckily, the engines restarted. Then came the longest 30 minutes of my life (at least up to that point) as Osborn, the co-pilot, and the engineer, frantically reread the manual, studied the valves and tried to figure out how to make the fuel transfer without sending us into the sea. Finally, we got it.

Our arrival in Goia was shock. The field was wet and muddy, and bordered by a great many parked B24s awaiting shipment to squadrons in need of replacements. After much gunning of the engines to get through the mud, we shut down, turned over the keys to what we thought was going to be "our plane," and became replacements ourselves awaiting assignment to a squadron. At that moment, our training ended. I felt full of anticipation and pride in the Air Force. I had been through the most efficiently run 18 months of my life. The training had been intensive, with no wasted motion. I doubt there was any way to bring a raw inductee to Goia ready for combat in a B24 in less than 18 months.

Squadron assignment came the next day. Trucks took us about 50 miles to the 449th Bomb Group, 716th Bomb Squadron, at Grotalia near Taranto. The field was a single dirt runway, 5,000 feet long. A bombed-out metal hangar, left by the Italians, stood at a distance from the runway. Squadron headquarters was a small Italian house. A screened shed served as a mess hall, another broken-down peasant house was the Officer's Club, and a makeshift shack built of crates, tin and sandstone blocks was the shower and latrine. There was, of course, no hot water. Living quarters were tents, pitched on bare dirt, arranged by squadron on one side of the field. Inside were four army cots and a lantern. It rained a lot, especially in the winter, and turned our tent floors to mud, miring the cots halfway up the legs. Food consisted of K or C rations, plus large quantities of powdered eggs and stewed tomatoes. We never could figure out why we always had those tomatoes, but we heard it had something to do with downed cargo ships and keeping the war effort in France well supplied while Italy got second best.

Beginning on October 29, 1944 and ending on April 8, 1945, I flew 31 sorties and was credited with 47 combat missions. (I received double credit for some missions because the 15th Air Force considered them more difficult than others.) Total combat flying time was 232=45 hours for an average of 7=48 hours per sortie. I'm not positive, but I believe our loss ratio was about two percent per mission. That means that in 31 sorties, 62 percent were lost. The fact that I made it back to base all 31 times I attribute to a lot of luck-and a bit of skill. I was the only pilot on the base to achieve such a string of successful returns. (Some planes got damaged and some ran low on fuel at the end of missions, so many pilots had to land farther north in Italy.)

My first mission-a long one, with double credit-was to Vienna. Squadron policy required new command pilots to fly at least two missions with an experienced crew as a final check ride. I flew to Vienna as co-pilot with a second lieutenant who had already flown 12 successful missions. I remember thinking that he was very stable under pressure. We were flying in exceptionally tight formation with six other B24s, climbing slowly toward 25,000 feet at 160 miles per hour (the Air Corps did not use the nautical mile for measurement). With a full load of fuel-2800 gallons-the plane weighted slightly over 64,000 pounds at take off. We carried ten 50-caliber machine guns with eight in four turrets-tail, nose, belly and top. The other two were mounted singly, on swivel, at open windows in the waist and were hand fired. About one hour out, over the Adriatic Sea, we tested all the guns and armed the bombs. The usual load was eight 500-pound bombs or four 1000-pounders. From time to time, we carried fragmentation bombs, particularly for airfields.

As we progressed up the Adriatic toward Trieste and Yugoslavia, the weather worsened and visibility dropped. We were fired upon several times after crossing the coast and after about four hours were attacked briefly by fighters.

But the low visibility made it difficult for both enemy fighters and our own to find us. The weather got so bad that about 20 minutes away from Vienna, the mission was aborted. Our retreat was orderly but nerve-wracking, since we could barely see the planes in our own tightly formed squadron, much less those in other squadrons. Even though no attack took place, we still got double credit because of the grueling ten-hour flight in tight formation through terrible weather and the brief engagements from ground fire and enemy fighters. We dumped our bombs on alternative targets on the way back. My third mission (second sortie) took place under much the same circumstances, with no attack, two days later.

On November 6, with three missions under my belt, I rejoined my crew for our first combat effort together. The target was Moosbierbaum, a heavily defended oil-refining complex near Vienna. At four a.m., we were awakened from a cold, damp sleep in our tents by a sergeant who unceremoniously blew a police whistle and shouted, "Out of the sack and into the flak!". A police whistle! I had hoped at least for a bugle calling us to glory. In an agony of shivers, we groped for our clothing in the semi-dark of candlelight. We had electrically-heated suits to wear on missions, but had to dress as if we didn't in case of electrical failure at 25,000 feet, where the temperature was minus-50 degrees. Complete with knives and pistols, the whole rig was very cumbersome. We waddled out of our soggy tents at 4:15 a.m. to a waiting truck for the ride to Group Headquarters. Red Cross beauties served us coffee and donuts before the 4:45 a.m. briefing.

The briefing was just like the movies. All the officers of the 449th Bomb Group scheduled to fly that morning, about 120 men, stood before a large stage with its curtains drawn. "Atten-hut," someone bellowed and in came the commanding Colonel. He gave us a few warm words and turned the stage over to the intelligence-briefing officer. This was the moment we found out where we were being sent. We waited anxiously, since some targets had extremely bad reputations for being heavily defended by accurate flak or fighters. When the curtains were pulled, dramatically revealing Moosbierbaum as our destination, there was an audible sucking in of breath, mingled with low curses. We had drawn one of the worst and longest assignments possible.

The mission proved to be every bit as tough as we thought. Flak was heavy, accurate and lasted a long time. It took us nearly six hours, flying in tight formation, to reach the target. The bomb run itself took about 15 minutes of very steady flying in our seven-plane box, flak exploding all around us. The open bomb door created drag, and the engine temperatures soared into the red as they labored to hold this load at the proper speed between 25,000 and 30,000 feet. I had no greater joy in life than to hear the bombardier shout, "Bombs away!". At the same time, I could see the bombs drop out of the Squadron Commander's plane just ahead of me, at which point he dove abruptly and steeply to confuse the flak gunners. We followed, heading home, nursing fuel all the way. We began to relax a little at about 10,000 feet, in the general neighborhood of the northern Adriatic. Out came cigarettes and C-rations-and it was amazing how good frozen, canned scrambled eggs and cheese could taste.

Though several of our squadron ran out of fuel and had to land further north, we made it back to base safely. As we passed over the base, the formation tightened up for the peel off and landing, a final salute to the commanding officer. Those with wounded men fired off red flares and went right in, so the waiting ambulances could attend quickly. After our landing, the crew chief found several holes in the plane-which made us feel even luckier at having completed our first mission-a 10-hour marathon-safely. We mounted a truck for the ride to the debriefing, and after detailed questioning about the mission, it was over. It was clear to all of us that getting through the ordeal of the 50 required missions was going to be very tough. We'd need good, disciplined behavior-plus a lot of luck. As the 10 of us stood there in the debriefing room, drinking coffee and contemplating the difficult road ahead of us, I promised them we would make it.

There isn't much point in trying to remember details about every mission. Sometimes we flew frequently and other times we had to sit out bad weather. On November 18th and 19th, we had no time off, flying a double and then a single, while from November 22nd to December 2 we sat out ten days worth of storms. There were enough crews in the squadron to supply good relief most of the time, and enough planes-about 10-so that we could put up a seven-plane squadron while doing maintenance on the others. From time to time this rhythm was interrupted by losses of crews and airplanes.

I clearly remember the most fearsome targets. The Brenner Pass at Bolzano (missions on November 12, December 29 and April 8) was frightening. The flak guns were mounted up in the mountains at about 8,000 feet, which put us only about 17,000 feet away. The Germans had their best weapons and gunners there because of the vital nature of the pass, with its bridges to the Italian front. The 88 mm shells would explode right in the middle of our formations and we never went without losses on these missions. On December 29, the plane just in front of me simply disintegrated in an explosion and I flew straight through the debris and smoke. Metal hit us everywhere, and just at "Bombs away!", we lost an engine. In order to mislead the Germans about our intended target, we had flown far north, turned 180 degrees and bombed Bolzano while heading south. Now, I fell out of formation and headed southwesterly in order to get over water near Portofino. We came back inland near Rome and landed at base with two dead engines, a plane full of holes-but, fortunately, no one hurt.

Another difficult target was only a short run to Ferrara, Italy. Dive-bombers and medium bombers had all failed to take out the rail bridge, so we were asked to try from high altitude. On November 22, we did, and were nearly blown out of the sky. We suffered losses in the squadron and my plane was full of holes, but again, none of my crew was hurt.

On Christmas Day 1944, our mission was to Innsbruck, Austria. This was our second of three to this target, the first having been two weeks earlier, on December 12. This was a difficult target-similar to Bolzano. Innsbruck lies at the northern entrance to the Brenner Pass and represented a major bottleneck through which all supplies to the German Army had to move. The rail yards were extensive. To keep this vital link open, the German defenses were strong, aided by natural defenses in the form of steep mountains on either side. This gave us only one avenue of attack, from the north to the south, and we were very vulnerable to 88 flak and fighters. Both were out in force on Christmas Day, and the squadron had heavy damage and some losses. Our luck was still good-holes but no injuries. We returned down the Adriatic, trailing scattered flak as we moved away from the mountains toward Venice. We relaxed and had what little Christmas dinner there was-failures in shipping had left us very poorly supplied.

That night, exhausted, with only 19 missions completed (and we received only one credit for this mission, though it lasted more than eight hours), I was sure I would never see another Christmas. I took a big drink of Scotch (some of our people had exchanged a case of beer for a case of Scotch with the British stationed on the other side of the field) and promptly went to sleep. Even on Christmas Day, drinking was never a big thing in my experience in the Air Corps. The constant lectures about the dangers of drinking and flying-especially given a pilot's responsibilities to his crew-kept us in line.

Weiner-Neustadt on March 16 was another horror story. This was a very long mission to an oil facility near Vienna, designed to put more pressure on the German fuel supply. (Throughout the winter of '44-'45, we alternated between hitting oil facilities and rail yards. Impaired transportation and fuel supply would finally shut down Germany's ability to fight; whereas the earlier campaigns in

'43-'44 against ball-bearings and munitions works and airplane factories had had only limited success.)

Our return from Wiener-Neustadt was typical-long and arduous. We were full of holes, and so was everyone else, though luckily, no one on our plane was hurt. This was my 40th mission and I was beginning to wonder how long my now-famous luck was going to hold. I had been recognized throughout the squadron as having the longest string of unbroken good fortune. While others crash-landed or were shot down or landed at other bases because of low fuel or damage, my crew and I returned to our base each time, landing smoothly despite battle damage, engine losses or flat tires. We returned three times on two engines, ten times on three engines and two times with a flat tire on the main gear. Landing a B24 with a flat tire on one side tends to turn the crew pale. The technique required holding the flat side off the ground as long as possible, holding the brake on the good side after touchdown and, as we slowed down, putting on power on the flat side along with full rudder on the opposite side. In spite of these measures, the plane would turn sharply into the flat side at the end of the rollout and we just had to pray that nothing worse would happen. It didn't with us.

On one long mission, the squadron had a new pilot flying his first mission as aircraft commander. I had met him only once. He, like the rest of us, was quite young, perhaps 19, though he looked younger. He was handsome and patrician in bearing and very likeable. As we returned from the mission, the squadron commander made his routine check with every pilot, asking especially about any wounded men and about fuel levels for the balance of the flight. The new man reported that he was low on fuel but could make it to base. The commander warned him to land elsewhere if his fuel got too low, but the new man wasn't about to drop out of formation. Fuel management was a matter of intense pilot pride; since it was poor formation flying that consumed more fuel.

After eight hours, we approached the field for our usual mission completed flyover before landing. I was flying number three on the port wing of the squadron leader and was first to peel off to the left in a steep, descending turn. If the turn was executed correctly, the big B24 would roll out of its 360-degree turn just over the end of the runway for the landing. Each plane followed closely. As one plane turned off the end of the runway, another was braking in the middle as a third was just touching down. As I turned off the runway at the end of my landing, I looked back and could see the new pilot, number four at land, at about 300 feet, in a steep turn to the landing strip. He never rolled out, though, and continued into the ground, left wing down, in a terrible cartwheel crash. There was no fire. He had run out of fuel on the final approach. The full crew of ten was lost.

The weather was bad that winter and kept us out of the air more often than we wanted. Finally, we were asked to fly single plane night missions for harassment purposes when the weather kept the squadrons down during the day. I volunteered for this duty, but before I was called on, a squadron-mate was sent up. The weather was bad all the way to Germany and back, and after nine hours, he came back, very low on fuel. It was about four in the morning and the ceiling was zero, with dense, low fog. The pilot made three passes over the field, hoping to be able to see it. Each time he was lower and lower. Finally, on the fourth pass, he came over my tent at no more than 30 feet. He was at least 200 yards east of the runway as he plowed into a tent area of another squadron. It was a disaster---at least 20 men were killed.

My last and 47th mission was on April 8, 1945, to Bolzano and the Brenner Pass again. Even though by then the Germans were quitting in Italy, the defenses at the pass remained intact. The mission was tough, but what made it worse was that I was sick. On the return, for the first time ever, I had to leave my seat and lie down on the deck, between bouts of throwing up. I managed to return to the pilot's seat for the landing. As I climbed out of the plane, the squadron doctor came by, looked me over carefully, and told me, "You have hepatitis. I've been watching you turn yellow for several days and wondering if I should stop you before today. I'm sending you to the hospital in Bari tonight."

Hepatitis, which came from drinking polluted water, was the scourge of the Mediterranean troops, just as malaria afflicted the Americans in the Pacific. The hospital had an entire ward devoted to the disease. Treatment was rest and boiled food. I was there for about three-and-a-half weeks, during which time Italy was cleared of Germans and I was transformed from the lucky senior pilot with only three more missions to go before I headed home in glory to just another replacement.

In early May 1945, fifteen pounds lighter from hepatitis, I was sent to the 456th Bomb Squadron at Cherignola, given a quick check ride and put back on active duty. Because the war was almost at an end, no more bombing missions were being flown. Instead, the Allied strategy was to move armies east across the Venetian plain as fast as possible to secure as much territory as possible before the Russians moved in. The Russians had already occupied most of the Balkans and parts of Austria, but Trieste, Istria, parts of Slovenia and all of northern Italy were not as yet claimed. The American and English troops could not move rapidly over the bombed-out roads and bridges, so the bombers became supply ships. We improvised with planks over the bomb bay doors and loaded the planes with artillery shells, munitions, rations and other necessities. We had no good way to compute the weights or prevent the shifting of these new cargoes, and the result was that we lost a few good men at the very end of the war, just because of improper loading. That almost happened to me when my first load of 105 mm artillery shells shifted aft at takeoff. It took every bit of strength of two pilots to pull the tail up and prevent a stall. We flew to an open farm field northeast of Venice to discharge. The field was surrounded with disabled planes whose nose wheels had broken in the soft ground. I made ten such deliveries over a period of six days and that was the end of my active war career. At the end of May 1945, I received orders to take a plane and go back to the U.S. I had been in combat from October 1944, to May 1945. Grueling missions to Moosbierbaum, Prijepolje, Ariano, Florisdorf, Morauska, Salzburg, Bronzda, Linz, Brod, Hall, Fuime, Brescia, Komarom, St. Paul, Zagreb, Neuburg, Cheb/Oberschon and St. Polten would begin to fade from memory. It would be years before I actually realized that I had "visited" Germany, Austria, Yugoslavia, Rumania, and Czechoslovakia in 1944-45. At the end of my tour of duty, I was promoted to Captain, awarded the air medal with eight oak leaf clusters and several campaign medals.

It was a long, slow victory journey home, through Africa, Brazil, Puerto Rico and Savannah. At Savannah, we were treated again like a replacement group. All of our cherished U.S. Air Corps property-the leather jackets, watches, pistols and other items of issue, which we had come to think of as our own-were taken back. And we were given a 30-day leave.

Back in Danville, my father paraded me all over town again, but this time as a war hero. I shook hands with every one of his employees and thanked them for working so hard in the war effort. I spoke to the local Rotary Club, the Kiwanis, and several mill employee gatherings. When the 30 days were over, I reported to Sioux Falls, S.D., a replacement depot, and after three or four weeks, was transferred to Walker Field, Kansas, a B29 training base. It was early August 1945, and before our training could begin, the bomb was dropped on Hiroshima, the war was over-and confusion set in.

Early in September, those of us with combat points were sent to Fort Meade, Md., for discharge. From there, discharge papers in hand still wearing my captain's uniform, I went to New York to meet my father, who was there on business. In his company's sales office, he introduced me to their advertising agent, Jack Cairns, Princeton, '24. It was he who persuaded me to go right to Princeton the next day to seek admission. The registrar was delighted to see me, since the campus had been cleared out by all the war programs. The fall term was only partially full, so, still in uniform, I was admitted as a sophomore to begin the new term around the beginning of October. So began my new and wonderful life as a student on the GI Bill at Princeton.

Russell Newton was born on April 18, 1924 in Montezuma, GA. Russ is an investor in Jacksonville, Florida where he and Joany reside.

SUBMARINE DUTY –
ALL WAS NOT WORK
AND NO PLAY

Leonard Robert Pavelka

USS Rasher (SS2690) - Patrol #8

Patrol from Midway to Subic Bay to Formosa, back to Subic Bay and on to the Gulf of Siam. War ended. Returned to Subic Bay. Left Subic via Pearl Harbor and through Panama Canal to Hudson River in New York City to hold open house for Navy Day. After about 10 days proceeded to New London, Connecticut, for D.E. commissioning.

While on submarine patrol we received a message to lifeguard an air strike by Mexicans flying P-47's against Takao (Steilino). Being on the surface we used a "Dumbo" (B-17) to alert us of any Jap planes. Suddenly a Jap plane dropped bombs on us. We dove (thankfully the bombs missed) and raised our periscope antenna. The message from "Dumbo" was "Are you damaged?" Thanks a lot noted our skipper in disgust.

On the surface charging batteries one night we were bombed by a Jap "Cherry" plane. The ocean was very fluorescent and we must have looked like a large ship since intelligence put out after the war said that this plane had reported sinking an American cruiser at this location and time!

Stopping a Siamese junk by firing a shot across her bow in the Gulf of Siam, the skipper sent our biggest and meanest looking ensign with a .45 pistol strapped on, over the side to board the junk and search her for anything she might be transporting for the Japs. The crew of the junk knelt and clasped their hands in a prayerful position. I guessed their prayers were answered since we ended up giving them clothes, canned hams and other items after we found no contraband. In exchange we dined on fresh red snapper exchanged for our gifts.

All was not work and no play. We had a chance to have R & R at the estate of a wealthy "beer baron" outside Manila. Being submariners we had fresh eggs, steaks, and other goodies so we had little trouble enticing army nurses from the local hospital to join us for cocktails and dinner.

En route from Subic Bay to Pearl Harbor I was given the job to navigate us home. Nearing Pearl Harbor we had the sad experience of watching an F6F "Hot Dog" for our group of subs. After several tricky maneuvers, he went into a steep dive and was unable to pull out. We were instructed to break off and search, which proved fruitless. Upon completion the skipper asked me if it was safe to cut across a certain area in order to catch up with the rest of the subs. I replied, "Yes, Sir", and then held my breath until we had transited those waters.

After mothballing Rasher, I served as aide and flag lieutenant to the Commander Submarines Atlantic Fleet stationed in New London, Connecticut. we flew to various bases in the command. On one occasion we were on our way to Panama in a DC-3 with the admiral, Operations Office Captain Tommy Dykers and others on board. Having little to do and getting bored during this long flight, I thought I would give these comrades instruction in the use of the parachute. Strapping the chute on I instructed my audience that if you have to jump, you yell "Geronimo" and pull the handle -- at which time I did and at which time the chute spread out in the plane! No court martial -- not even a reprimand.

My second boss admiral was a bachelor and had quarters in the B.O.Q. Sometimes on Sundays he would go to his office and dictate letters on the machine that, at that time, was a wax roll type. One Monday morning he buzzed me and asked me to take the wax roll containing his Sunday dictation down to the yeoman's for typing. As I left my office I was merrily swinging my arms and hit my hand holding the roll against the doorframe, cracking the roll very neatly. I asked the yeoman if he could transcribe from that damaged roll. Replying in the negative, I had to go to the admiral and tell him what happened. Admiral Fife calmly said, "Lennie, I don't spend Sunday afternoons dictating for you to break the rolls." Again, no court martial -- not even a reprimand.

Wanting to get back on the boats, I asked to be relieved. I Reported to Corsair in New London and also attended sonar school in Key West. While on overhaul with Corsair in Philadelphia I received a call from First Admiral (Wilkes) that he had orders to go to Germany and wanted me to go with him. Martha and I accompanied the Wilkes sailing first class on the Queen Mary. One of the chaplains who had served with the admiral previously was on board to see him off. Cocktails and conversation kept him occupied until he finally realized we were under way. Scrambling to the deck, he was led to a rope ladder so he could climb down to the departing tug.

Since Berlin was under blockade we had to travel in the "corridor" along with the planes airlifting mostly coal and flour to the blockade city. An Air Force C-47 with Air Force crew was assigned to the admiral.

There was a navy base at Bremerhaven but since there was no airfield there, we would fly into Bremen and motor from there. The field at Bremen was closed so our pilot (Wilbur Hall) would home in on the radio station in Bremen, break through the clouds, buzz the cows off the runway and land.

Flying into Templehof Airfield in Berlin, there was a narrow approach corridor with a graveyard on the starboard side. This made for exciting landings, especially when using GCA.

We had one captain on the staff whose greatest accomplishment seemed to consist of being able to reach into his shirt pocket, pull out his Zippo lighter, and light a cigarette all in one continuous movement!

We had just returned from North Africa and landed at Gibraltar when we witnessed a British Lancaster attempting a landing at La Linea, Spain. His outboard port engine was feathered, and as he approached for the landing, he suddenly pulled up and banked into his portside. The plane plummeted and burst into flames killing all seven crew. Having witnessed this tragedy, my wife said she was ready to make Gibraltar her home.

Many more experiences while stationed in Berlin including trips to Vienna, Stockholm, Oslo, Copenhagen, London, Paris and a motor trip from Brussels along the French coast to Marseilles. This included inspecting the heavy concrete U-boat pens the Germans had built as well as visiting the invasion points (Omha Beach, etc.). We spent one night at a small French hotel where the bartender insisted we sip many of his liquors. The admiral thought this a nice gesture and assumed this amenity was gratis. Much to his chagrin each of the "sample" drinks appeared on his bill.

One final note. We had acquired a longhaired dachshund while in Berlin. The blockade lifted just before we were to return to the states. We took the train to Bremerhaven and returned on the army ship Maurice Rose, but our dog flew back via KLM Royal Dutch Airlines!

Leonard Pavelka was born in Durhamville, New York on January 21, 1924. He graduated from the U.S. Naval Academy in June 1944. He resigned from U.S.N.R. in 1952. He was president of J.H. Churchwell Co., one of Jacksonville's oldest and most successful businesses. Lenny and Martha reside in Jacksonville, Florida.

FROM CIVILIAN
TO COMBAT
IN 12 WEEKS

Gilbert Rodman Porter, Jr.

On the morning of 7 December 1941, my father and I had gone bird hunting. When we returned around mid-afternoon, the entire block was ringed with army vehicles and soldiers. Since my cousin was in the National Guard which had been federalized, the senior officer told us of the attack on Pearl Harbor, instructed my cousin to get aboard, and they were off to Camp Blanding.

Thirty days later was my 15th birthday and on 30 January 1942, I received my Eagle Scout Badge. As an Eagle Scout I stood aircraft spotter watches.

In 1943 when a British tanker was sunk off of Apalachicola, an infirmary was set up in the National Guard Armory for the approximately 18 survivors. I volunteered to perform orderly duties. While in high school, I realized that I would probably be subject to military service. Knowing that my preference was the Navy, I became interested in naval aviation and was qualified for V5 Naval Flight Training upon graduation and enlistment.

Graduation came and my mother refused to sign my enlistment papers, since she felt 17 was too young to fly. My father tried to reason with my mother, that for the first two years I would be enrolled in Auburn University or Georgia Tech. I wouldn't start flight training until the third year. My mother held her ground that age 17 was too young to fly. My mother, however, had no objections to my going into regular naval service.

So, I enlisted and was sent to Great Lakes for six weeks of boot camp. Prior to graduation from boot camp, I requested to be sent to trade school. The CPO who interviewed me learned that I was an Eagle Scout, sent me to the sail loft, where another chief interviewed me, later handed me a pair of flags and put me through some simple sending /receiving exercises. Shortly thereafter we went through the same drill on the lamp with Morse code.

When the interview was over, the chief advised me that as an Eagle Scout I already knew more than the graduates from trade school, so my request for school was being denied. But since signalmen were needed in the fleet I was recommended for promotion upon graduation from boot camp to seaman first class signalman/striker.

Upon graduation I was given a 14-day leave, of which seven days were travel allowance with orders to Treasure Island, California for sea assignment. Two days after arrival I was given orders to report to USS Belleau Wood, CVL 24, which was in a shipyard for repairs after taking one of the first kamikaze's in the Pacific Theater at the Battle of Leyte Gulf. From the shipyard we proceeded to Alameda NAS to pick up Air Group 30, returning to the Western Pacific for duty.

The USS Randolph, on her first cruise to the Western Pacific, and several destroyers accompanied us to Pearl Harbor, where supplies, fuel and ammunition were topped off and we departed for the combat zone. Thus 12 weeks after I joined the Navy, I experienced combat, for which my mother never forgave the Navy Department.

We rejoined the 5th Fleet in clean up actions of the Philippines Campaign. From the raids on the home islands of Japan. Going North of the Arctic Circle and attacking Japan from the North. The Belleau Wood was one of seven light carriers converted from heavy cruiser hulls with no central heat or air conditioning. Thus the weather was brutal and severe when operating in waters North of the Home Islands.

In February, we participated in the invasion of Iwo Jima, providing air support. In between raids and chasing the Japanese Navy, we experienced a typhoon, which claimed all our airplanes, and a majority of our catwalks and AA guns. The most frightening moments came when we rolled/listed, first to starboard and then to port, 50-plus degrees. Ship specs indicated we could safely ride a 35 to 39 degrees list. During the starboard list, we took water down our stacks and lost two of our four boilers. For several minutes until the engineering department relit the boilers, we were at peril.

Those who stood watch on the bridge usually stood four hours on and four hours off, except when we were out of the combat zone. For those of us on watch as the full fury of the typhoon hit, we were confined to the bridge for approximately 30 hours, since it was too dangerous to leave. There was no inside passageway beyond the flight deck level. In addition to life belts, we tied lifelines around our waists chests to steel stouts on the bridge. Scary hours but outstanding seamanship by the ship's company under the leadership of Captain Wm. G. Tomlinson brought us through the typhoon with only the loss of one sailor.

After repairs and R/R at one of several exotic atolls, we it was back to raid on the Home Islands.

Then more R/R before the invasion of Okinawa which was on Easter Sunday, 1 April 1945. Intelligence reports indicated no surface naval defense of the island, so the skipper Captain Tomlinson gave permission for an Easter sunrise service on the flight deck. As an 18-year-old Christian, that will always be the most meaningful and memorable sunrise service ever.

At Okinawa, the Navy experienced the full fury of the Japanese kamikaze attacks. While many ships were attacked and either sunk or badly damaged, we came through the campaign without any damage, but lots of scares and near misses.

After R/R it was back to raids on the home islands. Later the fleet was ordered to Leyte in the Philippines for R/R and maintenance while preparing for the invasion of the home islands. While en route, the atomic bombs were dropped and we were ordered to return to Japanese waters for additional raids on selected cities.

During all this time, another issue that my mother could never understand was why I didn't come home, since the news media would report the 5th Fleet was relieved by the 3rd Fleet. My parents did learn of my whereabouts, since the late Hank Greenberg of baseball fame was a gunnery officer on the ship. A teammate of Greenberg's was a family friend. Thus when he got relieved and returned to the states he sent a message to my parents of our previous whereabouts.

Upon the Japanese surrender, the Navy ordered the USS Belleau Wood to proceed into Tokyo Bay to secure an anchorage for the USS Missouri. The scuttlebutt on board ship was that this was our reward for having the best navigator, (Cdr. Patterson), in the Pacific fleet. So on 1 September 1945, we proceeded to enter and chart the course into Tokyo Bay, securing the anchorage for the USS Missouri. On the morning of 2 September 1945, we weighed anchor and left Tokyo Bay to provide air coverage during the surrender ceremony. On the afternoon of 2 September, we returned to the anchorage and on 3 September 1945 we pulled fleet liberty in Tokyo.

Later we received orders to return to New York for participation in the Navy Day Celebration. However, before we got to the Panama Canal, we received orders to turn around and proceed to Pearl Harbor. At Pearl Harbor we leaned we were going to be converted into Magic Carpet Duty. So off went the air group and approximately one-third of ship's company. The hangar bay was converted into a huge dormitory. Three trips were made in returning troops to the USA before we returned to our home port in Alabama in January 1946. Later the ship was taken out of commission and placed in the Pacific Reserve Fleet.

Even though I had sufficient points for release from active duty, I volunteered to remain on the ship as a staff member producing "Flight Quarters," the history of the Belleau Wood. Prior to finishing the publication, the Navy offered me a promotion if I would return to sea as communications officer aboard an LST outbound for the

Asian/Pacific, however, I was ready to return home and begin my college education.

The Belleau Wood was a proud lady, earning 12 battle stars and a Presidential Unit Citation. My tenure on her earned me my Petty Officers Crow, four battle stars and the Presidential Unit Citation.

Rod Porter was born January 6, 1927 in Apalachicola, Florida. He graduated from the University of Florida. His career was in banking in Jacksonville. Rod and Demaris currently live in Jacksonville.

"OF HE AIN'T
DEAD, HE
SHOULD BE"

Moses Webb Pruitt

After 18 months of training, I received my wings on July 7, 1944 in Pensacola, Florida. One of the memorable experiences in Pensacola was crashing an SNJ on the takeoff of my first solo flight. The line mechanic had not filled the plane with fuel and when I reached 150 feet, the engine "conked out." My shoulder harness saved my life. As people gathered to see the wreck, a farmer spit tobacco and said, "If he ain't dead, he should be." I fortunately did not get pilot error, and after six weeks in the hospital, I was back in a plane to solo again.

Our squadron was commissioned at Naval Air Station, Atlantic City on December 1, 1944. We had a shore leave party the night before leaving for Groton, Connecticut, and the next day I had to fly at about 150 feet with the canopy open to "air out." The runway at Groton was partially closed down due to ice formations. After landing, my buddies assured me that I could be the designated driver of a 1939 LaSalle. I promptly hit the brakes, and the car slid into a department store window, and the mannequins fell over like bowling pins. Since I had not checked in with the skipper, he put me in hack for three days after the shore patrol delivered us back to the base.

While in Atlantic City, I had the privilege of talking to a young lady I met at the Chateau Renault Bar, and the next thing I knew we were bar hopping. The bartender had slipped me a mickey. I awakened without money and with clothes everywhere. Shortly after this, our flight surgeon was talking to this sweet thing in the same Chateau and I suggested that he leave her alone. Two thugs came up to me and assured me that I would be in concrete blocks in the ocean if I did not mind my own business.

We rode the train from Groton to Alameda, California and shipped out of Alameda on April 25, 1945 on the Crotain, a Jeep Carrier for Pearl Harbor, Guam and Saipan. We picked up the Lexington at Eniwetok. The squadron conducted daylight combat air patrols over Saipan and three air group strikes on the Japanese held island of Rota on August 6, 7 and 8, 1945. A fourth strike was initiated the morning of August 9, but was cancelled because word of the second atomic bomb striking Nagasaki reached us before takeoff. The war was over five days later. From Eniwetok the Lexington proceeded to Japan and Tokyo Bay. I had enough service points to come home on the Florence Nightingale, a crowded hospital ship. Aboard the LEX, I flew F-6-F's with VF-92.

We are now down to about 18 pilots of our original squadron of 55. We were scheduled to have our 56th reunion at Sea Island, Georgia in March 2002.

We had exciting, maturing days. Since the CO had put me in hack in Groton, as I was leaving the ship I told him that if I had any boys I would name them after him, and kick them in the "butt" every morning. Little did I know about the nice compliments he had written in my fitness report. You never can tell who your friends are.

This has been a few stories to go with a lifetime of experiences in the Navy.

Webb Pruitt was born in Jacksonville, Florida on April 7, 1924. He joined the Navy on October 27, 1944 – Navy Day.

"SIR, THIS AIN'T NO DEMOCRATIC NAVY"

Robert L. Read

Robert Rourk's admonition for a man to take a little time off as he gets older and devote the space to remembering the things that he did and that he will never do again, is sound advice. However, as he grows older, his memories of personal history need to be prompted and I thank you, Marvin, for your invitation to reflect on that wonderful part of my life that involved naval aviation.

My life has been blessed and filled with adventure and love and experiences beyond all expectations and dreams. Family, friends and abundance. God's love has enriched me beyond belief for which I give Him thanks and praise.

Growing up was a wonderful but rebellious experience as the only child of two loving but sheltering parents. High school was a mixed bag of social, academic and athletic trials, failures, and achievements. College was predictably similar. I majored in University of Virginia, SAE, campus politics and senioritis and minored in academics. I had the coke, beer, laundry and dry cleaning concessions for the house as well as the "Gold Card" football pool concession for the university. I waited tables for chow. Bridge, poker, and gin supplemented my dad's allowance and life was good!

Korea threatened us with the draft. Evelyn Perry, Duval County draft board chairman, and I became close and much correspondence was exchanged. I hovered on the brink of the draft. Perhaps I may have been a bit prevaricious in my quest for survival.

Naval aviation peeked my adventurous curiosity. Flying had always intrigued me and I was pretty good at things that required quick reflexes and thought. Having been rejected once for being vertically impaired, I went to another facility and when asked to weigh and measure myself passed the physical. The eye chart was a challenge. TECFOXLDPNH was the fifth line. That's the one they always chose. Pre-flight and primary were a blast. I loved it. I was made "spiffy checker" for Batt Three, Section Two and knew this was for me!

My mom hated it. My dad was proud but scared that I would "over do it." Everything wasn't roses. My best friend was killed along with several others at Saufley. I pulled escort duty, saw sorrow and tragedy and grew up. I still have a drink of Jamesons every St. Patrick's Day. To Sully!

The Marines were "selling" like crazy. "If you want jets, go USMC!" I was dumb but not stupid. I stayed Navy, got jet fighters and orders to VF-32 in Jacksonville! F9F8 Cougars -- Sweptwing, transonic. The latest and hottest! Had to leave one a memorable experience. Caterpillar Club, bad back, bad knees, but no regrets.

A cruise on the USS Ticonderoga CVA-14, straight deck, Essex class, WWII vintage and the most memorable experience. First night in the Med. Night ops. The Ads, Ajs - light and heavy attack - and VF-31 Banshee night fighters were up. We watched the launch and went to the wardroom to watch "Pickup on South Street" (why do I remember that?). About halfway through, we heard a "thud" above us and the ship made a max turn starboard. I left the wardroom went by my stateroom and got my flight jacket it was November. Then I walked up the catwalk onto the flight deck at the island. The ship was dark for night ops and the deck was slick from what I assumed was engine oil. I made my way toward the island when we "lighted ship."

The oil was blood. The flight deck officer had lost his legs. He was cursing and trying to stand up. Twelve of the flight deck crew were in pieces -- arms, legs, torsos severed. The crew was responding to the emergency but the scene was chaotic. I helped with the injured and did what I could. We mustered our crew to account for those who were there.

A young aviator in VF-31 landed hot, went through the Davis barriers and the net, wiped out part of the flight deck crew, all the port cat crew, hit the Banshee tensioned up on the port cat and went over the bow. The plane guard picked him up with a broken back. He spent two months in Landstul, Germany, Army hospital and was returned to duty in a nonflying status as permanent S.D.O. He was miserable. The crew was hostile. It was a sad, tragic, and a bad decision. I don't have dreams about it, but I haven't forgotten that night either.

We had a black steward's mate named Willie who had been in the squadron for years and had every venereal disease known to medical science. A junior officer came into the ready room and said, "Willie, gimme a ham and cheese sandwich."

Willie replied, "Sir, all we got is peanut butter and jelly." He said okay. G.D. it! The skipper came in and asked "Willie what kind of sandwiches you got?" Willie said, "Skipper, me got some fine ham and cheese."

The junior officer said, "Willie, G.D. it. You said all we had was peanut butter and jelly!"

Willie said, "Sir, it's time you junior officers learned this ain't no democratic Navy!"

I pulled Shore Patrol duty in Suda Bay, Crete, with a couple of senior petty officers. We were patrolling the red-light district -- off limits of course -- trailing two sailors from the Air Group. A girl from a balcony said, "Hey. Joe. Come up here and I'll give you something you never had before." The sailor turns to his buddy and says, "Hey, Chuck, haul ass, man, that girl wants to give you cancer!"

I spent the last part of my tour as an all-weather flight instructor because it always scared my mule to fly weather. "If you do the thing you fear, the death of fear is certain," I read somewhere. It worked. I haven't minded weather since.

My reserve squadron was VA-741 at NARTU Jax. A great bunch of guys! And the best aviators I ever flew with.

I could fill a computer with sea stories, but I'll stop with this. I have many friends -- frat brothers, social, business, Christian brothers -- but none so close as those with whom I risked it all!

Robert L Read was born in Atlanta, Georgia on March 4, 1930. He moved to Jacksonville, Florida when he was 15. He joined the Navy in March 1953 and was released in May 1959. In civilian life he is a very successful broker with Merrill Lynch.

THE WAR BEFORE CAPTURE – AND AFTER DETAINMENT

Oliver Valmore Robichaud

Things happen quickly and sometimes unconventionally in wartime. My situation is a case in point.

To begin with, before I ever met my future bride, I met her brother. We met in a drugstore in NC in 1941. I was in NC on maneuvers and my future brother-in-law was getting ready to enter the V-12 program at UNC. We struck up a conversation and in the true spirit of southern hospitality at its wartime best; he offered to take me to his home. That's where I met my future wife, Margie. She was just a baby then, but a precocious one who, though still in high school at the time, graduated early at the age of 15 and went to college. Margie was too young to go out with me when we first met, but we stayed in touch.

In the meantime, I was busy going through a variety of different training programs. The first was quartermaster school, then flight training, which I graduated from in 1942 in Selma, Alabama. After getting my wings, I went to multi-engine school and was finally assigned a B-17. With the assignment of a plane in 1943 I was sent to Florida in preparation for overseas deployment.

I had stayed in contact with Margie all this time, and when I was in Florida preparing for overseas deployment, I telephoned the then 17 year-old love of my life and proposed marriage. She accepted on the spot, over the telephone, and without first consulting her parents, even though she was still a minor and would need their permission. Her parents weren't too thrilled with the idea of their Southern Belle marrying a damn Yankee, but acquiesced for a number of reasons. Even though I was a Yankee, they thought I was a nice guy. Besides, Margie was away at college and all she would have to do to get married, with or without their blessing, would be to board a train and meet me in Florida.

With the blessings of Margie's parents, we were married in the base chapel in West Palm Beach in March of 1943. The marriage ceremony was followed by a small dinner at the George Washington Hotel, which was attended by the best man, Joe Mutz, an Army Nurse who was Margie's attendant, and the crew of my B-17. Within days of the wedding, Margie was back at school and I was headed for England and the war.

THE WAR BC
(BEFORE CAPTURE)

I departed from West Palm Beach with my bomber and my crew, headed for England. We stopped over in Puerto Rico for refueling and things just slid down hill from there; perhaps an omen of things to come? Someone had tried to sabotage the plane by mixing paint in with the oil.

While waiting for a replacement plane, a storm moved into the area, and by the time we took off, the weather was so bad that no sane person in peacetime would have taken off in such conditions. This wasn't peacetime and most of us, though sane, felt the invincibility of our youth. I underlined "most of us" because as we started out through the storm, our navigator had a nervous breakdown so I had to give the order to turn the plane around.

Back in Puerto Rico, I took my navigator to a flight surgeon who grounded him. I was assigned another navigator and this time was finally able to get underway for the war zone. We flew a southern route that took us by way of Africa for refueling. They wanted to detain us there because of a shortage of planes and pilots, but we finally were able to reach our destination of Horam, East Anglia, just north-northeast of London England.

I no sooner arrived at the base than they put me to work. It couldn't have been more than five minutes after my arrival that I was assigned my first combat mission, which was flown over Norway. At that time, the British weren't conducting any daylight bombing raids, only the Americans. We were constantly trying to dodge the flak that was fired at us. Add to that the fact that we had no fighter escorts, and you can see why we had a very high attrition rate for the Americans.

On July 23, 1943, after having flown just eight missions (two of which were turned around) and returning from a raid on Hanover, I caught the flak that sent me down. The plane was hit a couple of times: part of the tail was shot off and part of the right wing also. I put the plane into a nosedive to try to join a friendly group below in hopes of getting some protection and nursing the plane back to base, but I lost a couple of engines and kept falling behind the group. That's when I gave the order to bail out.

Thinking that everyone was out, I went to bail out myself and that's when I saw my bombardier, Bob Katz. He was just standing with his chute all unfurled and around him on the floor. I stayed with him until he got his chute gathered up and in his arms. He had a seat parachute and I had a chest one. We put our arms around each other and bailed out together. When we reached a certain level, I let go of him and his chute opened so he could land safely.

THE WAR AD
(AFTER DETAINMENT)

I landed in a cow pasture not far from the Holland border. I hit the back of my head when I landed and was out of it for a short time, but upon awakening, I spotted a barn and headed for it. Halfway there, some German farmers came after me with pitchforks and hit me all over the place. The women came soon after though, and helped me out by making the men back off and ease up on me. The women sort of surrounded me to protect me until the Wermacht came and picked me up on a motorcycle.

The German soldiers took me to the Burgermeister's office where some of my other crewmembers had already been taken. Graham Smith had been strafed when he bailed out and he died, but Charlie Cothran was there (wounded), Joe Mutz was there (wounded), Clarence Borchart was there (wounded), and George Kosturko was also there. I was wounded a little bit but never even mentioned it.

They tried to threaten one of my crewmembers. They knew that Bob Katz was Jewish and they said to me, "You know what we do to the Jews, don't you?" I got hit over the head with a rifle butt while trying to protect Bob.

After about eight days at the Burgermeister's office, the officers were separated from the enlisted members of the crew. The three of us who were officers were put on a train and sent to Stalag Luft 3 which was located in Sagan, Poland, about 20 kilometers from Auschwitz. Two of them were badly wounded and sent to a hospital, then repatriated. And then there was one.

At that time, since I was the only American there and they didn't have an American compound, I was placed in with the British. We did a variety of things to pass the time and maintain our sanity, but a prime concern was escape. To this end, one very important job was tunnel work. I was too claustrophobic to go down into the tunnel to dig, but I helped carry the dirt out into the outside compound. We carried it in the cuffs of our pants. Two or three guys would walk out together and sort of shuffle along while the one with the dirt in his cuffs pulled a string to release the dirt from the pants cuffs. It was tedious, but time was not a scarce commodity either.

After they built an American compound, I was transferred into it, where we had our own escape organization. We had three tunnels going at once: Tom, Dick, and Harry. Even though time was our most abundant commodity, we tried not to waste it. Our officer compound was rich in intellectual resources, from lawyers to a variety of educators, which were utilized to help us pass the time. In addition to having an array of classes, we also had our own governing body with a sort of pseudo legislature where I was the senator from Maine. Unfortunately, however, our legislators were powerless in trying to get us food stamps or government surplus rations.

The food, which came only twice a day, was primarily a watery soup containing bits of vegetables and potatoes. To go with the soup, we were given a bit of black bread that we referred to as sawdust bread. The Red Cross provided parcels that were supposed to be given to the prisoners once a month, but we were at the mercy of the camp commander. In our case, he decided not to hand them out. In January when we were forced out of Stalag Luft 3, we left behind a warehouse full of undelivered parcels; parcels from the Red Cross and parcels from the families at home.

I was shot down in July 1943, and not long afterward my wife found out about it in a very circuitous way. There was a ham radio operator in Presque Isle, Maine who monitored a frequency used by the Germans. The Germans would read off the names of prisoners who had been captured. This ham radio operator recognized the name from the list and tried to contact my mother, but she was out of town. However, somebody else in town knew where my wife was and contacted her. So she got the news about three weeks after I was captured. The Army never gave her the news that I had been captured. She got a telegram from the Army telling her that I was "missing in action and presumed dead," and that was it.

I was allowed to write my wife, and as soon as she got my address, she started sending food and toiletries every time she was allowed to, which was once every two months. These parcels couldn't weigh more than five pounds so she tried to put in a large quantity of dehydrated items and vitamins to maximize what she sent. She also tried to send me some clothing items, shoes, and overshoes, but these all came back unopened after the war. All I received was an occasional food package.

While in Stalag Luft 3, we used what ingenuity we had to survive mentally. Physically, things weren't too rough on us, except for the meager rations. We weren't used for labor the way some other prisoners were, so we had time to fill. We had our own housekeeping duties, and with the rest of the time we fashioned wings (replicas of our pilot's wings) for our self-esteem, we made eating utensils (dishes, cutlery, cooking pots) out of old tin cans, and we even made compasses for those who would try to escape. Bob Katz, whose printing looked like type, worked on forging papers for the ones who would try to escape.

Just when we had settled into a daily routine, they moved us. It was 1945, the Russians were advancing, and the Nazis didn't want to have 10,000 POWs released into the countryside to interfere with their war efforts, so, in the coldest weather I had ever experienced, we were marched towards another camp. The scene was one straight out of a twisted movie. It was sub-zero weather, and so miserably cold that one of the old horses died. The guard that was on him had to walk. The guard was so old and feeble that I even carried his gun for him. Escape would have been lunacy for we had no provisions and nowhere to go. We plodded along in the snow and cold for several days until we came to a barn where we were allowed to sleep. Then we plodded on again the next day and the next day and the next day -- so many that I don't remember how many.

We finally reached a railhead where we were loaded into boxcars. That was like trading one evil for another. We went from miserable to more miserable. The boxcars, which had previously been used to transport animals, had manure on the floor. This manure was covered with straw and we were packed in so tight that you couldn't lie down, you had to stand or sit on your ass. We were in there for about three days of misery. Once in a while we would receive a ration of sawdust bread to eat and that was it. We were given just one real potty break and the rest of the time, to relieve ourselves, we would just find a hole in the siding and urinate through it.

When we arrived in Mosseburg, at Stalag 7A, we all had to go through the delousing station and take a disinfectant shower. Other troops were also being brought in from different places to the north, in advance of the Russians, so we had a very busy, crowded camp.

We knew that the end of the war was near though. The Germans knew that the end of the war was near also. They were even starting to throw away their rifles because they knew it was essentially all over for them. The day before our liberation, I sat atop a building in Stalag 7A and watched the allies firing into our camp. They were just firing high, at the building tops, so I had to give up my perch for safety reasons.

The next day, I was lying in my cot, the latrine was overflowing, and Patton walked in. He could not believe that there were American officers being kept in those conditions. He told his aide that he wanted us out of there in 24 hours, and assured us that we would be out as soon as possible.

Twenty-four hours passed and there was no one around to help any of us, so I cut the fence wire and escaped from the Americans. When I went through the fence, I joined a tank outfit for a few days until they got me across the Rhine and connected with someone who was going into Paris by truck. In France, I tried to commandeer an airplane because I wanted to fly back to Horam and my 95th bomber group. They accused me of trying to steal the plane and were going to arrest me, but instead sent me to SHAEF Headquarters where, once I identified myself, they gave me some money and sent me down to Camp Lucky Strike in Le Havre. I was there on V-E Day. It was from Le Harve that I was finally able to cable Margie and let her know of my status. When she got the cable, she couldn't believe that I was finally free, and she fainted dead away.

THE TRIP HOME
AND POST WAR

At Le Havre I was put on a very crowded ship headed for Boston and given a blanket and whatever deck space I could find. I was finally heading home. As soon as I arrived in Boston I telephoned Margie, who was down in Charlotte, NC, to tell her that I would be taking the train to Charlotte and arriving at 8:30 the next morning. We didn't do much talking during the phone call, but mostly just cried and laughed.

When I got to Charlotte, I must have looked like just what I was, a newly released POW, because of the way Margie described her first sight of me. "I met the train at 8:30...and my God, what a sight. Somebody had given him some paratrooper boots and he had on Khakis. Even though it was the first party of June, it was cool, so he had an Australian bush jacket and German Afrika Korps cap. He weighed all of 95 pounds. He looked like a stick figure with these clothes on. But he was beautiful. I still feel it after all these years." Yes, it has been a lot of years. As of writing, we've been married over 58 years.

I guess everything after that was sort of anticlimactic. I was given six weeks R&R plus a week of counseling in Atlantic City then my choice of duty stations. I chose Craig for my first post-war duty.

After Craig, I had duty in a variety of stateside places such as Florida, Alabama. I dodged the Korean bullet, so to speak, because during that conflict, I was stationed at the Pentagon. I had what was called a critical AFSC, so they kept me at the Pentagon for five years.

From the Pentagon, I was transferred to Okinawa and put back in the saddle again. I flew B-29s, FA-16 pontoon boats and SA-16s. While assigned to the 581st Reconnaissance Group, I flew SA-16s into China to transport people out. After that I was assigned to an administrative position with the 51st Fighter Interceptor Wing.

When my tour of duty in Okinawa was completed, I returned to the states for my last duty station, which was the Air University at Maxwell Air Force Base. I retired from there in 1962 as a colonel.

Robi retired from the army air force in 1962 as a colonel. He joined the Massachusetts Mutual in agency management. He again retired and lives in Atlantic Beach, Florida, with Margie, the love of his life.

LIFE IN THE PACIFIC
ABOARD AN L.S.T

Bryant Brightman Skinner, Sr.

On December 7, 1941, I was a freshman at Davidson College. From that day on, as for everyone else in America, my life became more complicated.

In the spring of 1942, I volunteered for the Navy V-12 program and that summer was sent to the University of North Carolina at Chapel Hill to wait for acceptance at Midshipman School. While at Carolina we wore sailor suits and received considerable basic training. Naval officers who never wore a sailor suit missed a lot. We did while at Carolina, and never before in my life have I ever had more fun. Everybody loves a sailor! Whether in the gutter or on the sidewalk, friends were nearby.

In the winter of 1943, I left Chapel Hill and went to Camp McDonnough in Plattsburgh, New York. Plattsburgh was only a few miles from the Canadian border. The base fronted Lake Champlain. The night I arrived in Plattsburgh, the temperature was 20 below zero. To say the least, it was a little shocking to a Florida cracker.

I received my commission in June 1943 and, after knocking around awhile in Norfolk, was assigned to the Amphibious Forces and ordered to Fort Pierce, Florida, for small boat training. Our training there was to prepare us for future invasions of Pacific islands. We spent almost every night on the ocean in small boats, shuttling troops from transports to a mock invasion of the beach. Vero Beach, just six miles to the north, has a naval air base, and the men up there furnished air coverage for our mock invasions. They were pretty realistic.

After several months at Fort Pierce, I was assigned to L.S.T. 1009 (Landing Ship Tank) which had just been commissioned and was located in Norfolk. When reporting aboard, I was the youngest and lowest ranking officer, an ensign 20 years old. The complement of an L.S.T. was 10 officers and 110 enlisted men. Every sixth ship was assigned a doctor and a paymaster. We were fortunate to be the one, and I was lucky to room with the doctor who had just graduated from medical school as an obstetrician. He was a super nice guy, and we became close friends. The only time he had the chance to use his specialty was when our ship's cat was pregnant. Poor old doc was the laughing stock of the crew when all the kittens died within a few days after birth.

Because of my age and low rank, I was assigned all the duties no other officer wanted, the principal one being commissary officer. Our little ship had only three chief petty officers, but I was fortunate to have one assigned to me. Looking back, I'm proud I had sense enough to turn my division over to him and leave myself considerable time for acey-deucy and bridge in the wardroom.

Of the 12 officers, the captain, executive officer, doctor, paymaster, navigation officer and engineering officer, were not considered duty officers. That left six of us to run the ship on four-hour shifts as deck officers. I was a pretty conscientious young kid and took very seriously my four hours in the middle of the night on the bridge with everyone else below sound asleep.

After a month or so of getting our new ship outfitted, we departed Norfolk for New York, where our tank deck was loaded with submarine nets to guard the entrance to some port in the Pacific.

The cruising speed of an L.S.T. was only 11 knots. At that speed, it took us 10 days to sail from New York to the Canal Zone. A hundred or more ships were waiting for passage through the canal. We expected to get in line and enjoy at least a week of good liberty in Colon. We actually only got to stay one night. The next day, because we were to deliver submarine nets, they rushed us on through the canal.

About 20 days later, we arrived in Pearl Harbor. The charred hulks and battle-damaged landscape shocked us all. When leaving Pearl, we joined a small convoy and went to the Marshall Islands to deliver our submarine nets at Eniwetok. Those islands had taken a terrible pounding in our recapture of them from the Japanese. We were then loaded with damaged airplane engines, bulldozers, and other heavy equipment to deliver to the repair facilities in Pearl Harbor.

We then moved farther west, nearer the scene of action. Most of our time was spent picking up soldiers of the First Army and marines of the Fifth Division who had been involved in recapturing various islands from the Japanese. Even though they were tired and beaten up, we always enjoyed having them aboard for a week or so while we delivered them to some rest and recreation facility.

We were not in the middle of the invasion of Eniwetok, but close enough to feel the threat of the kamikazes who played such a big part in the battle. We found comfort in the thought that no self-respecting kamikaze would waste his life on a little L.S.T.

Just before the atom bombs were dropped, a devastating typhoon bore down on Eniwetok. We were caught at sea in the very middle of it. This was by far, for me, the most frightening experience of the war. All night long ships were going down around us, and I'll never know how we survived.

We were very nearby when the bomb was dropped on Nagasaki and the war ended.

Loaded with five million board feet of lumber and several hundred Seabees, we were one of the first ships to make a landing on Kyushu. The Seabees, with unbelievable skill, erected barracks in just a few days so the Marines could send in occupational troops. I was lucky to get assigned to the Marines and participate for a month or so in the occupational activities. This was the most fascinating part of my war experience. To move into little towns and take over from people who had never seen an American was an incredible experience. They had been told so many bad things about Americans, they could not believe when we treated them kindly. I wish so much I could have brought home just a tenth of the wonderful gifts I received.

I truly loved the Navy and the time I spent as a naval officer. Even though my naval career lacked the excitement of many who felt the intense heat of combat, I'm glad I was given the chance to do my little bit. If I prossess any admirable characteristics, I give the Navy a lot of credit for making a young man a little smarter and preparing him for the toughness of the world that lay ahead.

Bryant is a very successful real estate developer and investor. He and Betty reside in Jacksonville and Crescent City, Florida.

COMBAT FLYING
FROM A CARRIER IN THE
WESTERN PACIFIC

William Howe Skinner

WWII Military Experience 1941-1945

Date of Birth: April 4, 1919
Hometown: Jacksonville, Florida
Branch of Service: United States Naval Reserve
Unit or Squadron: VC 93 "composite squadron"
Dates of Service: July 1941 to September 1945

I enlisted in the United States Naval Reserve in June 1941, having been appointed a cadet for flight training. I had previously received my private pilot's license upon completing the government's Civilian Pilots' Training in Murfreesboro, Tennessee on February 15, 1941, while attending the University of the South at Sewanee, Tennessee.

My first orders were to report to the Miami NAS "E" Base in August 1941. "E" stood for elimination. At this base, after indoctrination flights and preliminary training, we either soloed or washed out. From there I went to NAS Jacksonville to begin my ground school training. During ground school we were designated Seaman 2nd class and studied everything from mechanics to meteorology. We also pushed planes around, cleaned windshields, cleaned heads (bathrooms) and did close order drill.

Flight training finally started on November 17, 1941, and I soloed on November 21. We were now full-fledged cadets. The Japanese attacked Pearl Harbor on December 7, 1941, and we were at war, and things intensified. We never wore civilian clothes again until after peace was declared in September 1945.

The Stearman bi-plane, the famous "Yellow Peril," became our classroom. We used a group of outlying fields from Jacksonville: Herlong, Fleming Island, Switzerland and Whitehouse. Thirty or 40 Stearman planes would take off in a cluster from Jacksonville and scatter to the various fields. After the Stearman we progressed though SNJs, OS2Us, and N2N seaplanes, and OS2U on floats.

I received my wings and commission as an ensign in the USNR on April 17, 1942, and was qualified as a VOVCS pilot, flying OS2U seaplanes, trained to search and spot battleships and cruisers. Each ship carried two planes and four pilots. We were to scout for enemy shipping and to give the coordinates for the targets that were over the horizon, and do anti-submarine work plus dive-bombing.

However, my orders were different. I was sent to Instructors' School, and then to Squadron 12, NAS Jacksonville. This was an intermediate squadron to take students from the Stearman into more advanced types with variable speed propellers, retractable landing gear, mixture control, flaps, and so on. It also included formation flying.

The most important thing that happened to me during my duty with Squadron 12, and for my entire life, was that I met a girl named Betty Bacon, who lived in Venetia, close to NAS Jax. I knew then, and it's been confirmed many times since, that the good Lord was guiding me.

At NAS Jacksonville, about November 1, 1942, I received orders to report to NAS Green Cove Springs, Florida. Here we taught basic aerobatics. I also had duties in the engineering department, and assisted in returning crashed planes back to the field. We learned that all the 100-octane gasoline had to be drained and dumped before a plane could be moved. Some of this was dumped into five-gallon cans, which I found was a wonderful tonic for my 1941 Ford.

On March 10, 1943 I was ordered to NAS Vero Beach to instruct in operational dive-bombing for students headed to the fleet. We flew Brewster-made SB2As. It was a large dive-bomber designed to replace the Douglas SBDs. The plane had many flaws in aerodynamics as well as mechanical flaws. We averaged losing one student out of every 10 in accidents. The plane was eventually abandoned in favor of the Curtis SB2C.

During this duty I made as many trips as possible to Jacksonville from Vero to date Betty Bacon. On one trip she agreed to marry me. On another I received so many mosquito bites returning to the base in the early morning from the train station, that I came down with malaria. When I thought I had recovered, I blacked out on a dive-bombing flight, so I applied and got 10 days sick leave, during which time Betty and I were married. We honeymooned in Gatlinburg, Tennessee, driving up on some of that 100-octane gasoline. That gasoline really flattened out the mountains!

I received orders at Vero to the fleet and went through field carrier landings, and then qualified in carrier landings on the USS Wolverine on Lake Michigan at Chicago on December 9, 1943. From there I was ordered to San Diego for assignment; so we drove to Jacksonville for Christmas before heading for San Diego, where I received orders to report to NAS Sand Point at Seattle, Washington. It was a roundabout way to get from Chicago to Seattle, but we covered the country in my '41 Ford. Incidentally, it was the last Ford model made by the Ford Motor Company until after the war.

On February 23, 1944 in Seattle, Composite Squadron VC 93 was formed and commissioned under the command of Lt. Cmdr. Chester P. Smith. It consisted of about 200 personnel (officers, crewmen and maintenance men). My assignment was as a torpedo pilot; the plane was a TBF and later a TBM, a Grumman-design made by Martin. The TBM was a torpedo plane capable of carrying a 2,000-pound torpedo, or four 500-pound bombs in a bomb bay plus two 50-caliber fixed guns forward, one 50-caliber turret, and a 30-caliber below.

The squadron was a new concept of putting fighters and bombers in the same squadron to fit the new jeep carriers. These carriers, with a designation of CVE, were actually a Kaiser liberty ship hull with a flight deck added, which caused it to always list to starboard after taking on a full load of fuel. We soon moved to the Naval Auxiliary Air Station in North Bend, Oregon for tactical training. We practiced gunnery, bombing, and torpedo dropping, along with group tactics.

When we were notified that the squadron would be moved to NAS Holtville, California for night flying, sometime in the near future, we decided that Betty, who was six months pregnant, should return to Jacksonville for delivery because of the uncertain timetable. So in the latter part of April she took the train from Portland, Oregon to Chicago, a three-day trip. She then flew from Chicago to Jacksonville, an all day trip with seven stops on the way.

After completing our training in North Bend, and Betty having delivered the baby, she met me in Yuma, Arizona, and presented me with a brand new six weeks old baby boy, William Howe Skinner, Jr. I found her staying with a friend who was living in an empty grocery store, set up as living quarters! We proceeded on to NAS Holtville where I reported for duty on August 24, 1944 -- the hottest place on earth except for one place in the Sahara Desert. We lived on the Mexican border in Calexico, California in a two-room motor court, with a desert cooler in one room to try to keep us cool. Betty had to wash diapers by hand on a scrub board, and hang them on a line to dry. As soon as she had finished hanging the last diaper, the first was dry, and she could take them all down and fold them. Primitive, but efficient.

After completing the night flying, we were then transferred to Los Alamitos, California on October 1. We found a little house in Bellflower, California, that we rented from a lady named "Cookie." She retained the use of one room. Gasoline was rationed, and we were always short gasoline coupons, but Cookie helped us by giving us some of her "C" coupons. We had been to the ration board for a few extra coupons, but they reminded me that a war was on, and refused. Cookie worked as a welder at the shipyard in Long

Beach, and her work was considered more important to the ration board than mine, so she had extra coupons and was very generous, and even gave us enough coupons to get Betty back to Jacksonville after I shipped out. The squadron training consisted of simulated strikes, amphibious support, field carrier landings, formation tactics and inter-type exercises. The senior TBM pilot failed to qualify, and in November I replaced him and became the senior bomber pilot and operations officer.

Finally, on December 1, 1944, we boarded the USS Shamrock Bay (CVE 84) for transport to the western Pacific. Our first stop was Oahu, Hawaii, where we were transported to Kaneohe on the north side of Oahu. We flew some night intercepts on friendly ships, some of them 150 miles away, which I, of course, had to lead to find the ship. My radar operator, Whitey Knowles, was essential. We would then drop flares and make dummy runs.

All during my time with VC 93 I flew with the best crew on board -- Donald Clancy, as turret gunner, and Alfred Knowles, as radioman-radar operator and belly gunner. These men were indispensable to our operation. Clancy was not only a good gunner but served as eyes in the back of my head, as well as my plane captain, keeping the plane in tip-top shape. He was also the squadron clerk and kept all the pilots' logbooks up to date. To reach a target the pilot used dead reckoning to navigate, but Whitey, as Knowles was called, could zero in on the target with radar, and was always our keenest eyes during antisubmarine patrols. I will always admire their courage in climbing in the back of a TBM, totally dependent on the pilot for their very lives, trusting they would return in one piece.

While at Kaneohe, we had a genuine Hawaiian luau, complete with the food cooked underground and with real Hawaiian hula-hula dancers. This was for the enjoyment of the entire squadron, officers and men. On December 26, 1944 we departed Pearl Harbor aboard the USS Long Island (CVE 1), and proceeded west on a zigzag course. We proceeded west across the international date line and a few days later crossed the equator. King Neptune came aboard and we were all initiated as Pollywogs by the Neptune Court. The proceedings got rougher and rougher until the captain finally had to call the ship to general quarters to calm things down. This was an experience not to be forgotten.

General Douglas McArthur had returned during the battle of Leyte Gulf, and the navy was engaged in the battle for the Philippines. We were to board another jeep carrier for the cleanup operation. The carrier, however, was damaged and had to return to the states for repair, so we were unloaded on Manus, then ferried over to Pityilu, a small island nearby. This was in the Admiralty Island group, just north of New Guinea. We flew a little, did survival training, but mostly the hours dragged on. We sought relief by building sailboats out of disposable gas tanks and whatever else we could find. We formed a kind of yacht club and had regattas in the lagoon. Bud Foster found an old rowboat and he, Doc Star and I patched it up, made a leeboard, rigged a sail and rudder and set sail. The tide had more effect on it than the wind. We didn't win any races!

On February 11, the squadron boarded the USS Barnes (CVE 20) for the Ulithi, in the western Carolines, to meet the USS Petrof Bay (CVE 80) for invasion of Iwo Jima. We arrived at Ulithi one day late, and to our dismay, missed the ship and the campaign. Thus we were settled in at a rest camp on Guam, recently taken back from the Japs. The wounded from Iwo Jima were being flown to the hospital on Guam. The doctors were swamped with the influx, so our doctor, Leon Star, jumped in to help the overburndened doctors and worked 18 hours a day until the campaign was over.

When Iwo was secure, the Petrof Bay retuned to Guam and we relieved the squadron on board, VC 76, much to their relief. We immediately set sail for Ulithi. This was when the fleet formed for the attack on Okinawa. Ulithi was a huge harbor surrounded only by a coral reef and a few small islands. One island was Mog Mog, and it was made into one huge bar, divided in the middle by a chain link fence. On one side was a bar for the officers, on the other a huge supply of ice cold beer for enlisted personnel. This is where I saw the largest pile of beer cans in the world! In the harbor there were innumerable ships from horizon to horizon. The ship's doctor made this comment about Ulithi: "If I had to give an enema to the earth, this is where I would do it."

On March 21, 1945 the fleet pulled anchor and headed north. One day out, with no warning, the ship hit a rogue wave that crashed over the bow, washed one seaman overboard, and injured several others who were working there. The destroyer following the Petrof Bay recovered the seaman's body and returned it to the Petrof Bay the next day. The ship's captain then performed a burial at sea. This only added seriousness to our nervousness about the upcoming invasion.

We hit and secured Karama Retto first. We bombed Karama Retto on March 24, Palm Sunday, to secure its harbor for our use in the attack on Okinawa. On April 1, 1945, Easter Sunday morning at daylight, our squadron, VC 93 from the Petrof Bay, along with a sky full of planes from other ships and an unending line of battleships and cruisers, which were pounding the coast, made glide bombing runs over the ships toward the shore. On one run, I even saw one of the shells from a battleship pass me as I was in my run. In addition there were an uncountable number of landing crafts filling the water between ships and shore like water bugs on a water trough, all headed to shore filled with marines and army units. The landings on the beach were uneventful and largely unopposed. The Japanese had set up defenses inland to form a trap for the invaders, which U.S. forces ran into when they moved inland.

While our fighters flew cover for this operation and also formed a picket line north of Okinawa to intercept kamikaze planes, we, in the bombers, supported the marine troops advancing in the northern part of Okinawa. I want to add that the sky over the entire island was so thick with airplanes that we had to abide by traffic rules somewhat as around a busy airport. After a couple of weeks, with the north secure, we turned our attention south to support the army, which had run into the main Japanese forces that were well dug in. We used both 100-pound and 500-pound bombs, and at times were dropping them within 100 yards of our troops. The Japanese had honeycombed the hills with caves and tunnels, and on strikes to hit these, we were armed with rockets.

This continued throughout April and May. We were occasionally diverted to make strikes on Japanese airfields such as Miyako or Ishigaki, which were located close enough to reach Okinawa or our ships. While at Okinawa, the Petrof Bay worked with five other jeep carriers, sometimes six, and moved as one. All jeeps would turn into the wind to launch simultaneously, each launching around 20 planes. This could put 120 planes in the air in 15 or 20 minutes. On these strikes, such as Ishigaki, all planes would form up into one strike force. For some reason, I often wound up leading this group to the target, which might be 100 or 150 miles distant. It was always a contest between ships as to who could get their planes in the air first, or get them back on the deck the fastest. One plane having trouble landing could keep the whole group in the wind and make all the captains very nervous about submarines.

It happened that I landed at Lantan Field on Okinawa on April 5, right after the field was made secure. This was to pick up a marine, Lt. Sassy, for an observation flight over the northern end of Okinawa. There were no signs of the enemy on that flight. The only problem in landing was dodging the bomb craters in the runway. My crewman, Donald Clancy, states from his journal that we were the first to land on Okinawa after the landings on the beach.

Other than flying through flack so thick the sky was black, I suppose the most nervous (scared) I became was on a flight back from Ishigaki, where I had been unable to release a 500-pound bomb. It was stuck on the rack in the bomb bay. After trying every trick I knew to shake it out of the bomb bay, I elected to land on the carrier with it rather than bail out. The ship's air officer and captain approved and cleared the flight deck as well as two decks down of all personnel except for the landing signal officer who would bring me in. A few days earlier a planed landed on a sister ship with a bomb and blew a huge hole in the deck. As it turned out my landing was uneventful, although I felt I hit the deck harder than usual, and it took a strong shot of brandy and a gallon of water to get the cotton out of my mouth.

My total duty overseas consisted of 78 carrier landings and 58 combat missions, for which I received a Distinguished Flying Cross and an Air Medal with four gold stars. The squadron and the ship received a Presidential Unit Citation. According to Navy release number C-1010898, "airmen of composite squadron 93 shot down 17 Jap planes, smashed 52 on the ground, and knocked out 86 enemy boats, 136 trucks and innumerable gun positions, mines, buildings and ammunition dumps." "The Petrof Bay (CVE 80) was launched January 5, 1944, commissioned February 18, 1944, and was decommissioned July 31, 1946. She was a Kaiser Class, which included CVE 55 through 104. A total of 123 escort carriers were commissioned from July 2, 1941, (Long Island CVE 1) to July 30, 1946 (Tinian CVE 123). Five Kaisers and one other were sunk."

A quote from "In Harms Way" by Doug Stanton: "Okinawa was Japan's Alamo, the only island standing between American forces and the final assault on Tokyo. Called Operation Iceberg, the U.S. attack on Okinawa was equal in scope to the invasion of Normandy, one year earlier. *The New York Times* would call the siege the final naval battle of World War II, the `most intense and famous in military history.' In total the Japanese launched nearly 2,000 kamikaze planes at a fleet of 1,500 American ships, the most powerful armada ever assembled." Also, from the book, "Generally speaking, however, the navy suffered its worst losses of the war at Okinawa, with 9,700 casualties, 4,907 of which were fatal."

On the May 30, 1945, upon completion of our work in the Okinawa campaign and with the island 99 percent secure, we were transferred to the USS Steamer Bay, CVE 87. On June 10 we proceeded north to do antisubmarine work, and fighter cover for the supply fleet supporting the armada involved in bombarding Japan in preparation for that invasion. At one point we were within 250 miles of Honshu, Japan, the closest any CVE had been to Japan. We left the Steamer Bay on July 18, 1945.

On August 3rd the squadron was ordered to return to San Diego for decommissioning, reclassification and leave. We left Pearl Harbor on August 4 for San Diego with plans to reform for the invasion of Japan. On August 6, 1945 the first atomic bomb was dropped on Hiroshima when we were half way to San Diego. The second bomb was dropped on Nagasaki three days later, on August 9. We arrived in San Diego on August 11, and I called Betty at 2 a.m., to let her know I was back in the states. On August 13, I returned to Jacksonville on leave, and the Japanese surrendered on August 14, 1945. So we left Pearl Harbor thinking we would soon be returning to the war, and by the time we got to San Diego everything had changed. What an historic time for us all! In 10 days our lives changed completely.

While in Jacksonville on leave, I found I had enough points to leave the service and did so in October 1945. My two brothers, Ben, Jr. and Cody, returned from service a few months later. Ben was a battery commander during the Normandy invasion of France and the Battle of the Bulge. Cody returned from occupational duty in the Philippines, after being commanding officer of the Training Command in Arkansas during much of the war. I started milking cows for a living before their return, and from a meager start of 18 cows, saved for us by our father, the three of us built Skinners' Dairy. We produced, processed, and distributed milk and it became a thriving business of 1,800 cows, 20 milk stores, a fleet of 40 trucks, and a milk plant capable of processing 30,000 gallons of milk and ice cream a day.

Now it's a pleasure to sit back and enjoy our children and their accomplishments. Bill is CFO of a group of real estate development companies. Lella is a whiz at computers and now has a business with a friend helping women in a stressful world. Dorothy is very involved with her husband's state of the art dairy business, Mecklenburg Farm, and has become quite a businessperson herself. Sarah is a veterinarian, with her own successful mobile veterinarian service.

Fifty-six years after the war, looking back, I have to say it was an honor to serve my country when it needed me. Tom Brokaw says we were the "greatest generation." There have been many generations that have safeguarded our freedom, beginning with our founding fathers. I feel my generation, facing what we faced, would turn to and live up to whatever the challenge. War is hell, but I was fortunate to serve in naval aviation, which was always a challenge and even a lot of fun, and I was able to come home alive to tell about my experiences.

"HIT THE BEACH
EASY. I JUST PUT
A CAKE IN THE OVEN"

Robert E. Sonntag, USNR

An LCT is a U.S. Navy landing craft 110-feet long with a 35-foot beam, shaped like a shoebox with one end that opens up as if it were hinged at the bottom. When the bow door opens, a load of four or five trucks can drive from the tank deck of the little ship onto the beach. LCT skippers were ensigns. That was me. There were 13 enlisted men. Those were the guys that made things work.

By July, 1944, our routines on LCT 643 at Omaha Beach had settled into a daily shuttle of troops and equipment from the liberty ships, anchored a half mile off the beach, to the beach itself. By this time the fighting was in the hedgerows far inland from the invasion beaches. One day I remember well. We had just picked up about 100 troops from a liberty ship and were headed into the beach to put them ashore.

As we approached the beach, our cook rushed up to the bridge from the galley. "Skipper," he yelled, "can you hold off from the beach for a few minutes?" "Cookie, what's up? We've got 100 infantry who need to get to their unit." "Well, OK. But hit the beach easy if you can. I just put a cake in the oven, and I don't want it to fall!"

In August our base of operations moved from the beaches to the port of LeHavre at the mouth of the Seine River. Approaching this famous old French port city for the first time we had a load of gasoline-2,000 jerry cans on the tank deck-10,000 gallons of high-octane explosive. About three miles offshore from the city a harbor pilot, a Frenchman, was put on board. We had never had a pilot aboard before. Why, I asked, was he necessary? The harbor, I was told, had been heavily mined by the Germans with "oyster mines." These babies sit quietly on the floor of the harbor, sense when a ship is passing overhead, then rise up to sock it.

Our harbor pilot knew where the mines were. We were able to dock safely, when I noticed the Frenchman's pitiful, ragged shoes. I went to my cabin and brought him a pair of new Navy fatigue boots I had just purchased. For you, I said, for getting us through the mine field. He was most grateful. Almost as relieved and thankful as was our crew!

The city was a mess-burned out German tanks and trucks, blown up pillboxes, a half dozen waterfront buildings, pretty much destroyed. And lying on its side, sunken in 50-feet of water at a dock not far from us, was the famous cruise ship Isle de France. My mother and father had sailed on this 800-foot luxury liner from New York to Europe, 25 years earlier, in 1919 on their honeymoon!

As usual, Ace Bowman, our quartermaster, was on the bridge with me that day. Ace looked at the Isle de France and the mess all around us and with his usual wry humor said, "Jesus, Skipper, what a place for a scrap drive!"

A year later, August 1945, and I was now the executive officer (first mate) on LST 500 in the Boston Navy Yard. An LST is three times the length of an LCT and carries five times the men and officers. It looks like a 300-foot bathtub. When the atom bomb ended the war, our LST was ordered to Fort Pierce, Florida. It was to be one weird assignment.

We were to pick up ammo of all sizes-left over from the war-haul it 90 miles out to sea and dump it. Now we were a garbage scow for 12-inch and 8-inch shells all the way down to thousands of cases of ammo of all calibers. With tens of tons of ammo aboard each trip, we had to "deep six" the stuff as quickly as possible and return to Ft. Pierce for another load.

I am the only naval officer who ever sailed one of these 300-foot bathtubs. Let me explain. Once out at sea, to get these tons of ammo out the bow doors by way of roller tracks, we soon learned that we could not head the ship into the wind. The waves would crash over the bow and flood the deck where these tons of ammo were carried. We had to put our stern to the wind before we opened the bow doors and started to unload. Then the dumping went a little better.

With our stern to the wind, we could set our engines at dead-slow speed. Still the waves sometimes flooded the tank deck. We simply were going too fast. Then I thought, why have the screws turning at all? If our helmsman were to swing the wheel-as needed-from hard starboard and back, we could sail this big bugger on a steady course before the wind. And that's what we did to the end of the project.

Name:	Robert E. Sonntag, USNR 341641
DOB:	October 6, 1922
Home town:	Evansville, Indiana
Service:	U.S. Naval Reserve
	September 1941, entered Naval ROTC at UNC, Chapel Hill
	August 1945, discharged, Lt. (jg), Jacksonville Florida
Ships:	LCT 643 and LST 500
Occupation:	Marketing exec and entrepreneur

MY LIFE
IN THE WILD
BLUE YONDER

George Brooks Stallings, Jr.

When I was born on May 12, 1918 in Jacksonville, Florida, I had no way of knowing that 23 years down the road I would be a pilot in the United States Army Air Corps.

This tale begins in 1940 during the first trimester of my last year in college at the University of Virginia. About November of that year I received my "Greetings" from the local draft board. It said that I would be allowed to finish college, but then to be ready for induction into military service. I had visions of becoming a foot soldier in mud-filled trenches. This was definitely not to be my cup of tea. I would see to that.

So, when I came home for the Christmas holidays, I decided to go to MacDill Field in Tampa to take the physical examination for the Flying Cadet Program of the United States Army Air Corps. Being only 22 years of age, and in good physical condition, I had no difficulty in passing the physical and being accepted in the Flying Cadet Program.

At this time I had never flown an airplane. So, I thought it would be a good idea to take some flying lessons before reporting to the Army. Laurie Young was a well-known flying instructor at the old Imeson airport, and his school was the logical place to learn the flying business. I first soloed in a Piper Cub and then moved up into an old Navy Fleet Trainer. This plane was quite similar to the PT-13 that I would be flying in Army flight school. When I arrived in the Army I had a slight jump on the young men who had never flown before.

On the 15th day of March of 1941 I took the oath for the Army at the Post Office Building, and shortly thereafter reported to the Army's Primary Flying School just north of

Jackson, Mississippi. The Army sub-contracted primary training to civilians. The airplanes belonged to the Army. They were biplanes with a blue body and yellow wings and tail. The landing gear was fixed and the propellers were fixed pitch. The field was commanded by a regular Army captain. A few enlisted men were there in charge of maintenance, but some civilians were employed in that capacity, also. Our flight instructors were employees of the Parks Air College of St. Louis, Missouri. They were tough and experienced professionals, and did a fine job of getting us through our introduction to military flying.

My primary training had a few added items that I could just as easily have done without. After a mere five hours and twelve minutes of flying, my instructor got us into a mid-air collision with another airplane below us, so he took over and leveled off. The other plane happened to be doing a chandelle (a climbing turn) and was headed for us on the right side. I thought we were goners. After the impact of the collision was over, I still could not believe we were alive. But, we were blessed. The lower left wheel of the other plane had caught our right tail wing, thereby shearing it off like it had been hit with a huge knife. The impact also cut the rudder cable on the right, making it difficult for the instructor to overcome the torque of the engine. His judgment was that we could not make it with two people in the plane so he ordered me to get out onto the wing and then dive into space.

At this stage of events I was so happy to still be alive that I was willing to do anything ordered. We were at about 3,500 feet in the air. One would think the Army would have given us some kind of preliminary instruction about the use of chutes. Wrong! All I knew about jumping was what I had seen in World War I movies, where the hero bailed out and counted to three before pulling the ripcord. Before I could get around to counting to three, I had reached terminal velocity.

At this point there is no sensation of falling at all. The feeling is more like floating on a cushion of air. This gave me a breather to take in what I was going to do next. Strangely enough I was in no big hurry to open the chute. I knew the wind was blowing from the west, because this was something the instructors instilled into us. I also knew that while falling my body was lined up with my head facing south. But, to the east I could see a formidable stand of pine trees that would make a disastrous landing area. Immediately below were plowed fields.

So, my decision was to hold on as long as I dared, because this would assure me of not being blown into the trees. It was the right decision, because I came down backwards in a plowed field. Chutes in those days were primitive compared to the ones today. They were round and not too much silk was there. It was like jumping off about a 10-foot platform when hitting the ground.

There was a real humorous side to this jump. By the time I had floated down to a few hundred feet above the ground, I saw some country people (obviously sharecroppers) looking up at the strangest phenomenon they had ever witnessed in all their born days. I hollered down to them to run ahead and help me out with the chute when I landed. They were so dumbfounded that they just stood there.

So, my landing was strictly a solo event. As I started to gather up the chute other airplanes from our group started circling at low altitudes, because they had witnessed this chute floating down over rural Mississippi. I walked up the hill with the gathered chute and the ripcord firmly locked in the grip of my right hand and I finally came to a farmhouse. It was not long after that my base sent out a series of vehicles to retrieve me.

Undoubtedly this event was the most spectacular the country people had ever seen. They must have talked about it with their friends and neighbors for a long time thereafter.

When I finally got back to the base, the welcome was that of a hero. Instantly, I became a legend of my fellow cadets. My upperclass mates had me retell this story many times. My fame even spread to the young ladies in Jackson. This also increased my social status, much to my approval.

What constitutes a "hero" is subject to a lot of definitions. In my case it was being in the right place at the right time under the right circumstances. At the time it was my greatest moment in the sun. Incidentally, I still have the ripcord. It is one of my greatest treasures. Every time I look at it I am made aware of the grace of God that let a 23-year-old flying cadet live to his present age of 83 wonderful years.

If the jump were not enough of an experience, two weeks before time to graduate from primary flying school, one of my fellow cadets and I come down with the mumps. The standard Army remedy for the mumps was to be confined to one's bed for two weeks. My only consolation was that I had a fellow sufferer with whom I could talk. Otherwise it would have been like being in solitary confinement.

When I finally got out of the infirmary, it was time to move over to Montgomery, Alabama for basic training. However, before I left, my instructor wanted to have a farewell celebration. For me this was a big mistake. Having a party after two weeks in bed with the mumps is a blueprint for a relapse. That is just what happened to me.

By the time I got to Montgomery, I was so ill I had to turn into the hospital at Maxwell Field. I must have stayed there a week or ten days before reporting for basic training. It was now almost a month since I had been in an airplane. As a result I had a difficult time adjusting to the BT-17 basic trainer. A low-wing monoplane is vastly different from a primary biplane. In primary we flew from the back seat. In basic and advanced training we flew from the front seat. I finally made it and graduated from the basic program. Here we had Army instructors who introduced us to such fun things as cross-country and night flying. I really thought I had "arrived" when I took my first solo cross-country flight. By the end of basic, we were really looking forward to advanced training where we would be flying the AT-6 (SNJ to you Navy guys). This airplane had a 900 HP engine, variable pitch propeller, and retractable landing gear. How could anyone go any higher than this?

My advanced flight training was taken at Craig Field in Selma, Alabama. Yes, I got there long before Martin Luther King! This field was really first class. The living quarters were the best yet. Gone were all the drills and parades we had in basic. This was where we got down to some serious flying. The biggest thing in advanced training was the exodus to Eglin Field, Florida for gunnery practice. Here we would be firing 50-caliber machine guns at moving targets, as well as fixed targets on the ground. But, my biggest thrill was getting checked out in a real fighter plane. This was the P-36, a vintage aircraft of the Army, which had been replaced by the P-40 and P-39. It would do 250 miles an hour...a fantastic speed for a student pilot. I also saw my first B-17. I think we had exactly 12 in the Air Corps at the time. One had to have the rank of major to fly it.

October 31, 1941 was the day set for graduation for the Class of 41-H. Several days before graduation I discovered what military bureaucracy was all about. Even though I had graduated from all three levels of Army flight training, it was discovered that I lacked five hours of flying, due to my illness in primary! So, I took an AT-6 and spent the better part of the day flying around Alabama to put in the five hours. I don't think those five hours of futzing around the sky in Alabama made me a better pilot, but the Army must have thought so. Anyway, I graduated in the top 10 percent of my class. This made the Army tap me for an instructor. Little did I know at the time that I would spend the rest of my military service teaching others how to fly.

Immediately after graduation I received my orders saying I would remain at Craig Field as an instructor in advanced training. I had to go through a short course in the Instructors School, and then I was ready for my first class of students. What a surprise it was to learn that my students would all be from the Royal Air Force (RAF). It was a relief to know that when I got them they had already been through primary and basic.

Most of these young Englishmen had never driven an automobile before they were shipped over to the USA for flight training. It was my understanding that these guys took a heavy toll on the instructors in the first two levels of flying. By the time they got to advanced, most of the truly dangerous ones had been weeded out.

Each instructor was assigned five students for the entire time they remained in Advanced Training. We gave each one of them one hour a day flying the airplane. This meant coming back to the flight line for each exchange of cadets. The best part of the job was that after completing five hours of flying/instructing, we were free of all other duties. While we were on daytime flying this was not too bad. But, the story at night was vastly different.

A special type of night training had to be provided because of the wartime conditions in England. Since the Germans were flying over England much of the time, night landing for the RAF had to be without landing lights. The system they used was to have hooded runway lights that could only be seen from a very low altitude. Without landing lights, the only way to put the plane on the runway was to literally fly it to the ground at a rate of descent of 500 feet per minute.

It was amazing to me the first time I did this that the tires and the landing gear reduced the impact with the ground to a tolerable bump. Upon impact the stick was eased forward and the throttle pulled all the way back. It was a pleasant surprise to me to find that most of these British students were good pilots and quite well educated. All in all, I think I had five different classes of these cadet pilots. Each class lasted about two months.

After we finished with the British students, from that time on we had nothing but Americans. As far as the life of flight instructor goes, it does not make much difference who is your pupil. The flying routine is the same. However, we did add a new program in advanced training. Craig Field began getting P-40's and P-39's after the first few classes of Americans. The idea was to get these students checked out in these fighter planes before graduation.

This was a job that caused me quite a bit of concern, because there is no way you can fly with a student in a single seat aircraft. Real fighter planes were a terrific step up for most students. So, we had to do everything possible to give instruction on the ground, and then trust to Providence that these guys would come back down in one piece. The first thing we did was to require a blindfold cockpit test, meaning that the student had to be able to touch any instrument on the panel while blindfolded.

As far as I can remember, only one student crashed and burned. Thank God he wasn't mine. He literally got so terrified that he could not slow the glide enough to make a landing. He came in too hot to put it down on the runway, and had to go around again. No amount of talking from the tower could calm him down. As he was going around for another of many attempts, he ran out of gas, rolled over and ended up in a fiery crash, which took his life.

After I had put in over a thousand hours instructing in advanced, I had the opportunity of moving up to four-engine bombardment aircraft as an instructor. My new base was at Smyrna, Tennessee, just 35 miles east of Nashville on the road to Murfreesboro. Here we had a fleet of both B-17s and B-24s. Our students in these planes were Americans who had already graduated from some form of advanced training.

Again I had to go through a short instructors course. My instructor was an old friend from Craig Field. At first I thought four-engine flying would be so great, but in reality, it was the most boring kind of instruction. We had five students each. In a large aircraft all the students can be aboard at the same time. Each day's flying gave each student one hour of instruction.

The good part of this job was that when the five hours were up, we were off for the rest of the day. The terrible part of the job was that we flew seven days a week. One day we flew in the morning, the next day at night, and the next day in the afternoon. This lousy routine kept up for the remainder of the war. By the time I got my orders saying the job was finished and I could go home...I didn't care if I ever saw another airplane. So, my years of military service were from March 15, 1941 through September of 1945.

After separating from the service I entered the College of Law at the University of Florida in September of 1946. By going to school all year round, I received my Juris Doctor degree in February of 1949. I practiced law in Jacksonville, Florida for 37 years thereafter. During that time I spent 10 years in the Florida Legislature as a member of the House of Representatives. After that period of time, I made the decision not to seek re-election. I then became General Counsel for The Florida Retail Federation and represented this group before the Legislature as its chief lobbyist for 13 years. After that I retired from law practice at the end of 1985. I have been fully retired ever since.

LEARNING MEDICINE
THE HARD WAY IN
THE SOUTH PACIFIC

George M. Stubbs

On December 7, 1941 I had just started my junior year at Emory Medical School. Due to our involvement in the war, summer vacation in 1942 was cancelled and our class was graduated in March 1943.

I was never comfortable not being in uniform. So I, and several of my classmates, elected to take our internships in the Navy. We were accepted and I was assigned to the National Naval Medical Center in Bethesda, Maryland.

Internships everywhere were cut to nine months, so in January I was assigned to the Recruiting Station in Jacksonville. I lived at the 310 Apartments (Ambassador Hotel) and we commuted to Camp Blanding six days a week to examine draftees, and played golf at Ponte Vedra on Mondays. I liked Jacksonville very much and returned years later.

In July 1944 I was assigned to Beach Battalion School at Camp Pendleton in Oceanside, California. The training was to set up beach party groups of about 30 sailors, two line officers, a medical officer and eight corpsmen. Each unit was assigned to an APA (Attack Transport) part of the amphibious forces. Our mission was to set up a beachhead with the invasion troops and my group was to give first aid and try to send casualties back to ships lying offshore that had hospital facilities. Each APA had four more doctors aboard for this purpose.

In October 1044 we were assigned to the USS Hocking, APA-121, a new ship waiting for us in San Pedro, California. I was on this ship from the first turn of her screw to the last.

We spent several weeks in shakedown off the California coast and in December set sail for Pearl Harbor. There we were told we were going to invade Iwo Jima, a place none of us had heard of.

Our transport division loaded a regiment of the Sixth Marine Divison at Hilo on the Big Island, made practice landings at Maui and Saipan and on February 19, 1945 landed on Iwo Jima. The island had been bombed, rocketed, blasted with 16-inch guns from the USS Tennessee at point blank, but that did not help a lot. We landed early on the first day. Only two divisions were to land and one was in reserve, but by the end of the first day all were ashore.

My beach party landed on Blue Beach (or something like that) but my corpsmen group was put on a pontoon 1000 yards offshore tied to LST-929. We accepted casualties from the beach and attempted to sort them out and send them to the hospital ships. Nothing worked out very well. We had a storm during the night and the pontoon broke loose. Fortunately we got aboard the LST. We then put all the casualties down in the tank deck and tried to care for them. It was really like being a Boy Scout. We had no blood, antibiotics, etc. All we had was morphine, dressings, sulfa powder and some I.V. fluids. It was a helpless experience. After about a week I helped set up a field hospital on the beach, then went back to Tinian where I met up with my old ship the PA-121. We were then sent to Ulithi (an atoll) for R&R (beer and softball) for a few days.

Then we went to Espiritu Santo in the New Hebrides to pick up the 29th Army Division for the invasion of Okinawa -- a bedraggled group who had been away from home too long.

On the way we crossed the equator. My head was shaved and my hair never grew back. We also anchored at Tulagi across from Guadalcanal -- a beautiful large island.

We made the invasion of Okinawa around Easter 1945. There were 1,200 ships in the invasion fleet. We landed our army group but did not set up a beachhead since the fighting was inland. We had some nighttime bombings and a kamikaze hit a ship next to us, a half-mile away.

We took casualties aboard and back to Tinian. I had the forward troop compartment full of combat fatigue cases, (I never thought of myself as a psychiatrist.)

We came back to San Francisco for two or so weeks (like being in heaven) then back to Okinawa. We were in Okinawa when the war was over. We then ferried troops from the Philippines to Korea twice, then to Shanghai and back to Los Angeles via Guam and Pearl.

On Christmas Eve 1945 I became senior medical officer on the ship and we set sail for Samar in the Philippines. We brought troops back to LA and then around to Norfolk, where we decommissioned the ship in May 1946.

On the trip from Samar to LA I did my first solo appendectomy. The surgery was on a young soldier and fortunately he survived. When I was an intern at Bethesda the hospital was the Navy's flagship. The Admiral insisted all interns take the exam for the Regular Navy. We would have had to stop breathing to flunk, so we were regulars. All that meant was that we were not separated after the war.

I spent about a year in Columbus, Ohio at the recruiting headquarters. Through the efforts of my father and Senator Claude Pepper, I was allowed to resign in May 1947 and return to Atlanta to continue my surgical training.

This may sound hokey to the present generation, but I feel that service to my country has made me feel better about myself, and though I did nothing spectacular I did what I was asked to do.

George Stubbs was born in Eatonton, Georgia on December 7, 1918. After practicing medicine in Jacksonville Florida, he retired and he and Beverly live at Ponte Vedra, Florida.

SUPPORTING THE INFANTRY
IN EUROPE WITH
HEAVY ARTILLERY

Herman Ulmer, Jr.

Without giving it a second thought, I signed up in my freshman year for R.O.T.C. My father was an infantry company commander in France in World War I, and was a firm believer in a strong national defense, a conviction which had rubbed off on me in my younger days. When I entered Princeton there was no doubt that I would try for a reserve commission through the R.O.T.C. program. In 1938, I had no premonition that I would go to war, but neither was I oblivious to events taking place in Asia and Europe. If it should become necessary to serve, I wanted it to be as an officer rather than in the ranks.

On June 16, 1942, with my Princeton diploma and a commission as second lieutenant in the field artillery, I headed home to Jacksonville to enjoy the 10 days of civilian life allowed by the Army before reporting for active duty at Ft. Bragg, North Carolina for a refresher course. During this period the engagement of Betty and me was announced, but wedding plans would have to wait. The country had been at war for six months and the future was just too uncertain to set the date.

After a few days at Ft. Bragg I was lucky enough to obtain five days leave at the end of the refresher course. Uncertain future or not, Betty and I made it to the altar on August 1. When my leave was up, orders awaited me to report to Ft. Sill in Lawton, Oklahoma, to take the battery officer's course. The Army next sent me to the 78th Infantry Division, which became my Army home until hostilities ceased. The division had recently been activated at Camp Butner, near Durham, North Carolina. Upon reporting, I was assigned to Headquarters Battery, 307th Field Artillery

Battalion equipped with twelve 105 mm howitzers, and given the usual duties of a new second lieutenant, such as mess officer and motor officer. After a few weeks, I received a surprise promotion to first lieutenant much sooner than I deserved it. In May 1943, our daughter, Jean, was born in Duke Hospital in Durham.

Halfway through Tennessee maneuvers, I was assigned in February 1944 as liaison officer with the 2nd Battalion, 311th Infantry Regiment, a position designed by the Army to provide an infantry battalion commander direct and fast communication with an artillery battalion. This turned out to be my permanent job for the duration. A few months later I received a promotion to captain.

After these maneuvers, came several months at Camp Pickett, Virginia, where we fine-tuned our training before going overseas. Since the artillery's sole purpose is to support the infantry, the brass thought it a good idea that we get better acquainted by sending the liaison officers and forward observers on special duty with the infantry. I spent three weeks as executive officer of G Company, 311th Infantry, where I had the exciting assignment one day of conducting bayonet practice (under the supervision of sergeants, of course!).

In October 1944, the division crossed the Atlantic in an uneventful voyage of convoyed troop ships and spent a few weeks on the coast of England. On a short pass to London I bumped into Bomber Elmer in front of the high altar in Westminster Abby. Neither of us knew the other was in the same hemisphere. Our sightseeing came to a halt while we went out on the town.

After crossing the Channel in an LST we moved into a front line position as part of the First Army on the edge of the Hurtgen Forest, three days before the Battle of the Bulge began. Our division was on the northern lip of the bulge. As the savage fighting a few miles to the south moved westward, threatening to envelope us, we remained in place for the next six weeks in relative quiet. I spent this entire time at my infantry battalion command post in the basement of a half destroyed house, 100 yards behind the front line where I planned to furnish artillery support if the tide started to come our way.

On January 30, when the Battle of the Bulge was finally over, we attacked out of our old positions in a raging snowstorm. My infantry battalion began a three-day bloody battle to take the small farming village of Kesternich, which had been heavily fortified by the Germans during the previous six weeks of inactivity. This was a house-to-house, street-by-street struggle in knee-deep snowdrifts. I was able to provide some artillery fire on targets that could not be seen, but when described by the infantry battalion commander, could be identified on my map. On the last day of the fight, the infantry was held up by machine gun fire from a house. The infantry colonel asked if I could put some artillery on the house, which was only about 100 yards down the street. I called my artillery fire direction center, gave the map coordinates of the house and waited for the shells to arrive. When they came, they were right on target. The infantry colonel complimented the artillery for its "beautiful" shooting. In nine more days of hard fighting, the division captured the strategic Schwammenauel Dam on the Rohr River. The infantry battalion I was with received a Distinguished Unit Citation for its outstanding action in the previous two weeks. In recognition of our part, the infantry battalion's Unit Citation Badge was awarded to me, my liaison section and forward observers. Also, I received a Bronze Star, recommended by my infantry battalion commander for heroic action at Kesternich, and an Oak Leaf Cluster to the Bronze Star on the recommendation of my artillery battalion commander for meritorious service over the two preceding months.

A month later, the bridge over the Rhine at Remagen was taken by the 9th Armored Division. The next day I rode across the bridge in my jeep along with the troops of my infantry battalion. The Germans were still able to fire artillery shells at the bridge. Traffic crawled and came to a standstill several times, leaving us like sitting ducks high over the Rhine. Fortunately, the Germans no longer had direct observation on the bridge. There were no hits while I crossed, but several near misses fell into the river by our side. Also a couple of their planes attempted to bomb the bridge, but again they missed the target and their bombs also dropped into the water.

The crossing was followed by several hectic days establishing the bridgehead in the picturesque tourist country east of the Rhine. I marched with my infantry battalion north near the bank of the river while my artillery battalion remained west of the river. The first morning after we crossed, I called on the radio for a fire mission without having any idea where the artillery battalion was. I requested a few white phosphorus rounds, the smoke from which established the fact that I was firing what artillerymen would call a 1600 mil T. This meant that a line from the guns to the target and a line from me to the target formed a 90-degree angle, a most unusual angle from which to conduct artillery fire.

Several days later, I accompanied the lead company of my infantry battalion on foot in a circuitous route to the Drachenfels, a mountain on the Rhine where legend has it that Seigfried slew the dragon. *Time magazine* reported that we bypassed it, but that was wrong. It would have been risky, if not impossible. It dominated the Rhine for miles, providing superb observation to the south, west and north. According to *National Geographic*, we captured it at bayonet point after two hours of stiff fighting, which also was wrong. The Germans had abandoned it. I walked up to the top with the infantry battalion commander and the point platoon of riflemen. A deserted restaurant at the summit contained a supply of pink champagne, which was enjoyed by all.

The next day we attacked and took the luxury resort Hotel Petersburg on another mountain across the river from Bad Godesburg. Here Chamberlain had met Hitler a week before their Munich conference. My forward observer and I found a bottle of Johnny Walker Black Label at the hotel bar.

We had just poured a stiff one when we heard what sounded like a counterattack against the hotel.

Leaving our drinks untouched at the bar, we entered the lobby where small arms fire was hitting the revolving front door causing it to spin wildly. We crawled across the carpeted lobby floor to a window to see what we could see, which was nothing. When the firing stopped, it turned out that it was three or four Germans who had been on outpost duty away from the hotel, returning for chow without knowing that the hotel had changed hands. Needless to say, we never got back to the drinks we had left on the bar. C'est la guerre.

After the Remagen Bridgehead, our division attacked into the Ruhr Pocket. There was some resistance at first, but it became spotty as we moved in. After 11 days, we went into First Army Reserve and I went to the Riviera for a week's rest.

The war ended the night I returned from the Riviera. I rejoined my artillery battalion, which began occupation duty. I became recreation officer which gave me the opportunity to supervise a swimming pool, publish a battalion newspaper and run a dance hall and a beer parlor which I named "Yankee Doodle Tap Room."

In November I enjoyed a voyage home through a wild north Atlantic storm. I arrived home on Thanksgiving Day 1945 after a year overseas and with three campaign stars: the Ardennes, Rhineland and Central Europe -- and happily no Purple Heart.

Herdy, as friends call him, was born in Jacksonville Florida on April 17, 1920. He was a very successful lawyer in Jacksonville.

FROM 90-DAY WONDER
TO THE STORMS AND STRIFE
OF WAR AT SEA

Thomas P. Ulmer

Following graduation from Princeton in 1940, I realized America's entry into WWII was inevitable. When *Life Magazine* communicated the commencement of the Navy's "90-day wonder" officer training program, I volunteered 18 months before Pearl Harbor and earned my commission as ensign at Northwestern Graduate School that December.

During five years of service with many diverse memories, two episodes stand out more indelibly than others. The first was rather traumatic and the second a fantastic experience. Aboard the USS Cornelian, a large yacht converted, not very effectively, by Miami Merrill-Stevens to a submarine patrol craft operating from the Florida coast down to South America, one night we encountered a mega-storm. The ship was pitching precariously and taking sheets of water over its bow. The gyrocompass processed and the magnetic compass swung wildly. Two men were struggling at the helm to maintain course and to keep from broaching. We had no radar. As officer-of-the-deck I was bracing myself and peering through the plate glass in the pilot house.

Suddenly, a giant wave catapulted sheets of "green water" against the pilothouse so violently it broke the plate glass into shards directly in my face, gashing my nose, the side of my left eye and hand. I bled freely and my quartermaster fainted at the sight! I was led below to quarters I shared with another officer. He also fainted! The pharmacist mate (no doc aboard) patched me up with a compress. A day or so later we made it back to port. The Opa Locka doc stitched the bridge of my nose and placed a clamp to close the gash by the left eye for five or six days. Fortunately, no shards damaged my eyes.

At a later date, I was captaining my sub chaser in the Pacific attached to the 5th Amphibious Forces! (I had seen action off Cape Canaveral early on when five merchant ships and tankers were torpedoed in one day by German U-boats).

But this vast armada of hundreds of American forces, battleships, cruisers, troop ships and LSTs moving together on Saipan was awesome to behold! My ship's station was at the "line of departure," just outside the coral reefs where GIs were being unloaded in the waves to the beachhead. Saipan proved very costly, for the Japs were deeply entrenched in pillboxes and caves. It took about six weeks to secure the island. I shall always remember and respect the sacrifices of the marines attached to the 2nd and 4th Divisions. Their losses were substantial.

To conclude, during five years of naval service, I realize how fortunate I was to return home in one piece. I never earned any medals or the Purple Heart from wounds from enemy action. The only wounds I had were caused by "the cruel sea!"

Horrible as World War II was, it stopped Hitler and the Japs and united America like it's never been united, before or since. I'm proud to have invested five years of my life in the most significant challenge of the 20th Century.

Thomas P. Ulmer was born in Jacksonville, Florida on January 21, 1916. He served in the U.S. Navy in antisubmarine warfare and in the 5th Amphibian Forces. He was on active duty from July 1, 1940 until October 1, 1945. Mr. Ulmer was a very successful realtor in Jacksonville.

LIVING A LIFELONG
DREAM OF BEING A
NAVY NURSE AT SEA

Betty J. Pisani Uptagraft

I was born 4-26-42 in Long Branch, NJ and wanted to be a Navy Nurse from the very first time anyone asked me that age old question; "What do you want to be when you grow up?"

I told everybody that I was going to be a navy nurse and serve on a battleship. I wasn't worldly enough to know that, at that time, women didn't serve on battleships. I also didn't know there was such a thing as a hospital ship where women did serve. It wasn't until a couple of years after my 1963 graduation from nursing school at what is now Orlando Regional Medical Center that I learned about hospital ships.

After about a year and a half of working in the hospital where I trained, I decided it was time to pursue my life long goal of becoming a U.S. Navy Nurse. Since things were heating up in Southeast Asia, it wasn't difficult to join and get a direct commission, and that's how civilian Betty Pisani was transformed into Ensign Pisani.

Officer indoctrination, for all nurses, took place in Newport, RI. It was there that I was supposed to have learned how to wear the uniform and play the part of an officer. To that end I was given training on topics ranging from the "chain of command," right marching, saluting (who, when and where), swimming, and behaving like an officer and a lady, to paraphrase a movie title.

After going through the five-week, accelerated indoctrination course (previous courses had been eight weeks), I headed for my first duty station which was the Great Lakes Naval Hospital in Waukegan, IL where I stayed from 1965-1967. After two years there, it was time for a change of duty station, and that's when I headed for Mare

Island, CA where the U.S. Sanctuary AH-17 (auxiliary hospital) was receiving its final fitting out and conducting its sea trials before heading to Vietnam.

After a year aboard the hospital ship in Vietnam, I was granted my request for duty in Orlando where the Navy was taking over an old WWII hospital from the Air Force. Having burned out on nursing in Vietnam, I finished the remainder of my commitment with the Navy in Orlando and got discharged on January 1, 1970 with the grade of Lt.

I then entered an entirely different field by getting a BA in English followed by an MA in linguistics, which allowed me to teach English to foreign students in an intensive English language program at the University of Florida.

1. THE LITTER/LETTER INCIDENT

I had been close to finishing rounds with Dr. Baxter when the call came over the mic, or ship's public address system "Naval Hospital, man your patient handling stations, all hands provide-one litter."

Whenever a "patient handling" call came over the speaker system, numerous people from all over the hospital ship were mobilized. Ship's crew as well as hospital crew were involved every time we received patients, whether by boat or helicopter which were the two most common methods. Occasionally we would receive ambulatory patients when we were in port, but this time we were cruising along the south China Sea off the coast of Vietnam, it was July, 1967, and a "patient handling" call, under these circumstances, always held the potential for a life or death situation.

It had been a good morning rounds so far, with no flare-ups from the customarily fractious young doctor who seemed to find joy in pushing his great weight around. So far this morning, though, he was in an unusually agreeable mood. When the call came, however, his mood swung swiftly. He was on triage duty and would have to interrupt rounds to respond to the "patient handling" call. As he heaved open the heavy ward door and lumbered off the ward, grumbling himself into a bad mood, I wondered if I would ever have just one morning of peaceful rounds with him.

Within 10 or 15 minutes, the ward door flew open again, letting back in an angry, red-faced, almost incoherent, cursing, Dr. Baxter. I didn't realize until he had traversed halfway across the ward, that his wrath was aimed at me as he waddled over, stared me in the face, and breathed fire and venom, interspersed with words such as "letter" and "your own time, not mine", and "helicopter pilots", and "Don't you ever let your social life interrupt my rounds again." With his anger spent, and sweat dripping off his jowls, he announced that he would finish rounds later, after a coffee break. I only hoped that I would be on such a break when he returned to finish rounds. He could vent the rest of his anger, whatever it was about, on someone else.

I shook my thoughts back to the patient care at hand, and resumed work because there were always dressings to be changed, medications and IV fluids to be administered, vital signs to be checked, and patients with names, and Moms and Dads and sisters and girl friends. These patients usually needed a little special attention to their psyche, not just to their blood, muscle, bone and skin.

Before long it was time for lunch so I headed down to the wardroom. Since I was a junior officer, I (mercifully this time) had to go to the early seating. When I got to my place at the table, I noticed that there was a white, legal sized, envelope with my name on it sitting under my napkin. Where had it come from? I hadn't heard anyone announce "mail call." Besides, when mail came in, ours was always distributed in nurses' quarters.

After Father Kelley invoked God's blessing on everyone and all our food, I ignored my ever -present lumberjack's appetite and immediately went to the curious envelope. When I opened it and started reading the letter from Stan McGhan, Jolly Green Giant helicopter pilot, the events of the morning became all too clear to me.

When the helicopter pilot had radioed the ship requesting permission to land, he was asked, by the ship's radioman, what he was carrying. The pilot must have replied that he was carrying one "letter", which the ship's radioman misconstrued as one "litter" (stretcher), and it just went down hill from there.

The letter had been directed to me, because I was the unofficial liaison between the Air Force Jolly Green Giant helicopter pilots, and the "Chorus Line of 29" nurses (plus two female Red Cross workers, and one female pharmacist). Our one mission, social mission, that is , was to plan parties. This particular letter contained the final plans for our very first party ashore, the date, times of arrival for the helicopters that would be transporting us ashore, ETA for our return, and contact person just in case we had to be called back early.

In order to legitimize the party, we had to include some doctors in the list of invitees, so, a week later when the helicopters came to pick us up, Dr. Baxter was one of the chosen waiting to go ashore and party. He was able to assuage (some would say, drown) his earlier anger in the punch which was served from a brand, new porcelain toilet bowl. The vessel from which that high-octane beverage was served didn't turn away any imbibers.

At the end of the evening, the otherwise fractious Dr. was in such a cheerful mood that he even helped plot the theft of the potty/party bowl. It wasn't so much a theft as a taking home of a party favor. After all, it was the hosts who helped us to load and transport the large white, American Standard toilet bowl, with the remaining punch still sloshing around in it, along with a few cigarette butts, some paper cups, napkins, and a few cocktail wieners.

He, the good and drunk doctor Baxter, along with some co-conspirators, brought the treasured white elephant back aboard ship and very ceremoniously placed it in the officers wardroom (dining room) where it became a receptacle for an odd assortment of elongated appurtenances over the next several weeks. Finally some other pranksters secreted it away and gave it a more suitable throne, perhaps in the bowels of the ship.

Although Dr. Baxter remained, for the most part, a disgruntled young man, the litter/letter incident became more humorous material for many ceremonies, speeches, and skits over the subsequent nine months that I had remaining aboard the Navy Hospital Ship, U.S.S. Sanctuary, AH-17. I didn't mind, though, because that letter was the start of many shore parties that the wonderful Jolly Green Giants planned and helped execute for us. They were gracious hosts, provided us with some much needed diversion, and always brought us back aboard our floating band-aid box safely, to serve another day with the likes of Dr. Baxter.

2. CLOTHES THAT GO CLUNK

Under the terms of the Geneva Convention, "Article (IV) relative to the Protection of Civilian Persons in Time of War, Geneva, 12 August, 1949", Article 3, (2), states that "The wounded and sick shall be collected and cared for." The terms of the Geneva Convention were still binding in 1967 therefore the Navy Hospital Ship, U.S.S. Sanctuary, operating in war time off the coast of Vietnam, was obligated to provide care to all the sick, injured, and infirm, friend and foe alike. To comply with these terms, we had a "People to People" ward which ministered to the needs of the sick and wounded from the civilian population of Vietnam. Since it was a cultural trait for well family members to accompany the sick to hospitals, this ward often resembled a circus, minus the three rings to control the activity. There were old men, young and old women, and children of all ages shuffling about in their bare or sandaled feet and chirping away in Vietnamese or French.

The civilian casualties usually came aboard while we were anchored off of DaNang or Chu Lai, and stayed with us while we cruised up and down the South China Sea and sometimes even went with us when we sailed for the Philippines to take on supplies, have repairs done, and get R&R. Very often these civilians came to us with little more than the clothes on their backs. As their condition improved and they became more ambulatory, we would have to find ways of providing clothes for them.

The wonderful Jolly Green Giant, Air force helicopter pilots, always solicitous of our needs, often asked if there was anything they could bring us. In desperation, we decided to enlist their help in getting civilian clothing for this partially ambulatory, partially bed-bound, floating humanitarian endeavor that was peopled with scantily clad, little people.

Not wanting to miss an opportunity to engage in hedonism, we also enlisted the Jolly Greens' help in getting us some of the "real thing" at the same time. Now, we had a geedunk (snack bar) on board ship that sold fresh popcorn, candy, and other snacks every afternoon, along with fountain colas, but these ship's colas never quite measured up. They were either too syrupy, too weak, or just too awful in flavor to satisfy the memory our taste buds held of the "real thing." When I placed the clothing order, I also asked that as many cans or cases of Coca Cola (we weren't a part of the "Pepsi generation") as they could scrounge up be placed in with the clothing.

True to their word, the Jolly Greens radioed the ship a few days later requesting permission to land in order to deliver a few boxes of "children's clothing." The very large Huey landed on our small helicopter deck and off-loaded, with much clunking and clanking, several boxes marked, "children's clothing", and earmarked to my attention.

The news of the clothing that went "clunk" reached me long before the boxes did, but luckily, those boxes were well-secured and any pilfering would have been all too obvious, so the clothes boxes with coke cans intact reached me safely. My roommate, who worked the "People to People" ward took charge of distributing the clothes while I stowed away the cokes in our locker. We would have enough to last us until we went back into Subic Bay, provided we rationed ourselves, and didn't get too gluttonous.

There was only one small downside to having all those cans of coke, which I had so neatly stacked in the bottom of my roommate's and my combined closet. Whenever we hit the slightest bit of rough seas, or even rolled from side to side in the waves, the cans clunked and clanged with ever roll of the ship. It had been not only a total waste of time and energy, but also a labor steeped in abject stupidity on my part, to think that all those cans would stay within their appointed limits.

Early the next morning, my poor unsuspecting roommate, forgetting all about the scrambled coke cans, hurriedly opened the closet doors wide so she could pull out a uniform for the day. She was almost buried in an avalanche of red and silver cans, careening out of control, out of their bounds, across the deck of our room, and into my semi-consciousness. I didn't have to work until evening. I should have been allowed to sleep longer. I wanted to get angry, but at whom? Wishing to console my roommate, I probably made the understatement of the day, if not the week. "You know, you don't have to re-stack them."

My roommate and I clunked and clanged our way up and down the South China Sea to the reassuring sounds that meant we still had some of the "real thing" in the bottom of our closet, clanging around with OUR clothing this time.

Although the "clothing went clunk" angered the CO at the time, he got many knots of the story at ensuing ceremonies and gatherings, much to my red-faced chagrin.

3. DINNER WITH THE CO, AND OTHER INCONGRUITIES OF WAR

I've never been able to become reconciled to some of the incongruities of war. The biggest incongruity for me has always been, rules of war. War itself conjures up images of mayhem, anarchy, and lawlessness. Conditions such as those don't have rules.

A major incongruity that confronted me daily was the wardroom ambiance aboard the Navy Hospital Ship, U.S.S. Sanctuary, AH-17. While cruising off the coast of Vietnam in `67 and `68, waiting to receive the wounded from the battlefield, I could hear the sounds of war being waged in the not-too-distant jungles while I dined in air conditioned comfort, seated at linen covered tables, eating such wonderful things as steak, pork chops, curried lamb, baked Alaska, and whatever else we planned for our menu. The brutal truth, however, was that one might get called away from such sumptuous fare at a moment's notice to receive the war wounded straight from the battlefield, with remnants of cold c-rations still in their shot up bowels; What a shameful disruption. Why couldn't the rules of war dictate that no fighting be engaged in during the dinner hours?

In the evenings, my roommate and I would sit out on the deck of the signal bridge, playing pinochle with our boyfriends. Seated on blankets and canopied by the stars, we could watch the tracers of war that were being fired in the not-so-distant jungles. We could listen to the sounds of gunfire while watching the lights from the tracers, and imagine we were back home at a 4th of July celebration instead of within earshot of killing and maiming.

I learned to live with these incongruities, and was eventually able to keep from cowering in shame when the Army nurses would come aboard, wearing their green fatigues and combat boots, to do some shopping in the ship's BX. I wasn't even embarrassed when one such Army nurse ecstatically exclaimed, upon finding a long sought item, "My God, you've really got Tampax!"

On special occasions we would have wardroom parties, and invite the CO, who normally ate in his quarters, and had his meals prepared by his own chef, and served by his own stewards, much like the early, ill-fated, South Pole expedition in which the British explorers went heavily laden with silver tea services, and other non-essentials. St. Patrick's Day, Easter, and the major Holidays, of course, commanded major celebrations to which the CO was invited.

What was unusual, though, was for the CO to invite a non-peer to his stateroom for dinner. It was not only unusual, but also unheard of, that is, until there were some visiting dignitaries whom the CO had invited to dine with him, and whom he thought he could please by having young females present in his stateroom during the dinner.

My invitation was hand delivered by the Chief Nurse, who informed me that I was expected to show up for dinner in the CO's cabin, in the uniform of the day, at the time noted on the invitation. No RSVP was required because the invitation itself was not really an invitation, but a direct order, which I must obey, albeit begrudgingly.

I dressed in the uniform of the day, and went to the CO's cabin, all too aware of the young, war wounded two and three decks below, and all the other young men out in the field, many of whom would become our next patients.

The evening was almost insufferable for me, and I felt like an inanimate ornament that had been brought in merely as window dressing. The CO and his three male guests conversed over, around, and through me and the other female ornaments who had also been brought in for decoration. The scenario was even more surreal than the everyday wardroom setting. There were more stewards per person when dining with the CO, the silver had a brighter shine to it than in the wardroom, and my uniform didn't have any blood or body fluid stains on it.

I can't remember what I ate, who the visitors were, or what the conversation was about. I do remember, however, that I tried to smile, and laugh at the appropriate times, while counting the seconds, minutes, hours, and decades (or so it seemed) until I could get out of that enclave of male dominance.

I couldn't believe my lousy, unlucky stars when, no more than two weeks later, I received another invitation (order) to dinner with the CO and another group of visiting dignitaries, politicians, representatives, reporters, journalists, or whoever. I couldn't believe that he wanted me back again. I never got a chance to engage any of the men in conversation, and all I did was sit there eating and smiling while churning on the inside.

I pleaded with the Chief Nurse, bless her soul, sympathetic messenger that she was, to please tell me how I could get out of the second invitation. She told me that there was no way out, short of death. I was 25 years old with a very strong wish to live, but also a strong determination not to repeat the miserable evening of two weeks ago.

The invitation had come one day in advance of the dinner which was certainly adequate under the circumstances. After all, what were the possibilities for a social life out in the South China Sea? The CO knew I would be home, and without plans to go out for the evening. Where in the Hell could I go?

Early the next morning, the day of what was to be my second dinner with the CO, the gods of "out maneuver the CO" were with me when I encountered the Chief Nurse first thing in the morning. Fortunately for me, I hadn't slept very well the night before, and must have looked a bit rough. The Chief Nurse, being the nurturing type, like most nurses, commented on my appearance. I seized the moment and seized my abdomen, feigning what I hoped she would be willing to imagine, given my demeanor.

When she told me that I didn't look too well, I didn't contest what she said. I implied with gestures and grimaces (but never really said) that I had some form of gastro-intestinal upset. She immediately informed me that she would have to find someone to take my place at dinner that evening. I had to seize my stomach again just to keep from laughing in sheer delight over my victory. The chief nurse, thinking I was about to vomit, continued to try and console me. I assured her that with a good long rest the remainder of the day that I would be ready for work the following day. Assured of my well-being, the chief nurse went off in search of another hapless ornament. I had found a way, short of death, to get out of a dinner invitation with the CO, and I never received another such invitation.

The incongruities of war continued, but his was one that I wouldn't have to be a part of ever again. I was free to sit on my gray, navy-issue blanket, out on the deck of the signal bridge while the Southern Cross shone bright in the sky, helping the moon to illuminate my pinochle hand. Though the tracers raced across the sky punctuated by intermittent gunfire, they never interrupted our game. The stakes were high because we were playing for Singapore Slings in Singapore, our next R&R port.

4. THE INSIDES
OF BOTH SIDES

It was February, 1968, and the TET offensive in Vietnam was drowning us with a river of wounded. We were working virtually non-stop, and the wards were so full that as soon as some poor young convalescent was well enough to recuperate unsupervised, he would be given a cot on the open deck of the U.S. Navy Hospital Ship, U.S.S. Sanctuary. I was hoping I wouldn't have to play musical beds again to accommodate another new patient that day.

My duty area was the surgical post op ward with a bed capacity of 26. The beds were actually bunk-style racks. Less than that even, because they were metal framed springs with the mattresses on top. These metal frames were attached to metal poles that ran from deck to overhead (floor to ceiling). These metal-framed springs were attached two high on the poles, bunk-bed style. When not in use, the bed frames could be triced up (folded up) out of the way to allow more maneuvering space around the ward.

This particular day, however, the only bed not occupied or triced up was the one right next to the nurse's desk. We rarely used it because, when down, it almost cut off the passageway between the ward and the treatment/medication room. This bed was at the extreme end of four rows of other similar bunks. The only time we could really justify using it would be if we had a patient who needed very close and constant supervision, and those patients either remained in the recovery room until they were stabilized, or were sent to the ICU (Intensive Care Unit) for longer term care.

But this was February, 1968, and the TET Offensive was creating a flood of war-wounded, so the recovery room had to move them out more quickly, and ICU was already overflowing. I got word that I would be receiving a very fresh (meaning just barely coming out of anesthesia) post-op patient who had multiple gunshot and shrapnel wounds to the chest, abdomen, and lower extremities. He had been operated on in all of those areas, had a chest tube in place, had multiple operative sites with the potential for bleeding, and had received some minor head wounds, for which he would require frequent assessment both surgically and neurologically. This was a patient who would need closer attention than the other patients on my ward, for a while.

We had prepared the lower bunk closest to the nurses' desk for this new patient, and as soon as he arrived, I began doing all the routine checks of dressings, drainage tubes, IV fluids, vital signs (Blood pressure, temperature, pulse, and respirations), and level of alertness.

I wasn't at all surprised on seeing that he was Vietnamese as it wasn't unusual to receive such patients. Over the course of the 10 months that I had been in Vietnam, we had cared for our own young American men, but also Australians, South Koreans, and other South Vietnamese soldiers.

This one, however, wasn't South Vietnamese (our ally). He was North Vietnamese, a VC or Viet Cong, or to be more precise, he was the enemy, and as soon as my corpsman, who was reading his chart, brought this to my attention, in my mind, the VC's eyes immediately began too look more slanted, more sinister, more threatening, more to be hated, and I wanted to walk away from him. I had 25 other sick or wounded young American men on that ward who needed and deserved my time and attention. Why did I have to spend one second on this dark-skinned little runt of a slant-eyed monster who had probably been responsible for some of the misery my young American boys were suffering? He was obviously different and didn't deserve any of my energy. With difficulty, I pushed the sinister thoughts aside so that I could concentrate on the job at hand.

Since this patient was in the lower bunk, I actually had to kneel down beside him to check some of the tubes and dressings. While kneeling down inspecting and checking, my back was turned to all of the other wounded American men on the ward. I could feel the eyes (25 pairs of them) of the other wounded men almost piercing through my turned back, and I wondered if they felt abandoned by me. I felt guilty for what I was doing, and wished that I didn't have to do anything for this enemy soldier. I struggled with my major moral dilemma for what seemed like hours but in reality was probably only seconds.

The symbolism was almost overwhelming for me. I was turning my back on my own people, not only symbolically, but also physically. Again, I shook my straying attention back to the job at hand. The blood on the VC patient's dressings was red, his limbs constructed of the same muscle and bone and blood vessels as the limbs of the young American men, and his lungs, wounded and struggling though they were, breathed air in the same manner as did American soldiers. It was then that I realized that the insides of both sides were the same.

This VC soldier stayed with us for several weeks, and although I don't know when it happened, sometime during his stay, the outsides of both sides started to look very much the same also.

5. U.S.S. SANCTUARY AH-17

The Red Rover, a side wheel steamer, was the very first U.S. hospital ship. It was built in 1859 and saw duty during the Civil War. Since the U.S. Navy Nurse Corps was not formed until May 13, 1908, that first hospital ship used civilian nurses and nuns to provide patient care.

All subsequent Navy hospital ships bore names indicative of peace and tranquility: Consolation, Relief, Solace, Samaritan, Haven, Repose, Refuge, and Sanctuary to name just a few.

The U.S.S. Sanctuary started as a merchant ship, SS Owl, but with the forthcoming invasion of Japan, she was converted to a hospital ship. She was launched 15 August, 1944, fitted out as a hospital ship, and commissioned on 20 June, 1945. Two months later she arrived at Pearl Harbor. By that time, hostilities with Japan had ended so she was ordered to Japan to pick up liberated POWs. On the way out of the harbor at Wakayama, Japan, she encountered the incoming Fifth Fleet Flagship, the battleship New Jersey. Who would have guessed that these two ships would again see duty together some 23 years later in nearby waters off the coast of Vietnam.

After transporting POWs from Nagasaki, Okinawa, and Guam, the Sanctuary finally set sail back to the United States where she was decommissioned at Philadelphia Naval Shipyards on 15 August, 1946.

Twenty years later she was modernized, outfitted with a helicopter deck, and re-commissioned on 15 November, 1966 for duty in Vietnam. She arrived in Da Nang Harbor, Vietnam 10 April, 1967 and began a five year deployment in the South China Sea. Except for brief visits to various Asian ports for upkeep and R&R, Sanctuary spent her entire deployment cruising up and down coastal Vietnam. Wounded, both civilian and military, friend and foe, were flown straight from the battlefield by helicopter. After just one year of duty in Vietnam, she had admitted 5354 patients, treated 9,187 as outpatients, and received 2,500 helicopter landings. On 23 April, 1971, the Sanctuary sailed out of Da Nang Harbor for the last time, heading back to the United States.

Hospital ships are a unique command in that they have two commanding officers. The ship, naturally, has its Captain or Commanding Officer with a full complement of ship's crew under him. The hospital, likewise, has its own commanding officer who oversees the entire hospital crew of doctors, dentists, nurses, corpsmen, and, in our case, two Red Cross workers.

Betty got out of the Navy after serving just five years. Since the Vietnam experience had left her burned out on nursing, she decided to choose another career.

She got a bachelor's degree in English, a master's degree in linguistics, and certification to teach English as a second language.

Her new career led her to teach English to foreign students at the University of Florida for a number of years. She has now come full circle, so to speak, and is doing private health care.

DECODING THE SECRET
MILITARY MESSAGES
OF THE JAPANESE

George Washington Varn II

My clearest recollection of three years of our war was spending eight hours a day, six days a week at a long table filled with pages and pages of 30" x 30" paper with multiple columns of five digit numbers which I was adding up and dividing by three. The purpose of this was to read the highest security Japanese naval code, which we did through the war. It was boring, tiresome, and enormously useful. For most of the war we knew what the Japanese were going to do, where they would do it, and when.

It all began for me one spring day late in my senior year at Harvard when I was telephoned and asked to come to an office at the Dean's. It was very mysterious, and I couldn't find anything out about it, but I was told that under no circumstances was I to mention it and please be on time. When I got there, I was ushered promptly into a waiting room where I received a lecture that what I was going to hear was ultra-secret, and that I hadn't heard it anyway. After three different doors getting the same thing I finally met the great astronomer Dr. Donald Menzes, who asked me if I would be willing to try out for a super-secret cryptanalytic job in the Navy. I could not tell anyone what I was doing, and I must somehow manage to take a course which required several hours a week of work without letting anyone, teachers, friends, roommates or what have you know anything about it.

Throughout the rest of the spring I labored with this and eventually was told, that, subject to an FBI scrutiny, I would be accepted. From what I later learned there must have been half a dozen agents who combed through everything I had ever done anywhere and eventually decided I was a safe risk.

While this was going on I skipped graduation and worked in Washington with an economics professor waiting for my commission to come through, which it eventually did in about mid-July as I remember it. One day I was a civilian in the Office of Export Price Control, and the next day I had a uniform on and reported to the Navy Department where the same kind of a procedure went through as before.

Our office in Washington ran all the time, of course, and we were on a three-shift basis. It was staffed liberally with mathematicians, philologists, and so forth. Most of them could have been replaced by ordinary bright teenagers because none of us knew anything about Japanese, and what we were doing was simply high level adding and dividing. It was a fascinating group of people, however, largely from eastern colleges. The young people were a wonderful mix of seniors, men and women, and was really the finest bunch of bright people that I was ever around.

What we were doing was so super secret that we had to pretend that we were ordinary line officers, and this was difficult when nobody in the group knew much about any ship bigger than a rowboat. The results of what we were doing were then so highly classified that only a very few top admirals were informed, and only one person could take the information to specific places in the White House.

It was many years after the war before there was any information about this, and even today when I see it in writing I get a funny little twitch in my back. Nevertheless it has been thoroughly written about, and there's even an organization of ex-OP-20-G, which was the name that we couldn't even whisper during the war.

Fortunately, the regular Navy personnel had made great steps toward decrypting the Japanese naval code, so that its methods and so forth were pretty well thoroughly understood, and there was the ability to read a great amount by the time the war started. It was really a fairly simple system, which involved a codebook with five digit numbers representing places, words, and the Japanese equivalent of our alphabet, the Kana. A message would be encrypted by personnel using these five-digit numbers and they would then go to a huge book of hundreds of pages which were made up of random five-digit numbers and begin at a certain location and take these numbers and add them to the code so that they got an unintelligible resulting number. Our job then was to reproduce the codebook, and also the thousands and thousands of random five-digit numbers. Fortunately the Japanese used an anti-garble system for their code so that every code word was divisible by three. Mathematically any number whose digits add up to a number divisible by three is itself divisible by three. Thus 303 can be divided by three, but 302 cannot. In working with this then we instantly learned to determine whether a number was divisible by three or not, and even today I catch myself looking at license plates and all kinds of things and seeing whether they "scan" or don't. What we had to do was to reproduce the codebook, get the additive numbers, and break the system for determining where the message began and where it ended. Naturally the Japanese did not use the same books all through the war, but fortunately for the most part, due to the problems of supply and so on they did not change everything all at once except either once or twice that I can remember. Even then, the Japanese are so methodical, that one can predict a great deal of what they are doing. Furthermore, with all the ships in the Navy getting the new books and so on it was inevitable that somebody would lose them, or would make a mistake and use one of the wrong books and so forth so that we could get an inkling to what was happening when the changes were made.

We would work at long tables with reams of paper which had overlaying messages lined up one after the other and we would try to find a number that would make everything in the column turn into something divisible by three. Most military messages tend to be fairly stereotyped, and as a result we usually knew pretty much what a short message was likely to be saying anyway and if we had any inkling of the code we could work from that. In addition to place names and stereotyped words such as arrival, and departure, there would be times when something would be spelled out in Kana, which is the syllabic Japanese morpheme basis. For example Jacksonville is written in Romanized Kana as Jiyakusonbiru. If we ran upon this and knew what it was we could very easily pick up several lines of additives.

Originally we had a unit in Belconnen, Africa, staffed by the English; one in Melbourne staffed by Americans and Australians; one in Pearl, and the one in Washington. Naturally the idea of staying in Washington for the war did not suit me, and by that time I was ready to get out if I could but nobody ever left this unit. Obviously the dangers of anyone giving information about this were so overwhelming that it wasn't tolerated. I applied for transfer to everything that I could think of, and routinely it got not further than the desk of the chief who handled the paperwork.

After I had been in Washington for a couple of months or so the Navy decided that everyone who had a commission needed to have some kind of rudimentary background in what the Navy was about, and we were all sent to indoctrination school (Dock school). The one I was assigned to was at Harvard, and when I got there I was assigned exactly the same room that I had had as a freshman, but under circumstances that were obviously quite different. As a freshman I had a roommate and we each had a private bedroom and there was a living room. In the Navy we had double-decker bunks and I can't remember whether there were four or six of us living there. The Navy did its best to make us into good Navy people, mainly by insisting that if we didn't shape up that we could be turned into enlisted men. This did not get very far with me because after all the trouble they had had getting me into this unit I felt pretty certain they weren't going to toss me out. In any case I guess this got across to the superiors because after I had been there some three weeks or so there was a hurry-up call from Washington that I had to go back, and I was granted some kind of a certificate saying that I had been to school for the required two months.

Back in Washington the war progressed, and I wanted to get out of Washington some way if I possibly could. I applied for overseas and in the early spring I was transferred to Pearl Harbor.

I arrived in Pearl in the spring of 1943, about 15 months after the attack. There was still a lot of evidence of what had happened, and the harbor itself had a lot of junk ships still in it. When we first got there, however, there had not been much building and we were housed in old officer's quarters which were pretty good. After a year or so there they managed to put up a lot of BOQs and we moved in under considerably less than luxurious conditions.

Our shift in Pearl was two day, two evening, and two mid-shifts. We never had more than 24 hours off for the rest of the war.

As I have said the work was boring, but extremely successful. We knew a great deal about ship movements, and the typical messages that we decoded were merchant ships telling when they were leaving somewhere and when they were arriving and we could easily predict their route and send a sub to sink the ship. The Japanese Merchant Marine was effectively wiped out by the combination of information acted on by a superb sub force.

We usually knew where their Navy was, and where they were headed. In April, 1943, we read a highly secret dispatch which had said that Admiral Yamamoto, the architect of the attack on Pearl Harbor and First Admiral of the Japanese fleet, was going to fly around to some of the islands they had captured in the Pacific. We were able to chart his itinerary, and one leg of his journey put him just within the 400-mile range of our fighters. Sixteen planes were dispatched, and his plane was shot down. Yamamoto was probably the brightest young man in the Japanese Navy command, and his death was a serious blow to their effort. It was also a great shot in the arm for us.

As I said earlier we were reading a lot of the Japanese code before the war ever started. The Navy had a number of career Japanese code people who were superb and who knew the Japanese mind in and out. I have always felt that we certainly read at least some of the traffic that was sent just before the final attack reached Pearl. Of course the Japanese Navy exercised radio silence up until the time the planes were launched, but it took several hours for the planes to get to Pearl, and once their radio silence was broken at all I feel certain that we could have read at least parts of it. The regular Navy officers who had been in code work before the war clammed up completely whenever they were asked about this, and they never admitted that there was any intercept. Whether the crypt office itself was at fault because it was an early Sunday morning, or whether the admirals and generals were either asleep or on the golf course, I never found out, but it seemed to me there was a good chance that we read at least some of it.

Eventually I got to Guam, and was working on some other code work of my own, which gave some useful information during bomb raids. We were very close to Saipan, which is where the planes took off for the run to Tokyo. I remember well the night that Enola Gay took off. That was the only thing that was probably more secret than what we were doing, and none of us knew anything about it. As everyone in the Navy knows, enlisted men always know more about operations than officers. Chiefs run the Navy. My yeoman came to me and told me that a plane had taken off carrying an atomic bomb. I gave him a ten-minute lecture on why an atomic bomb was impossible and I finished just about the time the radio dispatches began to come in from Tokyo.

My main recollection of Guam is that there was an officer's liquor ration of two quarts of whiskey a week. We were allowed also to substitute five bottles of wine (including champagne) for each bottle of whiskey. Since this was clearly more alcohol than most of us would consume, the Seabees developed a scheme of making souvenirs of war relics and selling them to Navy officers, not for money, but for bottles of whiskey or wine, which they then promptly bootlegged to enlisted men at exorbitant prices.

After the war I went back to Pearl and waited about a month for a ship to return home. There was nothing for me to do except to check in every few days, so I got to see a great deal of the Hawaiian Islands during that month. As everyone can remember it was always possible to hitch a ride somewhere or another. In any case after about a month I was put on a Navy flattop and made a very uncomfortable seven-day trip back to San Francisco, quartered in a gun compartment. It didn't matter; we were on the way home.

Because of the point system I still had to server another three or four months and was sent to Charleston where some of the old OP-20-G people were working, and in one of the offices, which turned out to be publicity, a bit different from what I had been doing, I looked across the room and saw the most beautiful girl I had ever seen in my life, a WAVE in the Public Relations Office. I decided she was for me. It took a little more work than I anticipated, which  included convincing the commander in charge of the office that I was the world's gift to journalism when the last time I had written anything for publication was when I was editor of my high school paper. I convinced him so thoroughly of how good I would be that he sent me to take charge of an office elsewhere in the Navy yard, but fortunately the beautiful girl had enough time to come and do a lot of my work for me. She had more points than I did, and was getting out in a few weeks so the assault had to be rapid. It was, we did, and have lived happily ever after.

George Varn was born on December 1, 1920. He and Betty live in Jacksonville. George is active in the various Varn Timber and Investment Companies.

FIGHTING ACROSS
EUROPE WITH THE
42ND RAINBOW DIVISION

George William Whitmire

At the age of 17, when I entered the engineering school of Alabama Polytechnic Institute in the winter quarter of 1942-43, I had no inkling of the disjointed career, both academic and military, that awaited me.

Alabama Polytechnic Institute (now Auburn University), with its strong military heritage, mandated enrollment in the Army Reserve Officers' Training Corps (ROTC), so I enrolled and chose the artillery branch.. All that was needed to get a degree and a commission was to complete four years of university study, four hours a week of military field training, five hours a week of physical training and two weeks of active duty at the end of both the sophomore and junior years.

By taking 23 hours per quarter most quarters, I was, in the spring of 1944, a first quarter junior, and well on my way to achieving my dual goals of college degree and Army commission. I had the rank of second lieutenant in advanced ROTC, was in command of a platoon, and was receiving $25 per month pay.

At the end of the spring quarter I headed to Ft. Benning to complete my two-week active duty summer requirement, and this is when things started to unravel. In January of this same year, Major Sutton, a decorated veteran of Guadalcanal, advised me to choose either the infantry or the armored branch of the military because, according to him, no additional artillery officers would be needed. He also advised me that after the summer of 1944, I would probably no longer be deferred from active duty.

Armed with this rather grim information, I decided to enlist in the Army at Ft. McPherson, Georgia in June 1944.

With Major Sutton's help, it was arranged for me to attend Officer Candidate School (OCS) after completing infantry basic training. For this training, I was sent (in August 1944) to Camp Blanding, Florida, which was, at that time, the largest infantry training replacement center in the country. As acting, noncom platoon leader, I was in command of 40 recruits and a barracks building. Despite this command position, I was still required to participate in all of the rigorous training. The most memorable and challenging aspect of this training was the five-mile forced march in platoon formation, which had to be completed in 45 minutes while wearing full battle gear.

After completing just 12 of the 14 weeks of basic training, I was pulled out of field maneuvers and transported back to base. Another bump in my career road had come along in the form of the Battle of the Bulge. I was given orders to report to Ft. Mead, Maryland, and from there was transported to Camp Kilmer, New Jersey, to await ship transport to Europe. After sailing to Marseille, I was transported across land to Epinal in the frozen foothills of the Vosges Mountains. The sounds of artillery bursts and the flashes of night flares welcomed me to the war. The next morning I received orders to the 42nd Rainbow Division, which was on the front line in combat several miles to the northeast. This division was an assault division, and, as a member, I was about to embark on a long line of campaigns, each with a story unto itself.

It was during the attack on Schweinfurt, the most heavily defended city in Germany, that I was wounded. Early in the morning of April 11, 1945, I was slightly wounded in the thigh, then later that day I was wounded severely enough to require five months of hospitalization and rehab. Victory in Europe (V-E Day, May 8, 1945) was on the horizon, and a new career awaited me over the horizon and beyond the Army.

For his services in combat, I was awarded the Infantry Combat Badge with Silver Laurel Leaves, the Bronze Star medal, the Purple Heart, the ETO medal with three Bronze Stars and the ETO Victory Medal. I was also entitled to wear the Rainbow Division patch on my left shoulder and the Seventh Army patch on my right shoulder.

The following is a brief summary of the major battles that I participated in during World War II, that I wrote to my six grandchildren on December 16, 1998.

This date, December 16, 1998 marks the 54th anniversary of the Ardennes-Alsace Campaign, which was one of the most costly battles of World War II for the U.S. Army, which incurred approximately 134,000 casualties. To your generation, this campaign is better known as the "Battle of the Bulge & Nordwind."

As you know, I served in the 42nd "Rainbow" Infantry Division, which traces its roots back to the Civil War, and is one of the most highly decorated and famous divisions in the U.S. Army.

The following is a brief chronology of the major battles, which I fought in:

BATTLE OF THE BULGE – NORDWING
DECEMBER 16, 1944 - JANUARY 18, 1945

We were in defensive positions southeast of Hatten and in the town of Kaltenhouse (Hagenau) France against the elite German 10th S.S. Panzer Division and 21st Panzer Division. Our battalion was awarded the Presidential Unit Citation for repulsing the enemy with heavy losses.

HARDT MOUNTAINS
MARCH 15, 1945

We were in the first assault wave against the German main line of resistance in the Hardt mountains where we advanced through mine fields and small arms fire, and then we repulsed a German counterattack that night in hand-to-hand combat. The German units were the 221st Volksgrenadier Regiment of the 6th S. S. Mountain Division.

SIEGFRIED LINE
MARCH 18, 1945

We were in the first assault wave on the Siegfried Line where we broke through the outer defenses and destroyed a large concrete pillbox and a 75-mm cannon, which had blocked our tanks from advancing to the rear of the Siegfried Line.

THE RHINE RIVER CROSSING
MARCH 28, 1945

Our battalion was attached as an Armored Infantry Battalion to Task Force I, Combat Command A, 12th Armored Division for the crossing of the Rhine River on April 1, 1945 (Easter Sunday) and destroying the German positions in front of Wurzburg, Germany.

WURZBURG
APRIL 2, 1945

Our armored column advanced to the east of the city and then north on the rubble filled road parallel to the Main River against sniper and small arms fire until we encountered heavy fire from an 88 mm battery, located in an apple orchard on a hill approximately 1,500 yards on our left flank. We dismounted and attacked and destroyed this battery and supporting infantry, and then advanced to our objective north of the city.

SCHWEINFURT
APRIL 10-11, 1945

Our armored column was ordered northeast to block the autobahn from Schweinfurt to Nuremberg, which was to the Southeast of Schwebheim. Our company, with a platoon of tanks, was the last unit to dismount and ordered to attack through a heavy forest to a planted tree farm.

I was in the lead platoon to cross the firebreak and we came under small arms fire, which began at approximately 1800 hours. This was followed by intermittent artillery fire throughout the night. We were surrounded on all sides except to the rear when at approximately 0700 hours we received heavy fire from several enemy batteries, which is known as a "TOT" (Time on Target), fire at will mission. In this battle, our company suffered over 100 casualties out of 190 men and two tanks were knocked out. Our objective was accomplished but with an unacceptable loss of soldiers, of which I was one.

CASUALTIES

During the above-described battles, our company suffered over 250 casualties out of the original company of approximately 190 men, which includes the replacements.

AWARDS

Among my awards are the Bronze Star Medal, Purple Heart Medal, E.T.O. Ribbon with 3 Bronze Service Stars, and the Combat Infantryman's Badge.

NOTE

Before the war ended on May 8, 1945, the division participated in the capture of Nuremberg, Dacha, and Munich, Germany.

In 1946 G.W. Whitmire married Frances Elizabeth Stephens, and they had three children. After graduating from Auburn Uiversity's School of Engineering in 1947, he returned to Jacksonville and joined his father's contracting and construction business, Whitmire Tank Company. It was sold in 1966 but he retained the real estate leasing business. He later joined the Atlantic National Bank, and was executive vice president for real estate and mortgage lending when he stepped down in 1986. He continued as a consultant with the bank until 1993. He is a past member of the Rotary Club of Jacksonville, the Florida Engineering Society, the Association of General Contractors, and the Auburn Alumni Engineering Council. For over ten years he served on the congressional committee which selects nominees to the U.S. Military Academy at West Point.

FLYING THE CORSAIR
IN KOREA, THE ATLANTIC
AND INDOCHINA

Ben H. Willingham

I have tried to put together some comments on my experience with old "hose nose."

My first introduction to the F4U was at Brown Field, an old NAAF in Chula Vista, California shortly after I finished flight school. The date was 21 March 1951 and the aircraft was an F4U-4, BuNo 68527. I remember this flight as if it were only yesterday. It was a very pleasant day without a cloud in the sky. I had heard of the Corsair's reputation and after flying the F6F and the F8F, I thought I could handle anything that wore a propeller. I had been given a very brief introduction to the aircraft by an old WWII pilot (he must have been at least a full LT, which to a fresh Ensign was impressive) who basically told me to be careful as this beast had a temper of its own. I did not have as much difficulty in taxiing as I had anticipated and thus, thought all of the stories I had heard about the difficulty in flying the Corsair were wildly overrated. I was cleared for takeoff and cautiously put the throttle forward, felt the torque and realized my leg was not long enough to keep it straight on the runway. I reduced power and brought the airplane to an uneventful stop and taxied clear of the runway. The tower wanted to know if I had a problem. Of course I said, "no, all was fine; I just wanted to check something again." I adjusted the seat forward, the rudder pedals back toward me and added a bit more rudder trim and announced I was again ready for takeoff. This time, I managed to take off without difficulty although it may not have been as straight as I might have liked. I flew around the area for about an hour to familiarize myself with the feel of the plane and returned for a series of landings. I don't recall the landings being either good or difficult. One clearly needed time in this aircraft to feel at home. Fortunately, I had the chance to fly it for about 25 hours before I was involved with any formation tactics. Then it was like, one day it clicked and I suddenly felt as if I had been flying the Corsair forever.

VF-791, a reserve squadron from Memphis, Tennessee, had been recalled for service in Korea. They had just arrived in the San Diego area for training prior to deployment on Boxer, I was attached to VF-791 for training and ultimately for deployment with them. All of the pilots in the squadron had been in WWII, were inclined to disregard the formalities of Navy life and were one great bunch to fly with. No one seemed to be concerned that I had so few total hours or that my time in the Corsair was less than about 40 hours. They took me under their wing and taught me their form of tactics. I think I learned more about flying in the next two months with these reserves than in all the time I had spent in the training command. Finally time came for FCLPs and CARQUALS and I can honestly say, I was ready and it went without difficulty. Their LSO could have brought a Greyhound Bus aboard ship; he was that good. At the end of the training period, we were ready to go. We went aboard Bataan (CVL-29) for the trip to Pearl. Boxer had already deployed on 2 March 1951 and had been on station off of the East Coast of Korea for about 60 days but had returned to Pearl for replenishment and maintenance. We transferred to Boxer and departed for Korea where we relieved Valley Forge (CV-45) and operated in the Korean area for 5 ½ months until Valley relieved us again. During this time, I flew 76 missions, a total of 172 hours with 81 traps. VF 791 never lost an aircraft or pilot on its deployment to Korea in spite of weather and flying conditions that must have been some of the worst in the world along with the fact that 10 of us were fresh young aviators just out of training. We flew the missions as they came up without regard to rank or experience.

With VF-791, we flew exclusively close air ground support missions. This involved low altitudes, difficult navigation and heavy loads. The F4U-4 would carry 4,000 pounds on the centerline and wing mounts. The –5, which we had a few of, would carry even more but the additional 200hp in the engine hardly compensated for the additional 1,000 pounds or so that were added to the load.

Boxer was due to arrive back in San Francisco on 24 October 1951 and I was to be reassigned, as the reserves were likely to be released from active duty. When we reached Pearl again we were told that several of the squadrons on Valley were short on experienced close air ground support pilots. We were asked if anyone would like to volunteer to fill in vacancies. I made one of the dumbest mistakes of my life and said, yes, I would be willing to go over and join VF-96, flying the F9F-2. This lasted only a few days since I was an experienced F4U pilot and had not jet time. I was temporarily loaned to a Marine squadron, VMF-243, flying F4Us until I could transition into jets. After my nine months with the reserves, I found I had landed in a different world. In spite of the fact that I was now a second tour combat pilot and had considerable experience, I was still a Navy Ensign and thus, at the very bottom of the totem pole. I was a wingman and my opinion was of no value and not welcomed. During the brief time I was with the Marines, I flew an additional 21 missions, 31 hours and 16 traps. This short time was by far the most dangerous, not because of the mission but rather the attitude of those in the squadron. The Marines lost numerous pilots and aircraft often because one did not know what the other was going to do next and every move was based on seniority, not who could do the job. Wingman left their leaders and the leaders lost their wingman due to maneuvers that were difficult to follow or flying too low on the target for the wingman to escape damage from their own bombs or napalm. Rather than the big family feeling I had in the reserve squadron, it was everyone for himself. I am just glad that my time with them was short and that I survived.

Fortunately, this temporary duty was soon over and I was put with VF-96, a regular Navy squadron. Although, this was an improvement over the Marines, it was not at all the same as being with VF-791. At least I was into jets but that is another story.

In November 1953, Boxer (CV-21) returned from her fourth and final Korean deployment. I was detached from VF-96 with orders to Corey Field in Pensacola to instruct in the SNJ, something I did not want to do. When I had initially received my orders, I had written BuPers requesting anything but the training command. I had hardly arrived home on leave when I received a telegram asking me to call BuPers in Washington. When I reached the individual I was asked to call, I was told I was on the list of qualified close air ground support pilots. If I was interested, there was an interesting opportunity if I were willing to volunteer to become an instructor/advisor to various foreign countries that had recently purchased surplus American aircraft and carriers. I know one should never volunteer but I think I would have volunteered for Antarctica to avoid going to Corey Field and sit in the back seat of a SNJ trying to teach some student how to fly. This sounded like something that would really interest me. Anything would be better than the SNJ. Anyway, I said, "Yes sir, when do you want me?" Three days later I was in Oceana. My initial assignment was with the Royal Dutch Navy flying F8Fs and as most of them spoke English and had a good flying background, this went well. After about three weeks, we departed for Den Helder, Holland where the Dutch have their main naval air facility. The Dutch had purchased a surplus CVL, now named the Karel Doorman after their famous admiral that was killed in the South Pacific in 1942. Since we had been several days enroute to Holland, we stared off with FCLPs at Den Helder following which we went aboard the Karel Doorman for two weeks of training in the North Sea and Atlantic. All went well and we had no accidents or other difficulties. All too soon, my brief tour with the Dutch came to an end and I returned to Oceana just after Christmas 1953.

When I arrived back at Oceana, I was informed that I was now to work with the French Navy (Aeronautique Navale) flying F4Us. The French had purchased new F4U-7s and were training new pilots at NAS Oceana. Unlike the Dutch, the French did not speak English and their flying skills were limited, at best. They were seriously in need of instructors and advisors that could train the pilots in both carrier operations and close air ground support activities. We started working on basic formation flying, a concept that was foreign to the French. They seemed to have a congenital fear of getting close to another aircraft. The quality of their flying would have caused the average U.S. Naval Aviator to be purged from the program if he had performed as poorly as they had. Anyway, they were the customers as they had purchased several surplus aircraft carriers and a variety of other worn out, surplus aircraft, including the F6F, SB2C, SBD and F4U-1s. Each time I complained to my naval contact, I was told I was the instructor and that I should teach them to overcome their weakness. Thanks.

This really turned into a great challenge. They spoke no English and at that time, I did not know a word of French. Since there were about forty of them and only very few of us, we started to learn French while training them in the Corsair. In a surprisingly short time, I found I could make myself understood in primitive French. After about six weeks, the initial training was finished and we left for Tunisia where we could go aboard one of the French carriers to continue training and help them qualify as carrier aviators so they could fight against the Algerian guerrillas from the waters around Algeria.

We arrived in Karouba, Tunisia and were preparing to go aboard R-92 Arromanches (British built CVL type carrier). At this time, matters in Indochina were changing. The fighting had been in progress since the end of WWII and generally remained in a stalemate. The Viet Minh had been attacking in guerrilla fashion all over Indochina without a defined battlefield or front. In order to keep the Viet Minh from gaining control of northern Laos and the middle and lower Mekong River Valley, the French began to reinforce their garrison at Dien Bien Phu in November 1953. As this was a strategic location between Hanoi in northern Vietnam and Louangphrabang in northern Laos, it became the focus point of both sides. The Vet Minh were counting on the French people getting tired of the continuing losses and great expense and had finally agreed to start negotiations in Geneva in the Spring of 1954. The French decided to bring in their forces from Africa, thinking if they put more military pressure on the Viet Minh, they would force them to negotiate more seriously.

Thus the change in plans that would take me from North Africa to Southeast Asia. We had brought all of our aircraft on board Arromanches where we were told we were being sent to Tourane (Da Nang), Indochina to help defend against the Viet Minh. We left the aircraft on board the carrier. The USAF transported us from Tunisia to Tourane. After what seemed like a month in the air in R5Ds, we finally reached Tourane in February 1954. The US had sent AU-1s down from Japan for us to use until our aircraft arrived from Africa. The AU is a low level version of the F4U. It had a powerful engine but no supercharger and would not get above about 20,000 feet. It would carry a large quantity of napalm or bombs but at slow speed. Although it had many of the F4U-4/7 characteristics, it was sluggish and not responsive making it difficult to bring aboard ship. Anyway, we picked them up at the French Air Force Base at Bach Mai (just outside Hanoi) and after considerable FCLP practice, we went aboard R-96 LaFayette (nee USS Langley, CVL-27). We were to conduct close air ground support activities against the Viet Minh in various areas where the French had been under attack. At this point, the French garrison at Dien Bien Phu was coming under increasing pressure and the French paratroopers arrived to defend the garrison. They soon found themselves surrounded and all logistics were air lifted to Dien Bien Phu. We began to fly support missions for the paratroopers trying to hold back the Viet Minh. There were three airfields at

Dien Bien Phu, all in a valley below the ridges. The French were surrounded and in a hopeless position as the Viet Minh held the high ground and were firing down on them. We flew three or flights a day, dropping napalm trying to force the Viet Minh to withdraw. Several weeks after our arrival in country, Arromanches arrived carrying our F4U aircraft. We happily turned our AU's over to the French Air Force and picked up our F4U-7s. After the short experience in the AU's, we really appreciated what a fine aircraft the new-7 was.

We were there as advisors to brief and teach. The three Americans attached to the ship would alternate flying into Dien Bien Phu to meet with the ground troops to determine where our targets and priorities were located. After this, we would work out a strike plan and brief the various flights. Our responsibilities should have ended here, as we were advisors. In reality, we would lead several four and eight aircraft flights into the valley each day. By this time, my French had improved to the point where I could curse with the best of them and brief the flights without great difficulty. We would launch and at the point we reached the target area, we were fortunate if half of the flight would actually follow us into the strike. In all fairness to the French, these pilots were not qualified to fly the F4U after so little total flight time or actual time in the F4U series aircraft. They had had only the limited training we gave them at Oceana in close air support. Although they had dropped practice bombs and napalm on the ranges in the Chesapeake Bay area, this was in a training environment and totally different from the game we were now playing. They lost relatively few pilots and most of these to flying accidents caused by inexperience. The Viet Minh began a major offensive in late April and Dien Bien Phu fell on 7 May 1994, the day before the peace talks were to begin in Geneva. After this, we continued to help the French in their general retreat until July when we were pulled out. We had operated from both the Arromanches and LaFayette with

American pilot/advisors and LSOs from February 1954 until July 1954.

Small things stay in my memory. The Arromanches was a British built carrier and to me looked quite different from LaFayette, an American built CVL. Our French pilots had a great difficulty telling them apart. The carrier skippers did not seem to have any appreciation of the pilot's problem in getting back to the ship and did not bother to tell us in advance where they would be going. We had a low frequency homing device that helped find the ship. When we returned, depending on the visibility, the French who did not have an American advisor leading them would head for the first carrier they found. Since we would fly several missions in a day, the French would land, refuel and rearm irrespective of which carrier they found. I would frequently fly from one carrier to the other to brief the group and lead them out again and at the end of the mission bring them back to the correct carrier. In the USN, a pilot landing on the wrong boat would catch hell from his shipmates but in this group, any landing anywhere, was considered a success.

During the short time I was in Indochina, I flew 187 sorties totaling 447 hours. We were frequently hit with small arm fire and machine guns but nothing that would be really dangerous, at least as long as it did not hit something vital. The Squadron, 14F, flew almost 1,500 sorties in 12 weeks. During this time, they lost six actual aircrafts and only one or two pilots to actual combat. I feel the limited losses were more a result of their not going in on the target and staying out of harms way than a credit to their flying skills. The anti-air defenses were nothing compared to what we had experienced in Korea or what was to come in Vietnam. In spite of our efforts, Dien Bien Phu was lost but we continued our close air support activities into July when the French realized they had had enough and reached an agreement to leave Indochina. The war officially ended on 20 July 1954.

The French had no idea why they were in this God forsaken area defending something they did not understand. Most of the soldiers on the ground were from the French

Foreign Legion and were not considered true French so most of the pilots really did not feel they had a dog in the fight. We had many philosophical conversations back on board the carrier. They were not necessarily bad pilots but they had very little training and no motivation to risk their lives for what they considered a useless cause.

The F4U-7 (the USA did not buy the –7 as the jets were arriving about the time it came out) was the absolute finest I have ever flown. Vought and removed all of the earlier unpleasant characteristics from the Corsair. It would respond easily to the torque on takeoff or wave off without difficulty. It had more power, much more controllability, larger all metal control surfaces and hydraulically folding wings. It had superchargers that would allow the aircraft to fly above 40,000 feet. The speed was almost up to the early series of jets.

On both carriers, we had American LSOs. On those occasions I landed in Dien Bien Phu, the number of Americans present surprised me. At the Officer's Club, everyone spoke English. As Dien Bien Phu was cut off and surrounded by the Viet Minh all of the supplies had to be brought by air. Americans flew all of the airlift flights of R4Ds, R5Ds, and R5Cs. The aircraft had no markings to identify them but were clearly ours. I always enjoyed my brief visits to Dien Bien Phu, as it was the only time I could speak English and be among fellow Americans.

As I look back on this experience, I have numerous thoughts. Without this experience, I would never have learned to speak French. Even though shipboard French is not appreciated in polite circles, this is a skill that has helped me greatly over the years and later was an instrument in my being sent to Europe to head the activities of a large American conglomerate where I ultimately met my wife, Erika. At the same time, I don't understand why we ever entered Indochina (Vietnam). We had amassed a great deal of experience fighting the Viet Minh. To my knowledge none of the many men that had served there with the French were asked about their experience before committing our troops to fight. As history has shown, we ultimately had the same lack of understanding of the cause as the French and, like the French, had to give up the struggle against Communism because we were not prepared to go in and fight it to a conclusion.

Ben H. Willingham was born on August 6, 1932 in Nashville, Tennessee. Graduating from High School at an unusually young age, I entered Georgia Tech in the fall just after my 16th birthday. After two years at Tech, I volunteered for the Navy Aviation Cadet program, entering the Navy at the old NAS Atlanta. After flight training in the Pensacola area, Memphis and South Texas, I received my wings in February 1951. After serving in the Navy for 8 years, I left active duty and returned to Georgia Tech to finish my education. Since leaving Tech, I have lived for 30 years in Switzerland where I have been active in international business.

ABANDONING THE WASP
IN THE SOUTH CORAL SEA

Downs Wright

Dearest Newt,

I have just finished a short airmail letter to you; it is supposed to go off in Noumea and is mainly to let you know that I'm O.K. This I'll bring back with me to you.

On Tuesday the 15th of September 1942 we got two torpedo hits in the Wasp. That sounds like a mild statement or an understatement of facts. No words and no living person can really describe what happened from the time they hit until we abandoned ship, picked up by destroyers and last saw her burning fiercely in the night. She did not sink until a "tin can" put another torpedo in her, but she was really burning.

The shock is beginning to wear off to a certain degree, but I have not slept to amount to a damn since then. I'll try to give you my impression of it all and I'll try to remember things I thought about. While I was lying on the stern listening to the bullets going off and bombs blowing up in the fire, I remember thinking about you and wondered if you'd ever know this was happening or, as you read this, that it had happened. When I was in the water and had just about hit my last strength, so tired I could hardly move, I found a mattress someone had thrown over. I found it would float me fairly well and I could rest. I lay there thinking about you again, wondered if I would ever see you and mother to tell you about it all and wondered too, if I could make that last quarter of a mile to a destroyer which had stopped to pick up survivors. I made it but the oil I had swallowed had just about sapped all my strength and will power.

We had launched 16 scouts and 8 fighters at 1420. I had landed at 1230 from a hop on which McBrayer the #3 in my flight had shot down a 4-engine Jap bomber. We were still in and around the ready room after the landings at 1430. Sometime about 1445 the hardest jar and explosion you can imagine shook us, followed I think about 2 or 3 seconds later by another. All the lights were out, just total Stygian blackness. I discovered I had been blown out of my seat over another and in between two seats. I managed to get up and the next I remember I was on the flight deck looking around. My leaving the ready room is only vaguely in my mind.

The torpedoes had been sighted from the flight deck and one had jumped completely out of the water or porpoised. They both hit just forward of the island structure on the starboard side. I had no idea they would jar a big ship like that. All but one of eight fighter's stationary on the flight deck had collapsed on the landing gear. The one that had not rolled over the side as the ship took a heavy list to starboard. The forward part of the hanger deck was like a furnace from bursting gas tanks. The ammunition began going off as it got hot and shrapnel was flying everywhere. The gasoline storage tanks blew out on the starboard side and the flame must have gone several hundred feet in the air; soon after this exploded, the forward magazine went up and shook the ship again. By this time we had stopped moving ahead and had backed down so that the wind blew all the smoke and heat off the port bow side. All light and communication had been knocked off so that orders had to be passed by the officers all along. We pushed the remaining planes over the side and over the stern. The order to abandon ship was then passed and men began jumping over. Several of the wounded and badly burned were helped down or lowered over the side. I saw several of the men that I could not recognize except by their clothes or uniforms; they had received flash burns that were horrible. The skin and flesh was actually falling off of them. Two or three should have been killed in the blast, they were still alive and able to walk but in awful conditions; they did die before or soon after being picked up by destroyers. There was no hysteria among the men; only once just before pushing the planes over was there any excitement and that was due to someone yelling "over the side with'em" meaning the planes and being misunderstood by the men, several hundred of whom were standing or lying down on the stern of the flight deck. Several of us took charge though and made everyone sit down and be quiet. There was so much noise from 5 inch shells and other ammunition exploding up forward that we could hardly hear, to say nothing of the roar of the fire. Anyway we pushed the planes over and began a very orderly abandon ship. Many men jumped before life rafts had been lowered and many jumped without life jackets. Shock is a terrible thing to see on men's and boy's faces. I cannot attempt to describe that. I went down a line on the port side of fantail with one of our mechanics with a one-man rubber boat or dingy that I got out of a plane. I also got the life rafts out of the other planes before pushing them over. Anyway I found, as soon as I got in the water that I had forgotten my shoes, that is, to take them off. I finally managed that and then to get the raft inflated. When we (the mechanics and I) got it inflated, about 10 or 12 people began hanging on the sides of it, so we could not get in at all. I let one boy who had no life jacket get in since he could not hold on in the oil that we were floating in.

I then discovered that we could not pull away from the ship since we were to leeward and she was drifting with the wind. There was one continuous roar of the fire raging from mid-ships to the forward end of the hanger deck and almost a continuous set of explosions going off and whining through the air. Several men were hit by these pieces, in the water, none seriously that I know of. I suspect that some were knocked out and drowned if not killed outright.

When we finally passed thru and under the smoke, heat, and blaze and reached the bow I thought we had a good chance of getting away and then I discovered oil burning on the water. We had to do some swimming and resting, more swimming, etc. to get our raft away from the fire, and covered with oil as we were it would have burned us at once.

Fortunately the oil on the water did not burn except along the starboard bow.

I remember discovering that my own life jacket was not fully inflated, so I blew it up tight and found I could get along without the raft to hold to. I shoved off and started swimming for the nearest destroyer, swimming and resting, but I got so very tired. I could look back and see the ole Wasp still afloat and not much list on (about 4 or 5 degrees I think) and down only about 5 to 6 feet by the bow. I could see an explosion now and then, but could not hear very well and I discovered some hours later that the blast had made me slightly deaf. She was burning from the island and bridge to almost the forecastle itself. I think we would not have lost her if it had not been for the fires that started so fiercely right after the torpedoes hit. The engine rooms and boilers were not damaged since the torpedoes hit too far forward. The forward locker room I'm told had brick knocked out and blowers were off until auxiliary power started up and this was only about a minute.

How many men we lost I do not know yet. Duncan, the destroyer I got on, picked up about 600, officers and men. We were all brought to Esperito Santo and transferred from destroyers to three cruisers that were with us. A check up was made here, but not as thorough as will be made when we are landed at Noumea. I suspect that we lost several hundred. The planes in the air must have landed aboard the Hornet, we don't know yet.

While I was lying on the deck of the destroyer I could see all our ships maneuvering and dropping depth charges. I saw a geyser of smoke and water go up amidships on the North Carolina about two miles away. A torpedo had hit her also. From this it looks as though we had run right into a nest of submarines. I'm not really surprised that we got torpedoed because we have been steaming around out here long enough for the Japs to get subs here by the dozens. Our higher command is too willy-nilly and definitely lacks initiative. All of us feel this way about it - that our higher in command is definitely not what it should be and should be changed. Changes are going to have to be made if we expect to win this war with the Japs, and we are losing it out here everyday.

I still can't quite realize that I'm safe and sound, but how thankful I am to be safe - as safe as being in Helena. Dick Flech was transferred about 6 weeks ago from here to Trinidad on inshore patrol. I can't realize either that I have lost everything I had. My pants, shirt, underwear, and socks are all I have. I don't have a penny. When I get back I'll have to buy all new uniforms and clothes. I had some things that were precious to me that I'll miss very much and can never be reimbursed for since they had no monetary value, only personal - the pictures of you, the letters to you on a day by day account of our activities, action etc, of which I had written well over 100 pages; I had bought you one of these new Parker "51" pens they had for sale on the ship and the little book of prayers mother gave me when I first went to school with a notation in it to me; all of my orders in my brief case, from my originals thru every ferry trip I had made. My log books, fortunately I gave you my other one to keep for me, and fortunate it is that I gave you the insurance policies. Our marriage certificate was in my brief case. Have not drawn much money so I'll be paid from July 1st all that I did not draw, that is, besides the allotments to you. I had planned to buy you a fur coat with this money for Christmas, but now I guess I'll have to put about half of it on uniforms and give the rest to you.

I expect that we will be put on a transport from Noumea and sent back to the States. This can't be too soon for me. How I want to see you now, you can only guess. Really can't think about it too much.

`Bye now
Your loving Downs

THE SECRETARY
OF THE NAVY
WASHINGTON

The President of the United States takes pleasure in presenting the NAVY CROSS to LIEUTENANT SPENCER D. WRIGHT, UNITED STATES NAVY for services as set forth in the following CITATION:

"For extraordinary heroism as section leader of an aerial flight during action against enemy Japanese forces in the Solomon Islands. During operations of the United States Naval and Marine Forces in support of the occupation of the islands, Lieutenant Wright's section, with superb coordination and relentless fighting spirit, destroyed six Japanese patrol planes and one motor launch off Gavutu Island. Pressing home his own attacks with persistent courage, maintained at great risk in the face of grave danger, Lieutenant Wright personally shot down three of the flying boats and destroyed one motor boat. In the same flight, he led a strafing assault on fuel and ammunition dumps, stores, motor vehicles, buildings and personnel on Gavutu and Tanambogo, thereby contributing immeasurably to the successful reduction and capture of those islands. His expert airmanship and loyal devotion to duty were in keeping with the highest traditions of the United States Naval Service."

For the President,
Frank Knox, Secretary of the Navy

Downs Wright was born in Newberry, S.C. May 24, 1913. He served on USS Wasp CV-7; VB-7 and VF-71. He was C.O. NAS Cecil Field in Jacksonville, Florida. Captain Wright U.S.N. (Ret.) died on May 5, 2001.

EMERGENCY
SURGERY IN THE
MID-ATLANTIC

Alexander Philip Zachella

Before I entered the Naval Academy, I had been interested in becoming a physician. As a matter of fact, I had one year of pre-med, at the University of Kentucky while on a football scholarship. So my interest in medicine goes way back. When I realized that I did not have the money to go to medical school, I decided to try for an academy appointment.

Upon graduation, I was assigned to the U.S.S. Greer (DD145), a four - stacker. My first job was an assistant engineering officer. In a few months the engineering officer was transferred to new construction and at the time of this story I was the Engineering Officer. We had been on North Atlantic convoy duty, but we were ordered to go to Casablanca to escort a fleet of empty LST's back to Norfolk, Virginia, after the North African invasions. We were on a zigzag course making about 8 knots and we were about at the Latitude 10 degrees North.

The convoy of LST's and our destroyer division were about halfway to Norfolk when one of my chief petty officers named Moon (his last name) reported to sick bay with a pain in his right abdomen. Fortunately, we had a doctor on board because we were the division flagship. Dr. Charles Herrick was a reserve officer called to active duty for the war. He was a general practitioner and had no surgery training except during his internship. We were cabinmates. He had the lower bunk because he was senior to me. He was a sailing enthusiast who had a desire to learn celestial navigation. So we made a deal. I would teach him to navigate if he would discuss medical procedures with me.

The pharmacist mate on board had become ill and we left him in the army hospital in Casablanca. So the doctor had no one to assist him. After examining Moon, Dr. Herrick concluded that he had acute appendicitis and surgery was absolutely necessary. We were at least 10-12 days from Norfolk. Dr. Herrick came into the ward room and says to me, "Zeke, we are going to have to operate on Moon."

My answer was, "What do you mean we?"

He said I need your help. I can't do it alone. So I said, "Okay, Doc. I'll try to help."

This was about 9:30 p.m. and we were in "darken ship" condition. All portholes were closed and there was little or no ventilation. All four stackers were direct current ships. Keep this thought in mind as it becomes important later. The temperature in the ward room was about 95 degrees. After Dr. Herrick had scrubbed we put Moon on the ward room table. Dr. Herrick had gown, masks and sheets he had sterilized ashore, and also a large steam sterilizer for his instruments. The "surgery team" included Dr. Herrick; me, the No. 1 assistant; the captain, Lt. Cdr. Maurice Cooper, USNR, taking blood pressure; the chief radioman counting sponges, and the chief steward, wiping sweat from our heads. Dr. Herrick had gone over the steps of an appendectomy with me, so I had a "rough" idea of what was about to happen.

The doctor gave Moon a shot of morphine, then administered the anesthesia with a spinal needle. It looked at least a foot long to me and I was not sure I would be vertical after Dr. Herrick inserted it in Moon's back. After a short time, he said to me, "Zeke, pinch Moon's toe to see if the anesthesia has taken effect."

I did, and we determined that he had no feeling in his lower body so the doctor was able to proceed.

Dr. Herrick told me he would make the incision and that I should take a hemostat with a gauze and line the incision with sponges to absorb the blood and to place the hemostats on the "bleeders." We proceeded through the abdominal wall into the cavity. The doctor then told me to get two retractors and hold the incision open so he could find the appendix. This I did, and after a long search the doctor identified the appendix and told me to get another hemostat and "gently" pick up the appendix so he could tie it off the main intestine and cut it off. I did as I was told and when I got the appendix out of the cavity, the doctor said it was discolored and looked as though it was gangrenous and would have ruptured if we had not removed it.

The doctor placed a "purse string suture" in the appendix and a suture above the "purse string" and cut the appendix between the two sutures. I then placed the severed appendix on the table. The doctor then cauterized the tip that had been formed by the cut and placed it into the intestine. At this point he pulled the "purse string" suture tight and tied it off.

Dr. Herrick asked the captain to take Moon's blood pressure. The captain had never taken blood pressure before. He went through the procedure and gave the doctor the reading. The doctor said, "Take it again captain, because if you are correct, we may as well quit!"

The second reading was much better. The doctor said, "Zeke, we are going to sew him up."

We took a count of the sponges to make sure we had all of them. The doctor took the first stitch and with this Moon started to move on the Ward Room table. The spinal was wearing off and Moon was beginning to feel pain. Up until this time, we had maintained good sterile condition. When the doctor took the second stitch, Moon got his left arm from under the sterile sheet and placed it smack on the incision. The doctor looked at me and said, "Zeke, he may as well have urinated in it."

He told me to take a pack of penicillin powder and sprinkle it into the incision. Then he turned to the Captain and said, "Captain, I am going to have to give him ether to put him out."

Being the engineering officer, I said, "We can't use ether because we have a motor generator just outside the ward room door."

If you know anything about a DC to AC motor generator, you know they spark. So I said to the captain, "We will have to shut down the radar or we could have an explosion." So we did the classic movie picture act. We got a tea strainer, gauze and ether. It did the trick; Moon was unconscious. With that, the doctor completed the task of sewing Moon up.

Moon slept in the doctor's lower bunk, the doctor slept in my upper bunk and I slept in Moon's bunk in the chiefs quarters. When we arrived in Norfolk 10 days later, Moon went on seven days leave and the doctor went to the Navy hospital for some R&R. He was a nervous wreck. It seems that one of the things they look for after an abdominal operation is for the patient to have a bowel movement.

Moon had been feeling badly for several days before he went to "sick call," so he had not eaten, therefore no "bowel movement." The doctor was sure he had contracted Ileus, an infection which causes a blockage of the intestine. Moon did not have Ileus. He had just not eaten. The doctor survived and so did Moon.

Seventeen months after graduation I was a J.G. and executive officer of the Greer (DD145). I think I was the first executive officer of a destroyer in our class. After three months as executive officer, I was transferred to the U.S.S. Ringgold (DD500), a twenty-one hundred tonner in the Pacific and relieved Broke Ensey '41 as executive officer. I was a lieutenant. I would like to know if anyone of our class was an executive on a destroyer before me. The Ringgold was with the fast carrier task forces in the Pacific.

Alexander Philip Zachella was born August 11, 1920 in Newport, Kentucky. He was graduated from the U.S. Naval Academy in August, 1942. During W.W.II he served aboard the destroyer U.S.S. Greer DD 145 and U.S.S. Ringold DD500. He resigned from the Navy in August 1953.

Zeke was a very successful executive with several large companies. He retired in Jacksonville.

Epilogue

There is one word I never saw used in the book and that is the word "scared."

No one wants to remember being scared and if we do remember being scared, we don't want to talk about it.

"Scared" is flying into enemy territory and flying on in to the anti-aircraft bursts where you know that some one is going to be hit; and no one can help another.

"Scared" is landing aboard you airplane carrier in the dark of night when you are just hoping you can pull it off once more.

Fear, nausea, and loneliness are not feelings that one share nor does one want to share with anyone. This is something no one writes of in this book, but it was there.

I do not think my fear, and I know my discomfort, can remotely compare with what many, many others lived trough; or did not live through. Among these are the marines and soldiers landing the beaches. They saw their comrades killed beside them. I am thinking of the troops in the mud and in freezing conditions in foxholes. Not only fear, but also the long periods of fatigue, no sanitation, and sometimes no food, were all suffered.

This part of the war we don't hear about; I don't believe we could understand it if we did.

This does not lessen the value of "Our War Stories" or the many other books on war experiences.

Thank God no one can understand the depths of another's fear and pain and agony.

Marvin Harper
Cdr. U.S.N.R. (Ret)

In 1941, after graduating from the University of Chattanooga, Harper entered the Navy. He was designated a naval aviator and served two tours in the South Pacific as a fighter pilot aboard U.S.S. Saratoga CV-3. He was awarded five air medals and the D.F.C. He received honorary retirement as Commander.

Upon release by the Navy, he entered the insurance business in Jacksonville, Florida, and is now retired in Jacksonville.